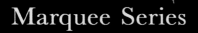

Microsoft® Windows 7

Nita Rutkosky

Pierce College at Puyallup, Puyallup, Washington

Denise Seguin

Fanshawe College, London, Ontario

Audrey Rutkosky Roggenkamp

Pierce College at Puyallup, Puyallup, Washington

Paradigm PUBLISHING

St. Paul • Los Angeles • Indianapolis

Contents

Managing Editor	Sonja Brown
Developmental Editor	Brenda Palo
Production Editor	Donna Mears
Cover and Text Designer	Leslie Anderson
Copy Editors	Susan Capecchi and Laura Nelson
Desktop Production	Ryan Hamner and Jack Ross
Proofreader	Laura Nelson
Testers	Amy McGuire, Rob Neilly, and Lindsay Ryan
Indexers	Ina Gravitz and Sandi Schroeder

Windows® 7 SECTION 1
Exploring Windows 7

Skills

- Navigate the Windows 7 desktop
- Perform the following actions using the mouse: point, click, double-click, and drag
- Start and close a program
- Open and close a window
- Shut down Windows 7
- Move a window
- Minimize, maximize, and restore a window
- Stack and cascade windows
- Use the snap feature to position windows on the desktop
- Change the date and time
- Use components of a dialog box
- Adjust the volume using the Speaker's slider bar
- Customize the Taskbar
- Add a gadget to the desktop
- Use the Help and Support feature
- Turn on the display of file extensions

Projects Overview

Your department at Worldwide Enterprises has received new computers with the Windows 7 operating system. You will explore the Windows 7 desktop; open, close, and manipulate windows; open a program; customize the Taskbar; add gadgets to the desktop; explore the online help for Windows 7; and turn on the display of file extensions.

Activity 1.1

Exploring the Windows 7 Desktop

The screen that displays when Windows 7 starts is called the **desktop**. This desktop can be compared to the top of a desk in an office. A person places necessary tools—such as pencils, pens, paper, files, calculator—on his or her desktop to perform functions. Similarly, the Windows 7 desktop contains tools for operating the computer. These tools are logically grouped and placed in dialog boxes or windows that can be accessed using the icons located on the desktop.

Project

SNAP

Tutorial 1.1
Exploring the
Windows 7 Desktop

At your department, new computers have been installed with the Windows 7 operating system. You decide to take some time to explore the desktop to familiarize yourself with this new operating system.

1. Complete the step(s) needed to display the Windows 7 desktop.

   Check with your instructor to determine the specific step(s) required to display Windows 7 on your computer at your school. You may need a user name and password to log on to the computer system. When Windows 7 is started, you will see a desktop similar to the one shown in Figure 1.1. Your desktop may contain additional icons or have a different background than the desktop shown in Figure 1.1.

2. Move the mouse on the desk and notice how the corresponding pointer moves in the Windows desktop.

   The **mouse** is a device that controls the pointer that identifies your location on the screen. Move the mouse on the desk (preferably on a mouse pad) and the pointer moves on the screen. For information on mouse terms, refer to Table 1.1 and for information on mouse icons, refer to Table 1.2.

FIGURE 1.1 Windows 7 Desktop

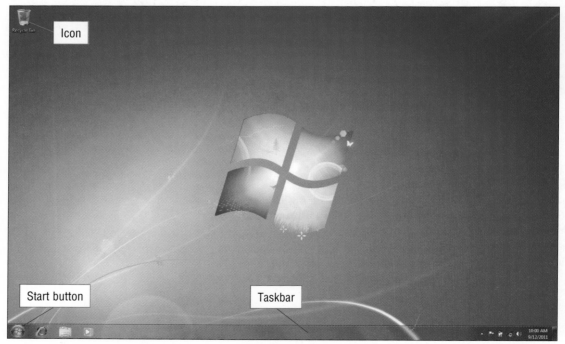

TABLE 1.1 Mouse Terms and Actions

Term	Action
point	Position the mouse pointer on the desired item.
click	Quickly tap a button, usually the left button, on the mouse once.
double-click	Tap the left mouse button twice in quick succession.
drag	Press and hold down the left mouse button, move the mouse pointer to a specific location, and then release the mouse button.

TABLE 1.2 Mouse Icons

Icon	Description
I	The mouse appears as an I-beam pointer in a program screen where you enter text (such as Microsoft Word) and also in text boxes. You can use the I-beam pointer to move the insertion point or select text.
⬉	The mouse pointer appears as an arrow pointing up and to the left (called the arrow pointer) on the Windows desktop and also in other program Title bars, Menu bars, and toolbars.
⬁ ⬀ ⬍ ⬌	The mouse pointer becomes a double-headed arrow (either pointing left and right, up and down, or diagonally) when performing certain functions such as changing the size of a window.
✥	Select an object in a program such as a picture or image and the mouse pointer becomes a four-headed arrow. Use this four-headed arrow pointer to move the object left, right, up, or down.
⬉	When you position the mouse pointer inside selected text in a document (such as a Microsoft Word document) and then drag the selected text to a new location in the document, the pointer displays with a gray box attached, indicating that you are moving the text.
⬉○	When a request is being processed or a program is being loaded, the mouse pointer may display with a moving circle icon beside it. The moving circle means "please wait." When the process is completed, the moving circle disappears.
👆	When you position the mouse pointer on certain icons or hyperlinks, it turns into a hand with a pointing index finger. This image indicates that clicking the icon or hyperlink will display additional information.

3 Move the mouse pointer to the bottom right of the desktop where the current day and time displays at the far right side of the Taskbar. After approximately one second, a pop-up box appears with the current day of the week as well as the current date.

To identify the location of the Taskbar, refer to Figure 1.1.

4 Position the mouse pointer on the Start button ⊞ on the Taskbar and then click the left mouse button.

> Clicking the Start button causes the Start menu to display. The Start menu contains a list of software programs and other options available on your computer. The menu is divided into two columns. Links to programs display in the left column and links to folders, the Control Panel, Devices and Printers, Default Programs, and Help and Support display in the right column. The bottom of the right column Start menu contains options for shutting down, restarting, or logging off the computer.

5 At the Start menu, point to *All Programs* and then click *Accessories* in the left column.

> To point to a menu option, simply position the mouse pointer on the option. Do not click a mouse button. Pointing to *All Programs* causes the left Start column to be replaced with a list of available programs. If the list does not immediately appear, click the mouse button. You may need to scroll down the list if the list is long to locate all available programs. Some programs in the list, such as *Accessories*, display with a folder icon. Clicking a program name with a folder icon expands the list to reveal the individual applications associated with the program.

6 Move the mouse pointer to *Calculator* in the expanded menu and then click the left mouse button.

> Clicking *Calculator* causes the Calculator tool to open and display on the desktop.

7 Close the Calculator by clicking the Close button [X] that displays at the upper right corner of the program.

8 At the Windows 7 desktop, position the mouse pointer on the *Recycle Bin* icon and then double-click the left mouse button.

> Icons provide an easy method for opening programs or documents. Double-clicking the *Recycle Bin* icon displays the Recycle Bin window. When you open a program, a defined work area, referred to as a **window**, appears on the screen.

9 Close the Recycle Bin window by clicking the Close button that displays at the upper right corner of the window.

10 Shut down Windows 7 by clicking the Start button and then clicking the Shut down button located at the bottom of the right column.

Options available from the right-pointing arrow next to the Shut down button include: switch to a different user account; log off or lock the computer; shut down and then immediately restart Windows (Restart); and place the computer in sleep mode or hibernate mode. Wait for Windows to power off the computer automatically. Important data is stored in memory while Windows is running and this data needs to be written to the hard disk before turning off the computer. In some cases, updates that have been downloaded automatically to your computer are installed during a shut down.

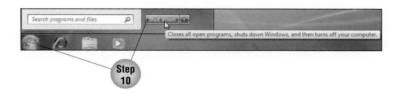

Step 10

Need Help?

Check with your instructor before shutting down Windows 7. If you are working in a computer lab at your school, a shared computer lab policy may prevent you from shutting down the computer. In this case, proceed to the next activity.

In Addition

Putting the Computer to Sleep

In Windows 7, Sleep mode saves all of your work and places the computer in a low power state by turning off the monitor and hard disk. A light on the outside of the computer case blinks or turns color to indicate Sleep mode is active. Reactivate the computer by pressing the Power button on the front of the computer case, or by moving the mouse. After logging on, the screen will display exactly as you left it when you activated Sleep mode. Sleep mode causes Windows to automatically save your work whereas shutting down does not save. Hibernate is an option designed primarily for laptops and is the lowest power setting. Hibernate saves open documents and programs to the hard disk and then turns off the computer.

Activity 1.2

Opening and Manipulating Windows

When you open a program, a defined work area, referred to as a *window*, appears on the screen. You can move a window on the desktop and change the size of a window. The top of a window is called the Title bar and generally contains buttons at the right side for closing the window and minimizing, maximizing, or restoring the size of the window. More than one window can be open at a time and open windows can be cascaded or stacked. The Snap feature in Windows 7 causes a window to "stick" to the edge of the screen when the window is moved to the left or right. When the window is moved to the top of the screen, the window is automatically maximized and when a maximized window is dragged down, the window is automatically restored down.

Project

You will continue your exploration of the Windows 7 desktop by opening and manipulating windows.

Worldwide Enterprises

SNAP

Tutorial 1.2
Opening and Using Windows

1. If necessary, turn on the power to your computer to start Windows. At the Windows 7 desktop, double-click the *Recycle Bin* icon.

   This opens the Recycle Bin window on the desktop. If the Recycle Bin window fills the entire desktop, click the Restore Down button ⬚, which is the second button from the right (immediately left of the Close button) located at the upper right corner of the window.

Recycle Bin

Step 1

2. Move the window on the desktop. To do this, position the mouse pointer on the window Title bar (the bar along the top of the window), hold down the left mouse button, drag the window to a different location on the desktop, and then release the mouse button.

3. Click the Start button on the Taskbar and then click *Computer* in the right column at the Start menu.

   If the Computer window fills the entire desktop, click the Restore Down button, which is the second button from the right (immediately left of the Close button) located at the upper right corner of the window. You now have two windows open on the desktop—Computer and Recycle Bin.

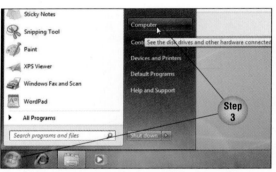

Step 3

4. Make sure the Title bar of the Recycle Bin window is visible (if not, move the Computer window) and then click the Recycle Bin Title bar.

   Clicking the Recycle Bin Title bar makes the Recycle Bin window active, moving it in front of the Computer window.

5. Minimize the Recycle Bin window to the Taskbar by clicking the Minimize button ▬ (located toward the right side of the Recycle Bin Title bar).

   The minimized Recycle Bin window is positioned below the Windows Explorer button (displays as a group of file folders) on the Taskbar. Notice the Windows Explorer button now appears with a button stacked below it.

Step 5

6. Minimize the Computer window to the Taskbar below the Windows Explorer button by clicking the Minimize button located at the right side of the Title bar.

7. Move the pointer over the Windows Explorer button (displays as a group of file folders) located near the left side of the Taskbar.

The two minimized windows are stacked below the Windows Explorer button. Resting the pointer on the Windows Explorer button causes a Thumbnail Preview of each window to display.

8 Click the Thumbnail Preview for the Computer window to redisplay the window on the desktop.

9 Rest the pointer over the Windows Explorer button on the Taskbar and then click the Thumbnail Preview for the Recycle Bin window.

10 Drag the Title bar for the Recycle Bin window to the top of the desktop until the window fills the entire screen and then release the mouse button.

> Dragging a window to the top of the desktop causes the window to automatically maximize. You may need to drag the window up toward the top of the screen for a few seconds until the shape of the window automatically expands to fill the entire desktop area. The Snap feature allows you to resize a window by dragging the window to the edge of a screen. You can also Maximize the window by clicking the Maximize button (displays as a square) adjacent to the Close button at the right end of the Title bar.

11 Drag the Title bar for the Recycle Bin window down from the top of the desktop to restore the window to its previous size before the window was maximized.

12 Right-click on a blank, unused section of the Taskbar and then click *Show windows stacked* at the shortcut menu.

> The Taskbar shortcut menu provides three options to display windows: *Cascade windows,* which places each window in a fanned, single stack with the title bars of each open window visible; *stacked,* which places windows in a horizontal stack with a portion of each window visible; or *side by side,* which places open windows next to each other.

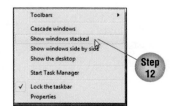

13 Right-click on a blank, unused section of the Taskbar and then click *Cascade windows* at the shortcut menu.

14 Drag the Recycle Bin window off the right edge of the screen until the window resizes to fill one-half the width of the screen and then release the mouse button.

15 Drag the Computer window off the left edge of the screen until the window resizes to fill the remaining width of the screen and then release the mouse button.

> The two windows are placed side-by-side. The Snap feature automatically resizes each window to fill one-half the screen.

16 Close each of the two windows by clicking the Close button (contains a white X) located at the right side of the Title bar.

In Brief

Move Window
1. Position mouse pointer on window Title bar.
2. Hold down left mouse button.
3. Drag window to desired position.
4. Release mouse button.

Stack Windows
1. Right-click an unused section of Taskbar.
2. Click *Show windows stacked* at shortcut menu.

Cascade Windows
1. Right-click an unused section of Taskbar.
2. Click *Cascade windows* at shortcut menu.

In Addition

Sizing a Window

Using the mouse, you can increase or decrease the size of a window. To change the width, position the mouse pointer on the border at the right or left side of the window until it turns into a left- and right-pointing arrow. Hold down the left mouse button, drag the border to the right or left, and then release the mouse button. Complete similar steps to increase or decrease the height of the window using the top or bottom border. To change the width and height of the window at the same time, position the mouse pointer at the left or right corner of the window until the pointer turns into a diagonally pointing double-headed arrow and then drag in the desired direction to change the size.

Activity 1.3

Exploring the Taskbar, Gadgets, and Dialog Box Components

The bar that displays at the bottom of the desktop is called the *Taskbar* and it is divided into three sections: the Start button, the task buttons area, and the notification area. Click the Start button to start a program, use the Help and Support feature, change settings, open files, or shut down the computer. Open programs display as task buttons in the task button area of the Taskbar. You can right-click a blank, unused portion of the Taskbar to display a shortcut menu with options for customizing the Taskbar. The notification area displays at the right side of the Taskbar and contains a clock and the program icons for programs that run in the background on your computer. Gadgets are mini programs you can add to the desktop that provide information at a glance. Display a gadget for information that you frequently use such as a weather update for your area.

Project As you continue exploring Windows 7, you want to learn more about the features available on the Taskbar and you also decide to experiment with adding a gadget to the desktop.

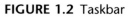
Tutorial 1.3
Exploring the Taskbar

1 At the Windows 7 desktop, click the current time that displays at the far right side of the Taskbar and then click *Change date and time settings*.

Figure 1.2 identifies the components of the Taskbar. Clicking *Change date and time settings* causes the Date and Time dialog box to display. Please refer to Table 1.3 for information on dialog box components.

2 Check to make sure the correct date and time display in the Date and Time dialog box.

If the date is incorrect, click the Change date and time button. At the Date and Time Settings dialog box, click the correct day in the calendar box. If necessary, use the left- or right-pointing arrows to change the calendar display to a different month. To change the time, double-click the hour, minutes, or seconds and then type the correct entry or use the up- and down-pointing arrows to adjust the time. Click OK when finished.

3 Click the Additional Clocks tab located toward the top of the Date and Time dialog box.

At this tab you can add the ability to show the current time for a second clock when you hover or click the mouse over the current time in the Taskbar. For example, you could show the time for Cairo, Egypt in addition to the current time for your time zone.

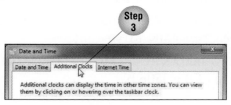

FIGURE 1.2 Taskbar

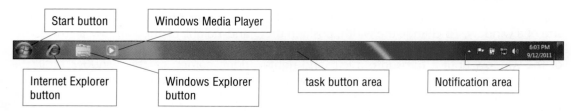

TABLE 1.3 Dialog Box Components (Each component will not be present in every dialog box.)

Name	Image	Function
tabs	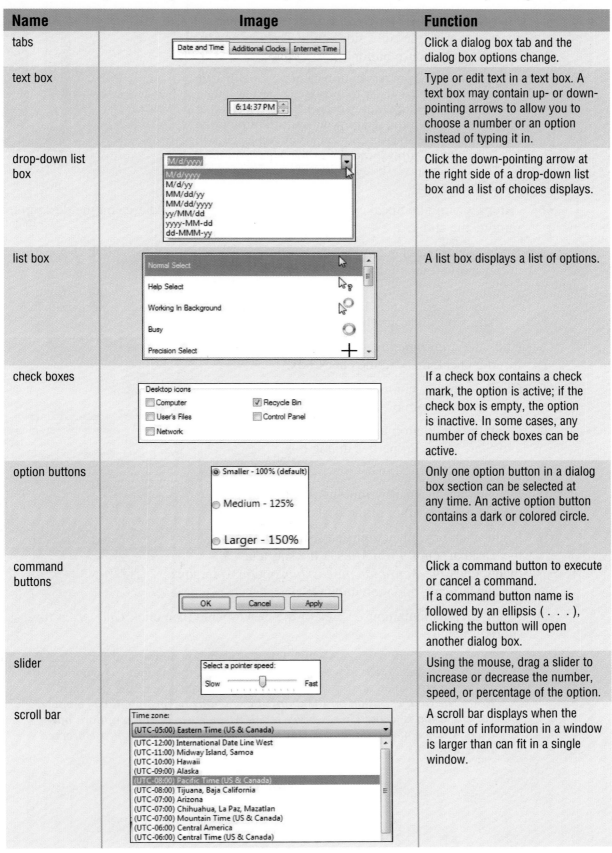	Click a dialog box tab and the dialog box options change.
text box		Type or edit text in a text box. A text box may contain up- or down-pointing arrows to allow you to choose a number or an option instead of typing it in.
drop-down list box		Click the down-pointing arrow at the right side of a drop-down list box and a list of choices displays.
list box		A list box displays a list of options.
check boxes		If a check box contains a check mark, the option is active; if the check box is empty, the option is inactive. In some cases, any number of check boxes can be active.
option buttons		Only one option button in a dialog box section can be selected at any time. An active option button contains a dark or colored circle.
command buttons		Click a command button to execute or cancel a command. If a command button name is followed by an ellipsis (. . .), clicking the button will open another dialog box.
slider		Using the mouse, drag a slider to increase or decrease the number, speed, or percentage of the option.
scroll bar		A scroll bar displays when the amount of information in a window is larger than can fit in a single window.

continues

4 Click OK to close the Date and Time dialog box.

5 Position the mouse pointer on the Speakers button located toward the right side of the Taskbar and then click the left mouse button.

> Clicking the Speakers button causes a slider bar to display. Use this slider to increase or decrease the volume. Click the Mute Speakers button located at the bottom of the slider if you want to turn off the sound. If the Speakers button is not visible, click the up-pointing arrow located near the left side of the notification area. This expands the area to show hidden icons.

Mute Speakers button

6 After viewing the Speakers slider, click in a blank, unused area on the desktop to remove the slider.

7 Right-click on a blank, unused section of the Taskbar and then click *Properties* at the shortcut menu that displays.

> This displays the Taskbar and Start Menu Properties dialog box with the Taskbar tab selected. Notice that the dialog box contains check boxes. A check mark in a check box indicates that the option is active.

8 Click the *Auto-hide the taskbar* option to insert a check mark in the check box.

9 Click the Apply command button located toward the bottom of the dialog box.

10 Click the OK button to close the Taskbar and Start Menu Properties dialog box.

> Notice that the Taskbar is no longer visible.

Step 8

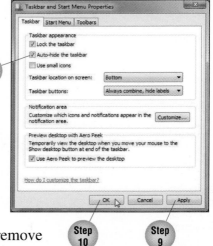

11 Display the Taskbar by moving the mouse pointer to the bottom of the desktop.

12 Right-click on a blank, unused section of the Taskbar, click *Properties* at the shortcut menu, click the *Auto-hide the taskbar* option to remove the check mark, and then click OK.

Step 10

Step 9

13 Right-click a blank, unused area of the desktop and then click *Gadgets* at the shortcut menu.

> The Gadgets window opens with a list of available mini programs for your computer. Clicking a gadget in the window causes the gadget to be added to the desktop in an area called the *Sidebar* (the right side of the desktop). *Note: The Gadget option on the shortcut menu may be missing if the computer you are using is located in a school setting where customization options have been disabled. If you do not see* **Gadget** *on the shortcut menu, please proceed to Activity 1.4.*

14 Double-click the *Calendar* gadget.

The Calendar program is added to the desktop with the current date displayed. By default, gadgets snap to the edge of the screen.

In Brief

Display Date and Time Properties Dialog Box
Click current time at right side of Taskbar and click *Change date and time settings*.

Display Speakers Slider
Click Speakers button on Taskbar.

Display Taskbar and Start Menu Properties Dialog Box
1. Right-click an unused section on Taskbar.
2. Click *Properties* at shortcut menu.

15 Click the Close button in the Gadget window.

16 Move the mouse pointer over the Calendar gadget to view the gadget customization buttons.

Customization options are dependent on the gadget program and some gadgets may not have any customization options.

17 Click the Larger size button (displays as an upward-pointing diagonal arrow) next to the Calendar gadget.

The Calendar expands to show the month above the current date.

In Addition

Using Gadgets While You Work

Additional gadgets are available from the Microsoft website. Click the link to <u>Get more gadgets online</u> in the Gadgets window to view a list of available gadgets that can be downloaded to your computer from the Windows website. For example, consider the following gadgets that can help you be productive at work:
* Add a gadget to show your upcoming appointments from Outlook.

* Add a traffic gadget to provide you with real time traffic conditions.
* Add a clock and customize the clock to display the current time for a different time zone if you regularly communicate with someone on the other side of the country or world.

Activity 1.4

Getting Help in Windows; Displaying File Extensions

Windows 7 includes an on-screen reference guide, called Windows Help and Support, that provides information, explanations, and interactive help on learning Windows features. The Windows Help and Support feature contains complex files with hypertext used to access additional information by clicking a word or phrase. Display the Windows Help and Support window by clicking the Start button on the Taskbar and then clicking *Help and Support* at the Start menu. At the Windows Help and Support window, you can perform such actions as choosing a specific help topic, searching for a keyword or topic, and displaying a Contents list of help topics.

Project

Tutorial 1.4
Getting Help

You decide to use the Windows Help and Support feature to learn how to customize the mouse. You will also turn on the display of file extensions to prepare for the next section with file management projects.

1. Display the Windows Help and Support window by clicking the Start button and then clicking *Help and Support*.

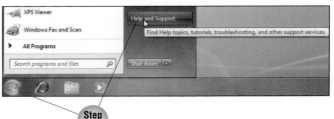

2. At the Windows Help and Support window with the insertion point positioned in the Search Help text box, type **customize the mouse** and press Enter.

3. Click the Change mouse settings hyperlink in the search results list.

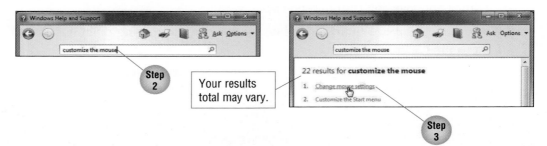

Your results total may vary.

4. Read the paragraph below the title *Change mouse settings* describing the options for customizing the mouse.

5. Click the Go to the Windows website to watch the video (1:56) hyperlink.

> You will need headphones to listen to the audio if you are watching this video in a computer lab that does not have speakers. If necessary, skip to Step 7 if you do not have headphones or cannot hear audio on the computer you are using.

6. At the Change mouse settings Windows web page, click the Play button positioned on the video player screen and watch the video.

7. Return to the Change mouse settings Windows Help and Support window by closing the Internet Explorer window when the video is completed.

8 Click <u>To change how the mouse pointer looks</u> hyperlink.

> The Help topic is expanded below the hyperlink to show the steps for changing the pointer appearance.

9 Read the steps and then click the <u>To change how the mouse pointer looks</u> hyperlink a second time to hide the content.

10 Close the Windows Help and Support window by clicking the Close button located in the upper right corner of the window.

> Worldwide Enterprises requires that employees work with the display of file extensions turned on. This practice helps employees identify source applications associated with a file and often prevents an employee from accidentally opening a file attachment in an email that is likely to contain harmful data.

11 Click the Start button on the Taskbar and then click *Computer* at the Start menu.

12 Click the Organize button in the toolbar and then click *Folder and search options* at the drop-down list.

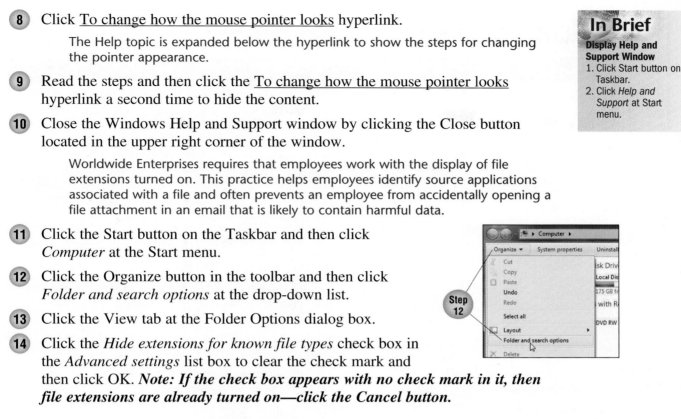

Step 12

13 Click the View tab at the Folder Options dialog box.

14 Click the *Hide extensions for known file types* check box in the *Advanced settings* list box to clear the check mark and then click OK. *Note: If the check box appears with no check mark in it, then file extensions are already turned on—click the Cancel button.*

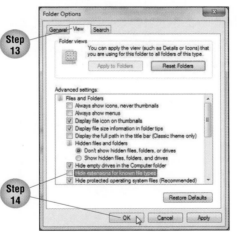

Step 13

Step 14

15 Close the Computer window by clicking the Close button located at the right side of the Title bar.

In Brief

Display Help and Support Window
1. Click Start button on Taskbar.
2. Click *Help and Support* at Start menu.

In Addition

Browsing Help by Topic Lists

You can locate Help information by browsing the Contents list of topics instead of typing key words in the *Search Help* text box. Click the Browse Help button (located next to the Print button) in the Windows Help and Support window toolbar. This displays the Contents list of Help topics. Click the hyperlink to a topic category in the Contents list and then continue clicking hyperlinks until you find the information you need.

Features Summary

Feature	Button	Action
close window	x	Click Close button on Title bar.
Computer window		Click Start button, click *Computer*.
Date and Time dialog box		Click time on Taskbar, click *Change date and time settings*.
Gadgets		Right-click unused area on desktop, click *Gadgets*.
maximize window	□	Drag window to top of screen or click Maximize button on Title bar.
minimize window	—	Click Minimize button on Title bar.
move window on desktop		Drag window Title bar.
restore window	□	Drag maximized window down or click Restore Down button on Title bar.
shut down computer		Click Start button, click *Shut Down*.
Start menu	⊕	Click Start button on Taskbar.
Taskbar and Start Menu Properties dialog box		Right-click unused location on Taskbar, click *Properties* at shortcut menu.
Taskbar shortcut menu		Right-click unused location on Taskbar.
Speakers slider	🔊	Click Speakers button on Taskbar.
Windows Help and Support window		Click Start button, click *Help and Support*.

Knowledge Check

Completion: In the space provided at the right, indicate the correct term, command, or option.

1. This mouse term refers to tapping the left mouse button twice in quick succession. _____
2. Click this button on a window Title bar to reduce the window to a task button on the Taskbar. _____
3. Click this button on a window Title bar to expand the window so it fills the entire screen. _____
4. Click the time located at the right side of the Taskbar and then click this option to open the Date and Time dialog box. _____
5. This is the name of a mini program that you can display on the desktop for information at a glance, such as a calendar. _____
6. Windows Help and Support is accessed from this button on the Taskbar. _____

Skills Review

Review 1 Opening and Manipulating Windows

1. At the Windows 7 desktop, click the Start button on the Taskbar and then click *Documents*. (If the Documents window fills the desktop, drag the window down from the top of the screen or click the Restore Down button located in the upper right corner of the window.)
2. Click the Start button on the Taskbar and then click *Computer*. (If the Computer window fills the desktop, drag the window down from the top of the screen or click the Restore Down button.)
3. Position the mouse pointer on the Computer Title bar, hold down the left mouse button, and then drag the Computer window so the Documents Title bar is visible.
4. Click the Documents Title bar to make it the active window.
5. Right-click on a blank, unused section on the Taskbar and then click *Cascade windows* at the shortcut menu.
6. Click the Minimize button (located toward the right side of the Title bar) on the Documents Title bar to reduce the window to a task button below the Windows Explorer button on the Taskbar.
7. Click the Minimize button on the Computer window to reduce the window to a task button on the Windows Explorer button on the Taskbar.
8. Point to the Windows Explorer button on the Taskbar and then click the Thumbnail preview for the Computer window to restore the Computer window on the desktop.
9. Point to the Windows Explorer button on the Taskbar and then click the Thumbnail preview for the Documents window to restore the Documents window on the desktop.
10. Drag the Documents window to the top of the screen until the window expands to fill the entire screen and then release the mouse button.

11. Drag the Documents window down from the top of the screen to restore the window to its previous size and then release the mouse button.
12. Drag the Documents window off the right edge of the screen until the window snaps to the right edge and fills approximately one-half the width of the screen and then release the mouse button.
13. Drag the Computer window off the left edge of the screen until the window snaps to the left edge and fills the remaining width of the screen and then release the mouse button.
14. Close the Documents window.
15. Close the Computer window.

Review 2 Exploring the Taskbar and Gadgets

1. At the Windows 7 desktop, click the time that displays in the notification area at the right side of the Taskbar and then click *Change date and time settings*.
2. At the Date and Time dialog box, click the Change date and time button. Click the right arrow in the calendar to display the next month (from the current month).
3. Click the OK button twice.
4. Click the Start button, point to *All Programs*, click *Accessories*, and then click *Notepad*. Notepad is a program used for creating and editing text files.
5. Close Notepad by clicking the Close button located at the right side of the Notepad Title bar.
6. Right-click a blank, unused section of the desktop, and click *Gadgets*. Double-click the clock gadget to add a clock to the desktop and then close the Gadgets window.
Note: If you do not see Gadgets *on the shortcut menu, then customization options have been disabled on the computer you are using. You will not be able to add a gadget to the desktop.*

Skills Assessment

Assessment 1 Manipulating Windows

1. Click the Start button and then click *Pictures*. (If the Pictures window fills the entire desktop, drag the window down from the top of the screen or click the Restore Down button.)
2. Click the Start button and then click *Music*. (If the Music window fills the entire desktop, drag the window down from the top of the screen or click the Restore Down button.)
3. Stack the two windows.
4. Make the Pictures window the active window and then reduce it to a task button on the Taskbar.
5. Reduce the Music window to a task button on the Taskbar.
6. Restore the Pictures window.
7. Restore the Music window.
8. Arrange the two windows side-by-side on the desktop with each window filling one-half the width of the screen.
9. Close the Music window and then close the Pictures window.

Assessment 2 Customizing the Taskbar and Adding a Gadget

1. At the Windows 7 desktop, display the Date and Time dialog box.
2. Change the current hour one hour ahead and then close the dialog box.
3. Display the Speakers slider bar, drag the slider to increase the volume, and then click the desktop outside the slider to close it.
4. Display the Taskbar and Start Menu Properties dialog box, change the Taskbar location on screen to *Top*, and then close the dialog box. (Notice that the Taskbar is now positioned along the top edge of the screen.)
5. Open the Gadgets window and add a gadget of your choosing to the desktop. *Note: Skip Steps 5–6 if* **Gadgets** *are not available on the computer you are using.*
6. Customize the gadget by dragging the *gadget* icon to another location on the desktop. If necessary, change other gadget options depending on the gadget you added. For example, if you added the Weather gadget, change the weather update to display the weather for your geographic location.

Assessment 3 Restoring the Taskbar and Removing a Gadget

1. At the Windows 7 desktop, display the Date and Time dialog box and change the date and time to today's date and the current time.
2. Display the Speakers slider bar and then drag the slider to the original position that the volume was at before you increased the volume in Assessment 2.
3. Display the Taskbar and Start Menu Properties dialog box and change the Taskbar location back to *Bottom*.
4. Remove the gadgets that you have added to the desktop in this section by right-clicking each gadget and then clicking *Close gadget*, or by moving the mouse over the gadget and then clicking the Close button that appears at the top right of the gadget.

Windows 7 SECTION 2

Maintaining Files and Customizing Windows

Skills

- Browse the contents of storage devices
- Change folder and view options
- Create a folder
- Rename a folder or file
- Select, move, copy, and paste folders or files
- Delete files/folders to and restore files/folders from the Recycle Bin
- Explore the Control Panel
- Use Search tools to find programs, folders and/or files
- Customize the desktop
- Change screen resolution

Student Resources

Before beginning the activities in Windows Section 2, copy to your storage medium the Windows folder on the Student Resources CD. This folder contains the data files you need to complete the projects in Windows Section 2.

Projects Overview

Worldwide Enterprises

You will explore options for browsing and viewing folders and files and then organize folders and files for your department at Worldwide Enterprises. This organization includes creating and renaming folders and moving, copying, renaming, deleting, and restoring files. You will also search for specific files and customize your desktop to the corporate computer standard.

Performance Threads

Organize files for Performance Threads including creating folders and copying, moving, renaming, and deleting files.

First Choice TRAVEL

Organize files for First Choice Travel including creating folders and copying, moving, renaming, and deleting files. Assist your supervisor by searching for information on setting up a computer for multiple users and how to work with libraries.

Activity 2.1

Browsing Storage Devices and Files in a Computer Window

Open a Computer window to view the various storage devices connected to your computer. The Content pane of the Computer window displays an icon for each hard disk drive and each removable storage medium such as a CD, DVD, or USB device. Next to each storage device icon, Windows provides the amount of storage space available as well as a bar with the amount of space used up shaded with color. This visual cue allows you to see at a glance the proportion of space available relative to the capacity of the device. Double-click a device icon in the Content pane to change the display to show the contents stored on the device. You can display contents from another device or folder using the Navigation pane or the Address bar of the Computer window.

Project

Worldwide Enterprises

You decide to explore the contents of the various storage devices on the computer you are using as you become familiar with the Windows 7 environment and are getting ready to organize your filing system.

Note: Before beginning the projects in this section, make sure you have copied the WindowsS2 folder from the Student Resources CD to your storage medium. If necessary, refer to the inside back cover of this textbook for instructions on how to copy a folder from the Student Resources CD to your storage medium such as a USB flash drive.

SNAP

Tutorial 2.1
Browsing Devices and Files

1. If necessary, insert into an empty USB port the storage medium that you are using for the files in this course. If an AutoPlay window opens with options for viewing the content on the drive, close the window by clicking the Close button located at the right end of the Title bar.

FIGURE 2.1 Computer Window

Address bar

toolbar

Organize ▾   System properties   Uninstall or change a program   Map network drive   Open Control Panel

★ Favorites
   ■ Desktop
   ■ Downloads
   ■ Recent Places

■ Libraries
   ■ Documents
   ♪ Music
   ■ Pictures
   ■ Videos

■ Homegroup

■ Computer
   ■ Local Disk (C:)
   ■ HP_RECOVERY (D:)
   ■ HP_TOOLS (F:)
   ■ KINGSTON (G:)

■ Network

Computer ▸   Search Computer

◢ Hard Disk Drives (3)
   Local Disk (C:)
   163 GB free of 222 GB

   HP_RECOVERY (D:)
   2.03 GB free of 9.00 GB

   HP_TOOLS (F:)
   0.99 GB free of 0.99 GB

◢ Devices with Removable Storage (2)
   DVD RW Drive (E:)

   KINGSTON (G:)
   1.84 GB free of 1.86 GB

The Content pane may vary depending on the installed devices and configuration of drives.

OFFICEWIN7LT   Workgroup: WORKGROUP   Memory: 3.00 GB
Processor: Intel(R) Core(TM)2 Duo ...

Detail pane

navigation pane

Content pane

2 At the Windows desktop, click the Start button on the Taskbar and then click *Computer* at the Start menu.

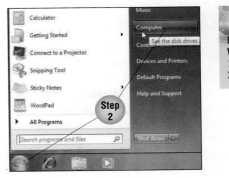

> The Computer window displays similar to the one shown in Figure 2.1.

In Brief

Display Computer Window
1. Click Start button
2. Click *Computer*.

3 Double-click the icon for the hard disk drive named *Local Disk (C:)*.

> The Computer window changes to show you the files and folders in the Content pane that are stored on the local hard disk drive assigned drive letter C:. Notice also that the Address bar in the Computer window updates to show the location where you are viewing *Local Disk (C:)* within *Computer*. You can navigate back using either the Back button or by clicking *Computer* in the Address bar.

4 Click the Back button to return to the previous list.

5 Double-click the icon for the storage medium upon which you copied the WindowsS2 folder. *Note: The screens shown in this section show* **KINGSTON (G:)** *as the storage medium in the Computer window. Your icon label and drive letter may vary.*

> USB flash drives are shown in the section of the Content pane labeled Devices with Removable Storage. Each device is assigned an alphabetic drive letter by Windows, usually starting at F or G and continuing through the alphabet depending on the number of removable devices that are currently in use. For example, if you had two removable devices inserted into two USB ports at the same time, one might be labeled G and the other H. Next to the drive letter, a label is shown depending on the manufacturer of the USB flash drive. If no manufacturer label is present, Windows displays *Removable Disk*.

6 Double-click the *WindowsS2* folder to view the contents of the folder in the Content pane.

7 Look at the Address bar and notice how the Address bar displays the path to the current content list: Computer ▶ KINGSTON (G:) ▶ WindowsS2. *Note: Your drive name and letter next to* **Computer** *may vary.*

> You can navigate to any other device or folder using the Address bar by clicking a drive or folder name, or by clicking the right-pointing black arrow to view a drop-down list of folders or other devices.

8 Click *Computer* in the Address bar.

9 Click the right-pointing arrow ▶ next to *Computer* in the Address bar and then click the drive letter representing the removable storage device with the WindowsS2 folder. For example, *KINGSTON (G:)*.

10 Click *Desktop* in the *Favorites* section of the Navigation pane.

> You can also change what is displayed in the Content pane by clicking the device or folder name in the Navigation pane. Click the white right-pointing arrow next to a device or folder name in the Content pane to expand the list and view what is stored within the item.

11 Close the Computer window.

Activity 2.2

Changing Folder and View Options

You can change the view to show the contents in various ways such as by size of icon, by list, by tiles, or by content. With the Content pane in Details view, you can click a column heading to sort the list or change from ascending order to descending order. In Activity 1.4, you displayed file extensions by opening the Folder Options dialog box and clearing the check mark for the *Hide extensions* *for known file types* option on the View tab. This turned on the display of file extensions when you were viewing a list of files. File extensions are helpful for identifying the program with which the file was created. Other ways in which you can customize the environment at the Folder Options dialog box include having each folder open in its own window, opening an item with a single-click, and applying the current view option to all folders.

Project You decide to experiment with various folder and view options as you continue to become acquainted with the Windows 7 environment and get ready to organize your filing system.

Worldwide Enterprises

Step 2

1 Click the Windows Explorer button [icon] on the Taskbar.

The Libraries window opens. For a description of libraries, please refer to the In Addition section at the end of this activity.

2 Click the drive letter representing your storage medium in the *Computer* section in the Navigation pane.

SNAP

Tutorial 2.2
Creating a Folder

3 Double-click the *WindowsS2* folder in the Content pane.

4 Click the down-pointing arrow next to the Views button located at the right end of the toolbar (displays with the ScreenTip *More options*).

5 Drag the slider to the *Large Icons* option and then release the mouse button.

6 Click the Views button once (click on the button and not on the down-pointing arrow) to change the current view.

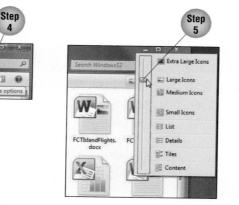
Step 4   Step 5   Step 6

7 Click the Views button again to change to another view.

Each time you click the Views button you change the current view by cycling through five view options: Large Icons, List, Details, Tiles, and Content.

8 With the folder now displayed in Details view, click the *Name* column heading to change the view to sort the list in descending order by name.

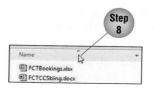
Step 8

9 Click the *Name* column again to restore the list to ascending order by name.

10 Click the Organize button on the toolbar and then click *Folder and search options* at the drop-down list to open the Folder Options dialog box.

11 Click the *Open each folder in its own window* option in the *Browse folders* section of the General tab and then click OK.

12 Close the Computer window.

13 Click the Windows Explorer button on the Taskbar and then click the drive representing your storage medium in the *Computer* section in the Navigation pane.

14 Double-click the *WindowsS2* folder.

> Notice that this time a new window opened with the WindowsS2 content list layered on top of the original window.

15 Close the WindowsS2 folder window.

16 Click the Organize button, click *Folder and search options*, click the Restore Defaults button located near the bottom of the General tab, and then click OK.

17 Close the Computer window.

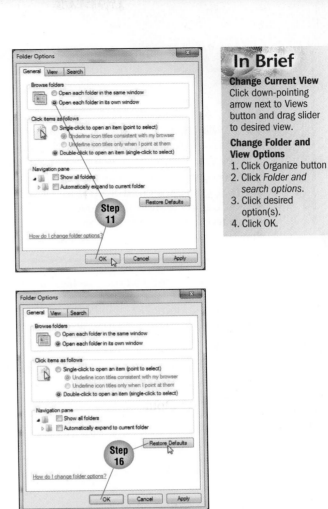

In Brief

Change Current View
Click down-pointing arrow next to Views button and drag slider to desired view.

Change Folder and View Options
1. Click Organize button
2. Click *Folder and search options*.
3. Click desired option(s).
4. Click OK.

In Addition

Windows Libraries

While browsing the Computer window you may have noticed a section in the Navigation pane with the title *Libraries*. Libraries are new to Windows 7 and are a tool you can use to keep track of and/or organize files that have something in common regardless of where they are stored. A library does not store the actual file but instead keeps track of locations where the source files are stored. When you click the library name in the Navigation pane, the library displays all of the files in the locations that it is keeping track of associated with that library. For example, in the Pictures library you could have Windows show you the contents of a Pictures folder on the local disk, from another folder on an external hard disk, and from a folder on a networked computer. Four default libraries are created when Windows 7 is installed: Documents, Music, Pictures, and Videos. You can create your own library and customize the locations associated with the default libraries. You will explore Libraries more in an Assessment at the end of this section.

Changing the Default View for All Folders

You can set a view to display by default for all folders of a similar type (such as all disk drive folders or all Documents folders). To do this, change the current view to the desired view for the type of folder that you want to set, such as a disk drive folder or a documents folder. Next, click the Organize button, click *Folder and search options*, and then click the View tab at the Folder Options dialog box. Click the Apply to Folders button in the *Folder views* section and click OK. Click Yes at the Folder Views message asking if you want all folders of this type to match this folder's view settings.

Activity 2.3

Creating a Folder; Renaming a Folder or File

As you begin working with programs, you will create files in which data (information) is saved. A file might be a Word document, an Excel workbook, or a PowerPoint presentation. Files on your computer may also be pictures or videos that you transferred from your digital camera. As you begin creating files, developing a system in which to organize those files becomes important so that you can easily retrieve a document or photograph when you need it. The first step in organizing your files is to create folders. Creating a folder is like creating a separate container in which you can place similar types of files.

File management tasks such as creating a folder, renaming a folder or file, and copying and moving files and folders can be completed at a variety of locations including at the Computer and Documents windows.

Project You need to organize files for your department at Worldwide Enterprises by first creating a folder.

SNAP

Tutorial 2.3
Selecting, Copying, Moving, and Renaming Files

1. At the Windows desktop, click the Start button on the Taskbar and then click *Computer* at the Start menu.

2. Double-click the icon representing your storage medium on which you copied the WindowsS2 folder.

3. Click the New folder button New folder on the toolbar.

    A new folder icon is added in the Content pane with the text *New folder* already selected.

4. With the text *New folder* already selected next to the folder icon, type **Revenue** and then press Enter. Note that as soon as you type the *R* in *Revenue*, the existing text *New Folder* is immediately deleted.

    This changes the folder name from *New Folder* to *Revenue*.

5. You can also create a new folder using a shortcut menu. To begin, right-click in a blank, unused area in the Content pane, point to *New*, and then click *Folder*.

6. With the text *New folder* already selected next to the folder icon, type **Contracts** and then press Enter.

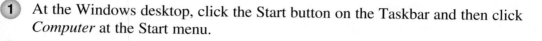
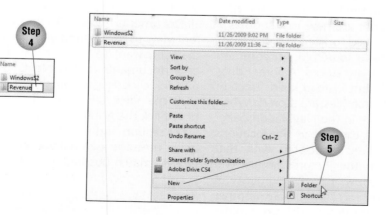

7. Click once on the *Revenue* folder to select the folder.

8 Click the Organize button on the toolbar and then click *Rename* at the drop-down list.

9 With the Revenue folder already selected, type **Income** and then press Enter.

> You can also use the shortcut menu to rename a file or folder.

10 Right-click the *Contracts* folder and then click *Rename* at the shortcut menu.

11 With the Contracts folder already selected, type **Administration** and then press Enter.

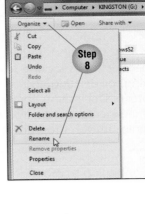

In Brief

Create New Folder
1. Display Computer window.
2. Double-click device on which to create folder.
3. Click New folder button on toolbar.
4. Type folder name, then press Enter.

Rename Folder or File
1. Display Computer window.
2. Navigate to desired drive and/or folder.
3. Right-click file to be renamed.
4. At shortcut menu, click *Rename*.
5. Type new file name, press Enter.

12 Double-click the *WindowsS2* folder.

13 Right-click the file ***FCTExcelSalesCom.xlsx*** and then click *Rename* at the shortcut menu.

14 Type **FCTSalesCommissions** and then press Enter.

> Notice when you rename a file that Windows does not select the file extension. Programs such as Microsoft Word and Microsoft Excel automatically assign a file extension to each document or workbook. These file extensions should remain intact. If you rename or remove a file extension by accident, Windows prompts you with a message that the file may no longer be usable and asks you if you are sure.

15 Close the Computer window.

In Addition

More about Organizing Files into Folders

Think of folders on the computer the same way you think of file folders in which you would store paper documents in your filing cabinet. Generally, you put similar types of documents into the same folder. For example, all of your rent receipts might be placed inside a file folder on which you have written the label *Rent* on the folder tab. Similarly, on the computer, you could create a folder named *Rent* and store all of the electronic copies of all of your rental documents within that folder. On the computer, a folder can have another folder stored inside it. The folder within the folder is referred to as a *subfolder*. For example, you may have thousands of pictures stored on your computer. Saving all of the pictures in one folder named *Pictures* would be too cumbersome when the content list contains thousands of images. You would be scrolling a long time to locate a particular picture. Instead, consider creating subfolders in the Pictures folder so that related pictures are grouped together in one place.

Activity 2.4

Selecting and Copying Folders and Files

In addition to creating and renaming files and folders, file management activities include selecting, moving, copying, or deleting files or folders. Open a Computer or Documents library window to perform file management tasks. You can use options in the Organize button drop-down list or shortcut menu options. More than one file or folder can be moved, copied, or deleted at one time. Select adjacent files/folders using the Shift key and select nonadjacent files/folders using the Ctrl key. When selecting multiple files or folders, you may want to change the view in the Computer window.

Project

Worldwide Enterprises

Tutorial 2.3
Selecting, Copying, Moving, and Renaming Files

Continuing to organize files for your department, you will copy files to the Income folder you created.

1. At the Windows desktop, open the Computer window.

2. Double-click the icon representing your storage medium on which you copied the WindowsS2 folder.

Step 2

3. Double-click the *WindowsS2* folder in the Content pane.

4. Click the down-pointing arrow next to the Views button located at the right end of the toolbar (displays with the ScreenTip *More options*) and then drag the slider to *List* at the pop-up list.

Step 4

5. Click the file named **WEExcelRevenues.xlsx** in the Content pane.

   Click once to select a file. Windows displays file properties in the Details pane at the bottom of the Computer window for a selected file and provides options to add or modify property information.

6. Hold down the Shift key, click the file named **WETable02.docx**, and then release the Shift key.

   Clicking **WETable02.docx** while holding down the Shift key causes all files from **WEExcelRevenues.xlsx** through **WETable02.docx** to be selected.

7. Position the mouse pointer within the selected group of files, right-click, and then click *Copy* at the shortcut menu.

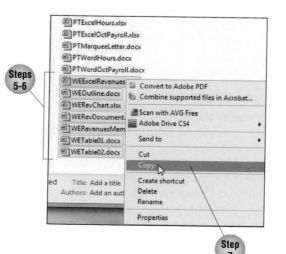

Steps 5-6

Step 7

8 Click the Back button located left of the Address bar.

9 Double-click the *Income* folder.

10 Right-click in the Content pane and click *Paste* at the shortcut menu.

> When a large file or large group of files is copied, Windows displays a message box with a progress bar to indicate the approximate time required to copy the files. The message box closes when the copy is complete.

In Brief

Copy Adjacent Files to New Folder
1. Display Computer window.
2. Navigate to desired drive and/or folder.
3. If necessary, change current view to *List*.
4. Click first file name.
5. Hold down Shift key and then click last file name.
6. Right-click in selected group of files and click *Copy*.
7. Navigate to desired destination drive and/or folder.
8. Right-click in blank area of Content pane and click *Paste*.

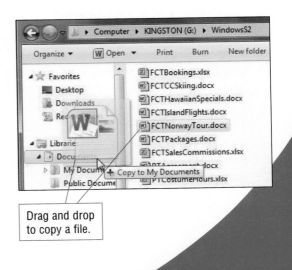

11 Click in a blank area of the Content pane to deselect the file names.

12 Close the Computer window.

In Addition

Copying by Dragging

You can copy a file or folder to another location using a drag-and-drop technique. To do this, open a Computer or Documents library window and display the desired file or folder in the Content pane. Position the mouse pointer on the file or folder to be copied, hold down the left mouse button, drag to the destination drive or folder name in the *Favorites, Libraries,* or *Computer* list, and then release the mouse button. By default, if you drag a file from one disk drive to another, Windows uses a Copy command. If you are dragging from one folder to another on the same disk drive, hold down the Ctrl key while dragging to Copy. Alternatively, you could open two windows and arrange them side-by-side on the desktop. In one window, display the files that you want to copy. In the other window, display the destination folder. Select the files to be copied and then hold down the Ctrl key while dragging the selected files to the destination window.

Drag and drop to copy a file.

Activity 2.5

Moving Folders and Files

Move files in a Computer or Documents library window in a manner similar to copying files. Select the file(s)/folder(s) that you want to move, position the mouse pointer over the selected file(s)/folder(s), right-click, and then click *Cut* at the shortcut menu. Navigate to the desired destination location, right-click a blank area in the Content pane, and then click *Paste* at the shortcut menu. You can also use the *Cut* and *Paste* options from the Organize button drop-down list.

Project

After further review of the files you copied into the Income folder, you decide to create another folder and move some of the files from the Income folder into the new folder.

1 At the Windows desktop, display the Computer window.

2 Double-click the icon representing your storage medium on which you copied the WindowsS2 folder.

3 Click the New folder button on the toolbar.

4 Type **Distribution** and then press Enter.

5 Double-click the *Income* folder.

6 Change the current view to *List*.

7 Click once on **WEOutline.docx**.

> Clicking once on the file selects the file name to identify the item that you want to move; double-clicking the file would instruct Windows to open Word and then open the document.

8 Hold down the Ctrl key, click once on **WETable01.docx**, click once on **WETable02.docx**, and then release the Ctrl key.

> Using the Ctrl key, you can select nonadjacent files.

9 Click the Organize button in the toolbar and then click *Cut* at the drop-down list.

10 Click the Back button at the left of the Address bar.

11 Double-click the *Distribution* folder.

12 Click the Organize button in the toolbar and then click *Paste* at the drop-down list.

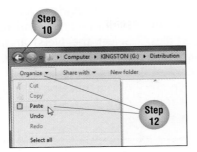

In Brief

Move Nonadjacent Files to New Folder
1. Display Computer window.
2. If necessary, change current view to *List*.
3. Navigate to desired drive and/or folder.
4. Click first file name.
5. Hold down Ctrl key, click each additional file name, and then release Ctrl key.
6. Click Organize button and click *Cut*.
7. Navigate to desired destination drive and/or folder.
8. Click Organize button and click *Paste*.

13 Click in a blank area of the Content pane to deselect the file names.

14 Click the Back button at the left of the Address bar.

15 Double-click the *Income* folder.

Notice the three files **WEOutline.docx**, **WETable01.docx**, and **WETable02.docx** no longer reside in the Income folder since Cut and Paste moves the files.

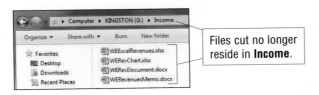

16 Close the Computer window.

In Addition

Displaying Disk or Drive Properties

Information such as the amount of used space and free space on a disk or drive and the disk or drive hardware is available at the Properties dialog box. To display the Local Disk (C:) Properties dialog box, similar to the one shown at the right, display a Computer window. At the Computer window, right-click *Local Disk (C:)* and then click *Properties* at the shortcut menu. With the General tab selected, information displays about used and free space on the drive. Click the Tools tab to display error-checking, backup, and defragmentation options. The Hardware tab displays the name and type of all disk drives as well as the device properties. The Sharing tab displays options for sharing folders and you can change user permissions at the Security tab. To enable quota management where you can assign space limits for each user click the Quota tab. View restore points at the Previous Versions tab.

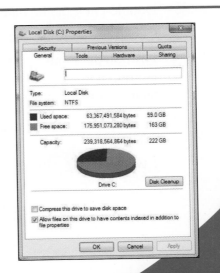

Activity 2.6

Deleting Folders and Files to the Recycle Bin

Deleting the wrong file can be a disaster, but Windows helps protect your work with the Recycle Bin. The Recycle Bin acts just like an office wastepaper basket; you can "throw away" (delete) unwanted files, but you can "reach in" to the Recycle Bin and take out (restore) a file if you threw it away by accident. Files or folders deleted from a hard disk drive are automatically sent to the Recycle Bin. Files or folders deleted from a removable disk, such as your USB flash drive, are deleted permanently. To delete a file or folder, display a Computer or Documents library window and then display in the Content pane the file(s) and/or folder(s) you want deleted. Select the file(s) and/or folder(s) and then press the Delete key on the keyboard, or right-click the selected files and click *Delete* at the shortcut menu. At the message asking you to confirm the deletion, click the Yes button.

Project

Continuing to organize your files, you will copy a file and a folder from your storage medium to the My Documents folder on the hard drive and then delete a file and folder to the Recycle Bin.

Tutorial 2.3
Selecting, Copying, Moving, and Renaming Files

Tutorial 2.4
Using the Recycle Bin

1 At the Windows desktop, display the Computer window.

2 Double-click the icon representing your storage medium on which you copied the WindowsS2 folder.

3 Click once to select the *Distribution* folder.

4 Position the mouse pointer over the selected folder name, hold down the left mouse button, drag to *Documents* in the *Libraries* section of the Navigation pane, and then release the mouse.

As you point to the Documents library in the Navigation pane, Windows displays the ScreenTip *Copy to My Documents*.

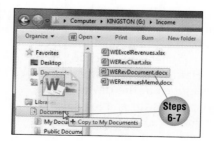

5 Double-click the *Income* folder.

6 Click once to select the ***WERevDocument.docx*** file.

7 Position the mouse pointer over the selected file name, hold down the left mouse button, drag to *Documents* in the *Libraries* section of the Navigation pane, and then release the mouse.

8 Click *Documents* in the *Libraries* section of the Navigation pane to display the files and folders associated with the Documents library in the Content pane.

> The Documents library displays the contents of two folders by default: My Documents and another folder named Public Documents. My Documents is the default folder in which files and folders are stored that are associated with the Documents library. You can add and remove folders associated with a library. You will learn more about libraries in an assessment at the end of this section.

9 Click once to select the *Distribution* folder.

In Brief
Delete File/Folder
1. Display Computer window and navigate to desired drive and/or folder.
2. Click file/folder to select it.
3. Press Delete key.
4. At confirmation message, click Yes.

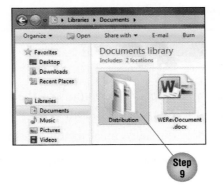

Step 9

10 Press the Delete key on the keyboard.

11 At the Delete Folder message asking if you are sure you want to move this folder to the Recycle Bin, click Yes.

Step 11

12 Right-click **WERevDocument.docx** in the Content pane and then click *Delete* at the shortcut menu.

13 Click Yes at the Delete File message asking if you are sure you want to move this file to the Recycle Bin.

14 Close the Documents library window.

In Addition

Dragging and Dropping Files/Folders

Another method for deleting a file or folder is to drag the file or folder to the *Recycle Bin* icon on the desktop. This drops the file you are dragging into the Recycle Bin. You can also select multiple files or folders and then drag and drop the selected items in the *Recycle Bin* icon on the desktop.

Activity 2.7

Restoring Folders and Files; Emptying Files from the Recycle Bin

A file or folder deleted to the Recycle Bin can be restored. Restore a file or folder with options at the Recycle Bin window. Display this window by double-clicking the *Recycle Bin* icon on the Windows desktop. A restored file or folder is removed from the Recycle Bin and returned to its original location. Just like a wastepaper basket can become overfilled with too much waste, the Recycle Bin can have too many files and folders stored in it. Emptying the Recycle Bin permanently deletes all files and folders. You can also delete a single file or folder from the Recycle Bin (rather than all files and folders).

Project You decide to experiment with the Recycle Bin and learn how to restore a file and then empty the Recycle Bin.

Worldwide Enterprises

SNAP

Tutorial 2.4
Using the Recycle Bin

1 At the Windows desktop, display the contents of the Recycle Bin by double-clicking the *Recycle Bin* icon.

Step 1

The Recycle Bin window displays similar to the one shown in Figure 2.2.

2 At the Recycle Bin window, change the current view to *List*.

3 Click once to select **WERevDocument.docx**.

Depending on the contents of the Recycle Bin, you may need to scroll down the Recycle Bin list to display this document.

Step 4

Organize ▾   Empty the Recycle Bin   Restore this item

☆ Favorites   📄 Distribution
💻 Desktop   📄 WERevDocument.
📥 Downloads

Move the selected items from the Recycle Bin to their original locations on your computer.

Step 3

FIGURE 2.2 Recycle Bin Window

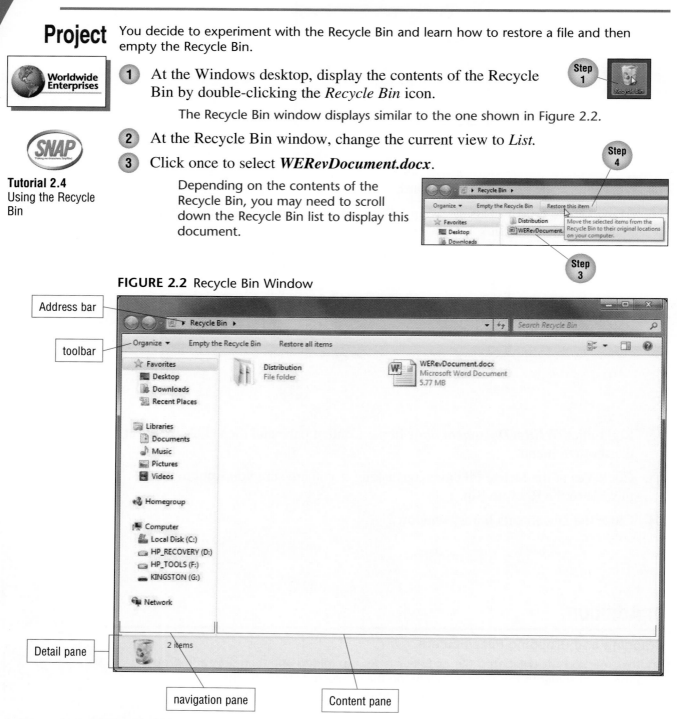

Address bar

toolbar

Detail pane

navigation pane

Content pane

4 Click the Restore this item button on the toolbar.

> The file is removed from the Recycle Bin and returned to the location from which it was deleted. Once a file or folder is moved into the Recycle Bin you are limited to the following options: Restore, Cut, or Delete.

5 Click once to select the *Distribution* folder.

6 Click the Restore this item button on the toolbar.

7 Close the Recycle Bin window.

8 At the Windows desktop, open the Computer window.

9 Click *Documents* in the *Libraries* section of the Navigation pane.

> Notice that the file and folder that you had deleted have been restored from the Recycle Bin.

10 Delete the file and folder you restored. To do this, click once on the *Distribution* folder, hold down the Ctrl key, click once on the **WERevDocument.docx** file name, and then release the Ctrl key.

11 Press the Delete key.

12 At the Delete Multiple Items message box asking if you are sure you want to move these 2 items to the Recycle Bin, click Yes.

13 Close the Documents library window.

14 At the Windows desktop, double-click the *Recycle Bin* icon.

15 Click once on the *Distribution* folder, hold down the Ctrl key, click once on the **WERevDocument.docx** file name, and then release the Ctrl key.

16 Click the Organize button and then click *Delete* at the drop-down list.

17 At the Delete Multiple Items message box asking if you are sure you want to permanently delete these 2 items, click Yes.

> To empty the entire contents of the Recycle Bin, click the Empty the Recycle Bin button on the toolbar. At the message asking you to confirm the deletion, click Yes.

18 Close the Recycle Bin window.

In Brief

Restore File/Folder from Recycle Bin
1. At Windows desktop, double-click *Recycle Bin* icon.
2. At Recycle Bin window, click file/folder to select it (or select multiple files/folders).
3. Click Restore this item button on toolbar.

Delete File/Folder from Recycle Bin
1. At Windows desktop, double-click *Recycle Bin* icon.
2. At Recycle Bin window, click file/folder to select it (or select multiple files/folders).
3. Press Delete key.
4. At confirmation message, click Yes.

In Addition

Showing or Hiding the Recycle Bin on the Desktop

You can choose whether the Recycle Bin icon displays on the desktop or not. By default, the Recycle Bin is shown on the desktop. To remove it, right-click a blank area on the desktop and then click *Personalize* at the shortcut menu. At the Control Panel, Appearance and Personalization, Personalization window, click *Change desktop icons* in the left pane. At the Desktop Icon Settings dialog box shown at the right, clear the check mark in the *Recycle Bin* check box and then click OK. Note the other desktop icons you can choose to show or hide at this dialog box.

Activity 2.8

Exploring the Control Panel

The Control Panel offers a variety of categories each containing icons you can use to customize the appearance and functionality of your computer. Display the Control Panel window by clicking the Start button and then clicking *Control Panel* at the Start menu. At the Control Panel window, available categories display in the Content pane. (By default, the Control Panel window opens in Category view. If your window opens in Large icons view or Small icons view, click the down-pointing arrow next to *View by* located near the top right of the Control Panel window and then click *Category* at the drop-down menu.) Click a category or hyperlinked option below the category and a list of tasks, a list of icons, or a separate window displays.

Project You want to know how to customize your computer so you decide to explore the Control Panel window.

1. At the Windows desktop, click the Start button and then click *Control Panel* at the Start menu.

   The Control Panel window displays similar to the one shown in Figure 2.3.

Tutorial 2.5
Exploring the Control Panel

2. At the Control Panel window, click the Appearance and Personalization hyperlink.

3. After viewing the tasks and icons available in the Appearance and Personalization category, click the Back button.

4. Click the Hardware and Sound hyperlink.

FIGURE 2.3 Control Panel Window

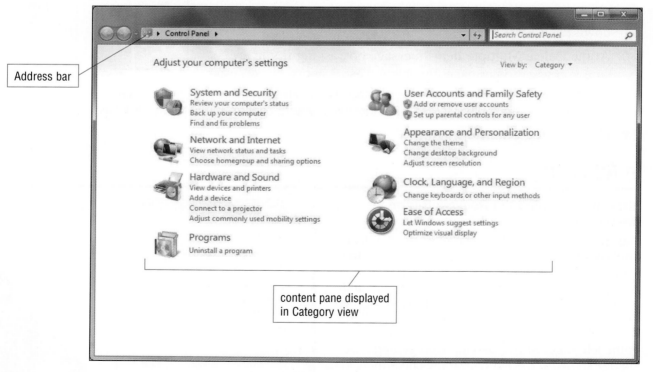

5 Click the <u>Mouse</u> hyperlink in the Devices and Printers category.

> This displays the Mouse Properties dialog box.

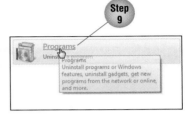

Step 5

In Brief
Display Control Panel
1. Click Start button.
2. Click *Control Panel*.

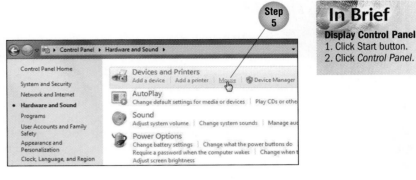

6 At the Mouse Properties dialog box, click each tab and review the available options.

7 Click the Cancel button to close the Mouse Properties dialog box.

8 Click the Back button.

9 Click the <u>Programs</u> hyperlink in the Content pane.

10 At the Programs window, click the <u>Programs and Features</u> hyperlink.

> This is where you would uninstall a program on your computer.

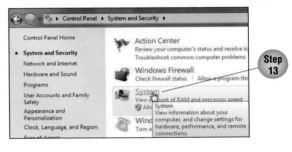

Step 9

11 Click the Back button twice.

12 Click the <u>System and Security</u> hyperlink.

13 Click the <u>System</u> hyperlink.

14 Maximize the window.

15 Close the Control Panel window.

Step 13

In Addition

Changing the Control Panel View

By default, the Control Panel window displays categories of tasks in what is called Category view. This view can be changed to *Large icons* or *Small icons*. In the Large icons view shown at the right, options for the control panel are shown alphabetically by icon name. To change from Category view to Large icons or Small icons, click the down-pointing arrow next to *View by* located near the top right of the Control Panel window (just below the Search text box) and then click the desired option at the drop-down list.

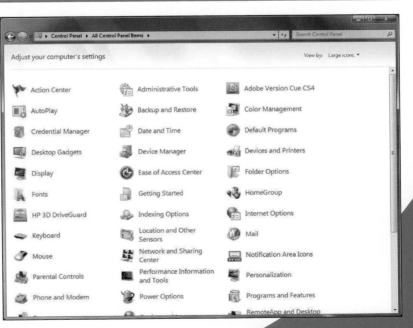

Activity 2.9

Using Windows Search Tools

Windows includes a *Search programs and files* text box at the bottom of the Start menu. You can quickly find a program or document by typing the first few letters of the program or document name. If your computer has many programs and documents stored on the hard disk, using the search tool allows you to locate what you need in a few seconds and with minimal mouse clicks. At the right of the Address bar in a Computer or Documents library window is a Search text box. Type the first few letters of a document you need to locate in this text box and the Content pane is filtered instantly to display items that match your criterion.

Windows performs fast searching because the operating system maintains an index in the background in which all of the key words associated with the programs and files on your computer are referenced. This index is constantly updated as you work. When you type an entry in a Search text box, Windows consults the index rather than conducting a search of the entire hard drive.

Project

You want to experiment with the Search capabilities of Windows to see how you can locate programs and documents more quickly in the future.

Worldwide Enterprises

SNAP

Tutorial 2.6
Searching for a File or a Folder

1. At the Windows desktop, click the Start button.

2. With an insertion point blinking in the *Search programs and files* text box located just above the Start button, type **calc**.

As soon as you begin typing an entry in the *Search programs and files* text box, Windows begins to display in the left column programs and/or documents that begin with the same letters that you type or that are associated with the same letters in a keyword. Notice that the Calculator program is shown below the heading *Programs* at the top of the list. Depending on the contents stored in the computer you are using, additional items may be displayed below *Calculator*.

3. Click *Calculator* in the *Programs* list at the top of the Start menu.

4. Close the Calculator window.

5. Click the Start button.

6. Type **snip** in the *Search programs and files* text box.

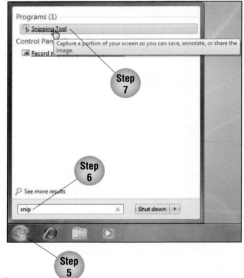

Windows lists all file elements stored on the computer you are using that are associated with the text *snip*, including the snipping tool, which is a program that you can use to create and save images from your screen.

7. Point to Snipping Tool displayed in the *Programs* list and read the ScreenTip that appears. Point to any other items in the list and read the ScreenTip.

8. Press the Esc key.

Pressing Esc clears the search results list and the *Search programs and files* text box.

9. Click *Computer* to open a Computer window.

10 Double-click the icon representing your storage medium on which you copied the WindowsS2 folder.

11 Double-click the *WindowsS2* folder and then change the current view to Large Icons.

12 Click in the *Search WindowsS2* text box located at the right of the Address bar.

13 Type **werev**.

As soon as you begin typing in the *Search WindowsS2* text box, Windows filters the list of files in the Content pane to those that begin with the letters that you type. Notice that the Address bar displays *Search Results in WindowsS2* to indicate that the files displayed that match your criteria were limited to the current folder. If you want to search other locations or by other file properties, click one of the option buttons located at the bottom of the Content pane below the title *Search again in*.

In Brief

Search for Programs or Document from Start Menu
1. Click Start button.
2. Type search criteria in *Search programs and files* text box.

Search for Document
1. Open Computer or Documents library window.
2. Type search criteria in Search text box.

Step 13

search results for files that begin with **werev**

14 With the insertion point still positioned in the Search text box, press the Backspace key to remove *werev* and then type **pte**.

The list of files in the Content pane is updated to display those files that begin with *PTE*.

15 Double-click the file named ***PTExcelOctPayroll.xlsx***.

The file opens in Microsoft Excel.

16 Close Microsoft Excel by clicking the Close button at the right end of the Title bar.

17 Close the Computer window.

In Addition

Using a Wildcard Character in a Search

When conducting a search you can type an asterisk (*) in place of any number of letters, numbers, or symbols within a file name to find files based on a pattern of characters. For example, typing ***hours*** would locate the files listed at the right in your WindowsS2 folder. Notice the pattern is that all files have *hours* in the middle of the file name but any number of other characters before and after *hours*.

PTWordHours.docx
PTExcelHours.xlsx
PTCostumeHours.xlsx

Activity 2.10

Customizing the Desktop

The Windows operating environment is very customizable. You can change background patterns and colors; specify a screen saver that will display when the screen sits idle for a specific period of time; or change the scheme for windows, title bars, and system fonts. Make these types of changes at the Control Panel Personalization window. Many companies adopt a corporate computer standard for display properties.

Project

SNAP

Tutorial 2.7
Customizing the Desktop

You decide to look at the customization options available for the desktop and set the screen resolution to the corporate standard in place for computers at Worldwide Enterprises.

Note: Before completing this activity, check with your instructor to determine if you can customize the desktop. If necessary, practice these steps on your home computer.

1 At the Windows desktop, position the arrow pointer on a blank area of desktop, right-click the mouse, and then click *Personalize* at the shortcut menu.

2 At the Control Panel, Appearance and Personalization, Personalization window, click the <u>Desktop Background</u> hyperlink located along the bottom of the window.

Make a note of the current background.

3 If necessary, scroll up or down the available images, click an image that you like, and click the Save changes button.

Click an image that you like at Step 3.

4 Click the <u>Screen Saver</u> hyperlink.

Make a note of the current screen saver name.

5 Click the button below *Screen saver* and then click *Photos* at the drop-down list.

A preview of the screen saver displays in the screen located toward the top of the dialog box.

6 Click the up- or down-pointing arrow next to the *Wait* text box until *1* displays.

7 Click OK.

8 Click the <u>Window Color</u> hyperlink.

Make a note of the color next to *Current color* below the color boxes.

9 Click the *Ruby* color box (last option in top row) and click the Save changes button. ***Note: Skip this step if your window does not display as shown below.***

10 Close the Control Panel window. Let the screen remain idle for one minute until the screen saver displays.

11 Move the mouse to deactivate the screen saver and then double-click the *Recycle Bin* icon.

Notice the Ruby color scheme applied to the Taskbar and the window borders.

12 Close the Recycle Bin window.

13 Reinstate the original desktop settings by right-clicking a blank area of the desktop, clicking *Personalize* at the shortcut menu, and then returning the Desktop Background, Screen Saver, and Window Color to the original settings.

In the next steps, you will set the screen resolution to *1280 × 800 pixels,* which is the corporate standard for all desktops at Worldwide Enterprises. Standardizing display properties is considered a best practice in large companies that support many computer users.

14 Right-click a blank area of the desktop and click *Screen resolution* at the shortcut menu.

15 At the Appearance and Personalization, Display, Screen Resolution window, look next to *Resolution* at the current setting displayed on the button. For example, your screen may be currently set at *1440 × 900.* If your screen is already set to *1280 × 800*, proceed to Step 17.

Screen resolution is set in pixels. **Pixel** is the abbreviation of *picture element* and refers to a single dot or point on the display monitor. Changing the screen resolution to a higher number of pixels means that more information can be seen on the screen as items are scaled to a smaller size.

continues

Click the button next to *Resolution* and then drag the slider bar up or down as necessary until the screen resolution is set to *1280 × 800*. If necessary, check with your instructor for alternate instructions.

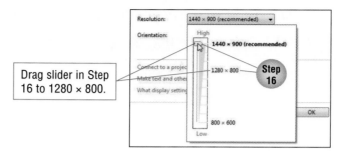

Drag slider in Step 16 to 1280 × 800.

Step 16

 Click in the window outside the slider box, click OK, and then click the Keep Changes button at the Display Settings message box asking if you want to keep the display settings.

> The screens in this textbook use 1280 × 800 screen resolution. If the computer you are using has a different screen resolution, what you will see on your screen may not match the textbook illustrations. For additional information, refer to the In Addition below.

In Addition

Windows Screen Resolution and the Microsoft Office Ribbon

Before you begin learning the applications in the Microsoft Office 2010 suite, take a moment to check the display settings on the computer you are using. The ribbon in the Microsoft Office suite adjusts to the screen resolution setting of your computer monitor. Computer monitors set at a high resolution will have the ability to show more buttons in the ribbon than will a monitor set to a low resolution. The illustrations in this textbook were made with a screen resolution display set at 1280 x 800 pixels. Below, the Word ribbon is shown three ways: at a lower screen resolution (1024 x 768 pixels), at the screen resolution featured throughout this textbook, and at a higher screen resolution (1440 x 900 pixels). Note the variances in the ribbon in all three examples. If possible, set your display to 1280 x 800 pixels to match the illustrations you will see in this textbook.

Appearance of Microsoft Word ribbon with computer monitor set at:

1024 x 768 screen resolution

1280 x 800 screen resolution

1440 x 900 screen resolution

Features Summary

Feature	Button/Icon	Action
Computer window		Click Start button, click *Computer*.
Control Panel window		Click Start button, click *Control Panel*.
copy selected files/folders		At Computer or Documents library window, select files/folders to be copied, right-click in selected group, click *Copy*, navigate to destination folder, right-click in Content pane, click *Paste*.
create new folder	New folder	At Computer or Documents library window, right-click, point to *New*, click *Folder*.
delete selected files/folders		At Computer or Documents library window, select files to be deleted, press Delete key, click Yes.
folder options		Click Organize button, click *Folder and search options*.
move selected files/folders		At Computer or Documents library window, select files/folders to be moved, right-click in selected group, click *Cut*, navigate to destination folder, right-click in Content pane, click *Paste*.
Recycle Bin	Recycle Bin	Double-click *Recycle Bin* icon.
rename file/folder		At Computer or Documents library window, right-click file or folder, click *Rename*, type new name, press Enter.
restore files/folders from Recycle Bin	Restore this item	At Recycle Bin, select desired files/folders, click *Restore this item* button in toolbar.
search for programs or documents	Search programs and files	Click Start button, type search criterion in *Search programs and files* text box; or, open Computer or Documents library window, type search criterion in Search text box.
select adjacent files/folders		Click first file/folder, hold down Shift key, click last file/folder.
select nonadjacent files/folders		Click first file/folder, hold down Ctrl key, click any other files/folders.

Knowledge Check

Completion: In the space provided at the right, indicate the correct term, command, or option.

1. Navigate to any other device or folder from the current device and folder using the Navigation pane or this bar in the Computer window. _____
2. Specify the option to open each folder in its own window at this dialog box. _____
3. Click this button on the toolbar to create a new folder in the Computer window. _____
4. Change the display of files and folders in the Computer window to List or Details using this button on the toolbar. _____
5. To select adjacent files, click the first file, hold down this key, and then click the last file. _____
6. To select nonadjacent files, click the first file, hold down this key, and then click any other desired files. _____
7. Click this button to display in the Content pane the files in the previous folder viewed. _____
8. Click this option at the Organize button drop-down list to move the selected files. _____
9. Files deleted from the hard drive are sent here. _____
10. Open this window to display a list of categories or icons in which you can customize the appearance and functionality of your computer. _____
11. Type a search criterion in this text box at the Start menu to locate a program. _____
12. Customize the desktop such as by changing the background, screen saver, and color option at this window. _____

Skills Review

Review 1 Browsing Devices and Changing the View

1. Open the Computer window.
2. Change the view to *Large Icons*.
3. Change the folder option to open each folder in its own window.
4. Display the contents of your storage medium.
5. Display the contents of the WindowsS2 folder.
6. Change the view to *Details*.
7. Close the WindowsS2 window.
8. Close the window for your storage medium.
9. Change the folder option to open each folder in the same window.
10. Change the view to *Tiles* and then close the Computer window.

Review 2 Creating a Folder

1. Open the Computer window.
2. Display the contents of your storage medium.
3. Right-click a blank area in the Content pane, point to *New*, and then click *Folder*.
4. Type **Worksheets** and then press Enter.
5. Close the window.

Review 3 Selecting, Copying, Moving, and Deleting Files

1. Open the Computer window.
2. Display the contents of your storage medium.
3. Display the contents of the WindowsS2 folder.
4. Change the current view to *List* if the display is not already set to List.
5. Click once on *FCTBookings.xlsx* to select it, hold down the Shift key, and then click *FCTPackages.docx*.
6. Right-click within the selected group of files and click *Copy*.
7. Click the Back button.
8. Double-click the *Worksheets* folder.
9. Right-click in the Content pane, click *Paste*, and then click in a blank area to deselect the files.
10. Click the Back button and then double-click *WindowsS2*.
11. Click *WEExcelRevenues.xlsx* in the Content pane, hold down the Ctrl key, and then click *WERevChart.xlsx*.
12. Click the Organize button and then click *Cut* at the drop-down list.
13. Click the Back button and then double-click *Worksheets*.
14. Click the Organize button and then click *Paste* at the drop-down list.
15. Click the right-pointing arrow next to your storage medium in the Address bar and then click *WindowsS2* at the drop-down list.
16. Click *FCTCCSkiing.docx* in the Content pane, hold down the Ctrl key, and then click *FCTNorwayTour.docx*.
17. Press the Delete key and then click Yes at the Delete Multiple Items confirmation message.
18. Close the Computer window.

Review 4 Renaming a File

1. Open the Computer window.
2. Display the contents of your storage medium.
3. Display the contents of the WindowsS2 folder.
4. Right-click *WETable01.docx* and then click *Rename*.
5. Type **WEPreviewDistribution** and then press Enter.
6. Right-click *WETable02.docx* and then click *Rename*.
7. Type **WEGeneralDistribution** and then press Enter.
8. Close the Computer window.

Review 5 Searching for Files

1. Open the Computer window.
2. Display the contents of the WindowsS2 folder on your storage medium.
3. Type *rev* in the *Search WindowsS2* text box.
4. Press the Esc key until the filter is cleared and all files are redisplayed.
5. Type *excel* in the *Search WindowsS2* text box.
6. Close the Computer window.
7. Click the Start button.
8. Type *word* in the *Search programs and files* text box. Notice the programs and files displayed in the Start menu.
9. Click in the desktop outside the Start menu to close the menu.

Skills Assessment

Assessment 1 Managing Folders and Files

1. Create a new folder on your storage medium named PerformanceThreads.
2. Display the contents of the WindowsS2 folder.
3. If necessary, change the view to List.
4. Copy all files beginning with *PT* to the PerformanceThreads folder.
5. If necessary, display the contents of the PerformanceThreads folder and change the view to List.
6. Create a new folder within PerformanceThreads named Payroll. (A folder created within a folder is referred to as a subfolder.)
7. Move **PTExcelOctPayroll.xlsx** and **PTWordOctPayroll.docx** from the PerformanceThreads folder into the Payroll subfolder.
8. Delete **PTMarqueeLetter.docx** from the PerformanceThreads folder.
9. Rename the file named **PTAgreement.docx** located in the PerformanceThreads folder to **CostumeAgreement.docx**.

Assessment 2 Managing Folders and Files

1. Display the contents of your storage medium.
2. Create a new folder named FirstChoiceTravel.
3. Display the contents of the WindowsS2 folder.
4. Copy all files beginning with FCT to the FirstChoiceTravel folder.
5. If necessary, display the contents of the FirstChoiceTravel folder and change the view to List.
6. Create a new folder within FirstChoiceTravel named Accounting.
7. Create a new folder within the Accounting folder named Commissions.
8. Move **FCTBookings.xlsx** from the FirstChoiceTravel folder into the Accounting subfolder.
9. Move **FCTSalesCommissions.xlsx** from the FirstChoiceTravel folder into the Commissions subfolder.
10. Delete **FCTIslandFlights.docx** from the FirstChoiceTravel folder.
11. Rename the file named **FCTPackages.docx** located in the FirstChoiceTravel folder to **FCTOregonNevadaPkgs.docx**.

Assessment 3 Managing Folders and Files

1. Display the contents of your storage medium.
2. Create a new folder named WorldwideEnt.
3. Display the contents of the WindowsS2 folder.
4. Copy all files beginning with *WE* to the WorldwideEnt folder.
5. If necessary, display the contents of the WorldwideEnt folder and change the view to List.
6. Delete **WEOutline.docx** from the WorldwideEnt folder.
7. Rename the folder named WorldwideEnt to WorldwideEnterprises.

Assessment 4 Deleting Folders and Files

Note: Check with your Instructor before completing this Assessment in case you need to show him or her that you completed the Activities within this section before deleting the folders.

1. Display the contents of your storage medium.
2. Delete the folder named Administration.
3. Delete the folder named Distribution.
4. Delete the folder named Income.

Assessment 5 Copying Folders from the Student CD to Your Device

1. Display the contents of the Marquee student CD that accompanies this textbook in the Computer window.
2. Display the contents of the Word folder in the Content pane.
3. Select all of the subfolders in the Word folder and copy them to your storage medium.
4. Display the contents of the Excel folder in the Content pane and then copy all of the subfolders in the Excel folder to your storage medium.
5. Display the contents of the Access folder in the Content pane and then copy all of the subfolders in the Access folder to your storage medium.
6. Display the contents of the PowerPoint folder in the Content pane and then copy all of the subfolders in the PowerPoint folder to your storage medium.
7. Copy the AudioandVideo folder to your storage medium.
8. Display the contents of the Integrating folder and then copy all of the subfolders to your storage medium.

Assessment 6 Searching for Information on User Accounts

1. You have been asked by your supervisor at First Choice Travel to learn about sharing your computer with other users. Your supervisor is considering adding an evening shift and wants to find out how existing computer equipment can be set up for other users. Using the Windows Help and Support feature, search for information on user accounts. *Hint: Type user accounts in the Search Help text box and press Enter. Consider reading the topic* **What is a user account?** *as your first step*.
2. Locate topics with information about the three types of user accounts: *Standard*, *Administrator*, and *Guest*. Specifically, your supervisor is interested in which type of account would be best suited for day-to-day work and why this type of account is your recommendation.
3. Create a new folder on your storage medium named WindowsEOS.
4. Compose a memo to your instructor that describes the differences between the three types of user accounts and then provide your recommendation for which type of account should be used for individual users on each shift.
5. Save the memo and name it **WS2-UserAccounts** in the WindowsEOS folder.
6. Print the memo.

Assessment 7 Searching for Information on Windows Libraries

1. You have been asked by your supervisor at First Choice Travel to learn about a new feature in Windows 7 called Libraries. Your supervisor is not sure about the difference between a library and a normal folder for managing folders and files. She wants you to find out how a library can be useful to her and how to create her own library and add folders to it. She also wonders if the default libraries Windows created can have other folders added to them. Using the Windows Help and Support feature, search for information on libraries. *Hint: Type libraries in the Search Help text box and press Enter. Consider reading the topic* **Working with libraries** *as your first step*.
2. Locate topics with information about libraries.
3. Compose a memo to your instructor that provides her with answers to the following questions:
   a. What is the difference between a library and a folder?
   b. How can I create my own library?
   c. How can I add or remove folders in a library?
   d. What is the limit on the number of folders that can be added to a library?
4. Save the memo and name it **WS2-Libraries** in the WindowsEOS folder.
5. Print the memo.

Internet
Microsoft®
Explorer 8.0

Nita Rutkosky

Pierce College at Puyallup, Puyallup, Washington

Denise Seguin

Fanshawe College, London, Ontario

Audrey Rutkosky Roggenkamp

Pierce College at Puyallup, Puyallup, Washington

Paradigm
PUBLISHING

St. Paul • Los Angeles • Indianapolis

Contents

Managing Editor   Sonja Brown
Developmental Editor   Brenda Palo
Production Editor   Donna Mears
Cover and Text Designer   Leslie Anderson
Copy Editors   Susan Capecchi and Laura Nelson
Desktop Production   Ryan Hamner and Jack Ross
Proofreader   Laura Nelson
Testers   Amy McGuire, Rob Neilly, and Lindsay Ryan
Indexers   Ina Gravitz and Sandi Schroeder

Care has been taken to verify the accuracy of information presented in this book. However, the authors, editors, and publisher cannot accept responsibility for Web, email, newsgroup, or chat room subject matter or content, or for consequences from application of the information in this book, and make no warranty, expressed or implied, with respect to its content.

Trademarks: Some of the product names and company names included in this book have been used for identification purposes only and may be trademarks or registered trade names of their respective manufacturers and sellers. The authors, editors, and publisher disclaim any affiliation, association, or connection with, or sponsorship or endorsement by, such owners.

We have made every effort to trace the ownership of all copyrighted material and to secure permission from copyright holders. In the event of any question arising as to the use of any material, we will be pleased to make the necessary corrections in future printings. Thanks are due to the aforementioned authors, publishers, and agents for permission to use the materials indicated.

Internet Explorer
Browsing the Internet Using Internet Explorer 8.0

Skills

- Visit sites by typing a web address
- Use hyperlinks to navigate to web pages
- Search for information using search tools
- Narrow a search using advanced search options
- Download content from a web page
- Evaluate content found on a web page

Projects Overview

Visit websites for two national parks. Search for websites pertaining to historical costume design. Use advanced search options to locate information on skydiving companies in the state of Oregon. Locate and save images of Banff National Park. Find information on Apollo lunar missions and evaluate the source and date of publication of the information.

Visit the home pages for the *New York Times* and *USA Today* and read a current article.

Search for and locate the web page for the Theatre Department at York University and the web page for the Department of Drama at New York University.

Locate a website for a snow skiing resort in Utah and then download an image from the web page.

Activity 1.1

Navigating the Internet Using Web Addresses

In today's world, the Internet is used for a variety of tasks including locating information about any topic one could imagine, communicating with others through email or social networking sites, and buying and selling goods and services. In this section, you will use Microsoft's Internet Explorer web browser to locate information on the Internet. A **web browser** is a software program that allows you to view the text, images, and other content that has been stored on a web page on the Internet. **Uniform Resource Locators**, referred to as URLs, identify web servers that have content on the Internet. A URL is often referred to as a **web address**. Just as you need a specific mailing address in order to identify your location to the post office, a web server has a unique web address that identifies its location to the Internet.

Project

Dennis Chun, the location director for Marquee Productions is gathering information for a new movie project. He has asked you to browse the websites for Yosemite National Park and Glacier National Park.

Note: Print instructions are not included in the project steps in this section. Check with your instructor to find out if you need to print the web pages that you visit.

SNAP

Tutorial 1.1
Browsing the Internet

1 Make sure you are connected to the Internet and that the Windows desktop displays.

> Check with your instructor to determine if you need to complete steps for accessing the Internet.

2 Open Microsoft Internet Explorer by clicking the *Internet Explorer* icon ⊙ located on the Taskbar.

> Figure 1.1 identifies the elements of the Internet Explorer, version 8, window. The web page that displays in your Internet Explorer window may vary from what you see in Figure 1.1. Refer to Figure 1.2 on the next page for descriptions of the tools available in Internet Explorer.

3 At the Internet Explorer window, click in the Address bar (refer to Figure 1.1), type **www.nps.gov/yose**, and then press Enter.

> For information on web addresses (URLs), please read the *In Addition* section at the bottom of the next page.

Step 3

FIGURE 1.1 Internet Explorer Window

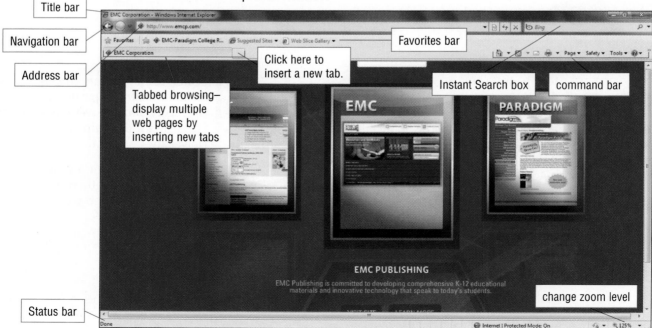

(4) Scroll down the home page for Yosemite National Park by pressing the Down Arrow key on the keyboard, or by clicking the down-pointing arrow on the vertical scroll bar located at the right side of the Internet Explorer window.

> The first web page that appears for a website is called the site's home page.

In Brief

Display Specific Website
1. At Windows desktop, click *Internet Explorer* icon in Taskbar.
2. Click in Address bar, type web address, press Enter.

(5) Display the home page for Glacier National Park by clicking in the Address bar, typing **www.nps.gov/glac**, and then pressing Enter.

> As you begin to type the first few characters in the Address bar, a drop-down list appears below the Address bar with the names of websites that you have already visited that are spelled the same. Matched characters are displayed in blue for quick reference. If the web address you want displays in the drop-down list, you do not need to type the entire address—simply click the desired web address in the drop-down list.

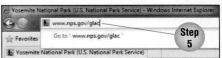

(6) Click the hyperlink to <u>HISTORY & CULTURE</u> displayed in the navigation area at the left side of the page.

> Most web pages contain hyperlinks that you click to connect to another page within the website or to another site on the Internet. Hyperlinks display in a web page in a variety of ways such as underlined text, text in a navigation bar, buttons, images, or icons. To use a hyperlink, position the mouse pointer on the hyperlink until the mouse pointer turns into a hand and then click the left mouse button.

(7) Scroll down and view the content on the History & Culture web page.

(8) Click the Back button on the Navigation bar to return to the Glacier National Park home page.

(9) Click the Forward button on the Navigation bar to return to the History & Culture page.

FIGURE 1.2 Browsing, Navigating, and Other Tools

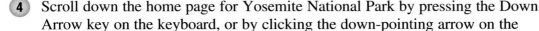

In Addition

Understanding URLs (Web Addresses)

URLs (Uniform Resource Locators) are used to identify locations on the Internet. The format of a URL is *http://server-name.domain*. The *http* stands for HyperText Transfer Protocol, the language used to transfer data within the World Wide Web. The colon and slashes separate the protocol from the server name. The server name in http://www.microsoft.com is *microsoft*. The last part of the URL is the domain to which the server belongs. For example, *.com* refers to "commercial," indicating that the URL is for a commercial company. Other domains include *.edu* for "educational," *.gov* for "government," and *.mil* for "military."

Activity 1.2

Finding Information Using Search Tools

If you do not know the web address for a specific site or you want to find information on the Internet but do not know what site to visit, complete a search with a search engine. A variety of search engines are available on the Internet, each offering the opportunity to search for specific information. One method for searching for information is to click in the Instant Search box, type a keyword or phrase related to your search, and then click the Search button or press Enter. Another method for completing a search is to go to the home page for a search engine and use options at the search engine's site.

Project

The research coordinator for Marquee Productions has asked you to locate sites with historical costumes for a new movie project. Specifically, she has asked you to locate information on Elizabethan and Renaissance costumes.

Tutorial 1.2
Searching for Specific Sites

1 With the Internet Explorer window active, click in the Instant Search box (currently displays *Bing*) located at the right end of the Internet Explorer Navigation bar.

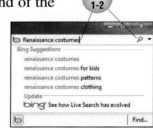

Steps 1-2

> Bing is Microsoft's online search portal and is the default search engine used. Bing organizes search results by topic category and provides related search suggestions.

2 Type **Renaissance costumes** and then click the Search button (or press Enter).

> As you begin to type, Bing displays search suggestions in a list below the Instant Search box. You can click a suggested phrase in the list instead of completing your typing. Characters in each suggested search phrase that match your typing are displayed in blue for quick reference.

3 Scroll down the search results list and click a hyperlink that interests you by positioning the mouse pointer on the hyperlink text until the pointer turns into a hand and then clicking the left mouse button.

4 Browse the content at the page you selected.

5 Use the Yahoo! search engine to find sites on Renaissance costumes by clicking in the Address bar, typing **www.yahoo.com**, and then pressing Enter.

6 At the Yahoo! website, type **Renaissance costumes** in the Search text box and then press Enter.

> As you begin to type, the Yahoo! search assist feature displays search suggestions in a list below the Search text box. Similar to Bing, you can click a suggested phrase in the list instead of completing your typing. Characters in each suggested search phrase that match your typing are displayed in another color for quick reference. Notice that Bing and Yahoo!'s suggested search phrases are different. Each search engine has its own way of cataloguing and indexing search terms.

Web	Images	Video	Local	Shopping	More

Renaissance costumes   **Web Search**

Search Assist: On | Off

medieval renaissance costumes
cheap renaissance costumes
plus size renaissance costumes
italian renaissance costumes
children's renaissance costumes

Step 6

(7) Click a hyperlink to a site that interests you.

(8) Use the Google search engine to find sites on Elizabethan costumes by clicking in the Address bar, typing **www.google.com**, and then pressing Enter.

(9) At the Google website, type **Elizabethan costumes** in the Search text box and then press Enter.

Notice that Google also provides a drop-down list of suggested search phrases based on the characters you typed. Additionally, Google includes the number of results for each suggested search phrase. This information is useful as you can see at a glance which search phrase will produce the most or the least links.

Step 9

Elizabethan costumes|	Advanced Search Language Tools
elizabethan costumes shakespeare	295,000 results
elizabethan costumes for women	162,000 results
elizabethan costumes for men	167,000 results
elizabethan costumes for romeo and juliet	55,700 results
elizabethan costumes to buy	107,000 results
elizabethan costumes romeo and juliet	30,600 results
elizabethan costumes for actors	100,000 results
elizabethan costumes for sale	126,000 results
elizabethan costumes pictures	121,000 results
elizabethan costumes hire	40,400 results
	close

(10) Click a hyperlink to a site that interests you.

(11) Use the Dogpile search engine to find sites on Elizabethan costumes by clicking in the Address bar, typing **www.dogpile.com**, and then pressing Enter.

Dogpile is a *metasearch* search engine. A metasearch search engine sends your search phrase to other search engines and then compiles the results in one list. You benefit by typing the search phrase once but accessing results from a wider group of search engines that index web pages. Dogpile provides search results from Google, Yahoo!, Bing, and Ask.

(12) At the Dogpile website, type **Elizabethan costumes** in the Search text box and then press Enter.

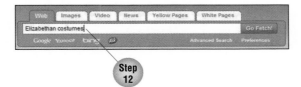

Step 12

(13) Click a hyperlink to a site that interests you.

In Addition

Adding Frequently Used Web Pages to Favorites

If you visit a web page on a regular basis, add the page to the Favorites Center or add a button to the web page on the new Favorites bar. To add the web page to the Favorites bar, display the web page and then click the Add to Favorites bar button (displays as a yellow star with a green right-pointing arrow) located next to the Favorites button. If the Favorites bar is not visible, right-click in an unused section between the browsing tabs and the Command Bar and click *Favorites Bar* to turn the toolbar on. If you prefer, you can add the website to the Favorites Center list. To do this, click the Favorites button and then click the Add to Favorites button at the Favorites Center. At the Add a Favorite dialog box that displays, make sure the information in the *Name* text box is the title by which you want to refer to the website (if not, type your own title for the page) and then click the Add button. The new website is added to the Favorites Center drop-down list. Jump quickly to the site by clicking the Favorites button and then clicking the site name at the drop-down list.

Activity 1.3

Refining Your Search Using Advanced Search Tools

The Internet contains an extraordinary amount of information. Depending on what you are searching for on the Internet and the search engine you use, some searches can result in several thousand "hits" (sites). Wading through a large number of sites can be very time-consuming. You can achieve a more targeted search results list if you hone your search technique by using the advanced search options offered by a search engine. Effective searching is a skill you obtain through practice. Look for an advanced search options link at your favorite search engine site the next time you need to locate information and experiment with various methods to limit the search results.

Project

SNAP

Tutorial 1.3
Researching Information

The stunt coordinator at Marquee Productions has asked you to locate information on skydiving companies in the state of Oregon.

1. With the Internet Explorer window active, click in the Address bar, type **www.yahoo.com**, and then press Enter.

2. At the Yahoo! home page, click the Web Search button | **Web Search** | next to the Search text box.

3. Click the more link located above the Search text box and then click *Advanced Search* at the drop-down list.

   Step 3

   Web | Images | Video | Local | Shopping | more ▾
   Answers
   Directory
   Jobs
   News
   Sports
   All Search Services
   Advanced Search
   Preferences
   Advertising Programs
   Page Tour
   About This Page

   © 2010 Yahoo! | Page Tour | P ... | Submit Your Site

   YAHOO!

4. At the Advanced Web Search page, click in the *the exact phrase* text box and then type **skydiving in Oregon**.

   This limits the search to websites with the exact phrase "skydiving in Oregon."

5. Click the *Only .com domains* option.

   Clicking this option tells Yahoo! to only display websites with a .com extension and to ignore any other extension.

6. Click the Yahoo! Search button.

   Step 6

   Advanced Web Search

   You can use the options on this page to create a very specific search. Just fill in the fields you need for your current search.

Show results with	all of these words		any part of the page ▾
	the exact phrase	skydiving in Oregon	any part of the page ▾
	any of these words		any part of the page ▾
	none of these words		any part of the page ▾

   Tip: Use these options to look for an exact phrase or to exclude pages containing certain words. You can also limit your search to certain parts of pages.

Updated	anytime ▾
Site/Domain	○ Any domain
	⦿ Only .com domains ○ Only .edu domains
	○ Only .gov domains ○ Only .org domains
	○ only search in this domain/site: .com

   Step 4

   Step 5

   Tip: You can search for results in a specific website (e.g. yahoo.com) or top-level domains (e.g. .com, .org, .gov).

(7) When the list of websites displays, click a hyperlink that interests you.

(8) Click the Back button until the Yahoo! Advanced Web Search page displays.

(9) Select and then delete the text *skydiving in Oregon* located in the *the exact phrase* text box.

(10) Click in the *all of these words* text box and then type skydiving Oregon tandem static line.

> You want to focus on websites that offer tandem and static line skydiving in Oregon.

(11) Click the *Any domain* option.

(12) Click the Yahoo! Search button.

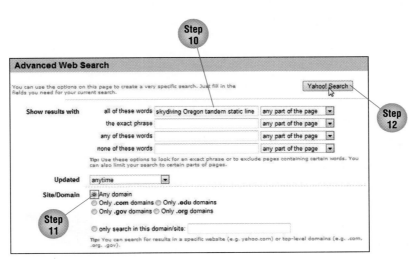

(13) When the list of websites displays, click a hyperlink that interests you.

In Addition

Displaying a List of Sites Visited

As you view various web pages, Internet Explorer keeps track of the websites visited. Display the History pane by clicking the Tools button on the Internet Explorer Command bar, pointing to Explorer Bars, and then clicking *History*. Click the timeframe for which the web page would have been viewed to expand the list and display the sites visited. For example, click *Last Week* to expand the list and view the pages that you visited within the past week. Click the desired hyperlink to revisit the page. At the top of the History pane, click the View button (currently displays View By Date) to change the order in which the history list is displayed. You can display websites in the History pane to *View By Date*, *View By Site*, *View By Most Visited*, or *View By Order Visited Today*. Click *Search History* at the View button drop-down list to search the websites in the History pane by keyword or phrase.

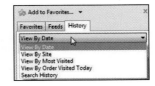

Activity 1.4

Downloading Content from a Web Page

Downloading content from a web page can involve saving to your hard disk or other storage medium images, text, video, audio, or the entire web page. Copyright laws protect much of the information on the Internet. Before using information or other media files you have downloaded from the Internet, check the source site for restrictions.

When in doubt, contact the website administrator or other contact person identified on the site and request permission to use the content. Finally, make sure to credit the source of any content you use that was obtained from a web page. Generally, you can use content from a website that is considered public domain such as government websites.

Project

The production manager of the new movie project at Marquee Productions has asked you to locate on the Internet a picture for Banff National Park and an image that shows a map of the park. She wants you to save the images as a separate file that she can insert into her presentation for the next production meeting.

Marquee
PRODUCTIONS

SNAP

Tutorial 1.4
Downloading Images, Text, and Web Pages

1. With the Internet Explorer window active, click in the Address bar, type **www.google.com**, and then press Enter.

2. At the Google home page, click the hyperlink to <u>Images</u> at the top left of the home page.

   Step 2

3. At the Google images page, type **Banff National Park** in the Search text box and then press Enter or click the Search Images button.

4. Browse the images that display in the search results.

   Your image may vary.

5. Position the mouse pointer over an image you want to download, right-click the mouse, and then click *Save Picture As* at the shortcut menu.

   The image that you choose may vary from the one shown here.

   Step 5

6. At the Save Picture dialog box, click *Desktop* in the *Favorites* section of the Navigation pane, select the current text in the *File name* text box, type **BanffPicture1**, and then click Save or press Enter.

   Step 6

7 Click the Address bar, type **www.dogpile.com**, and then press Enter.

8 Click the Images tab at the Dogpile home page.

9 Click in the Search text box, type **Banff National Park Map**, and then press Enter or click the Go Fetch! button.

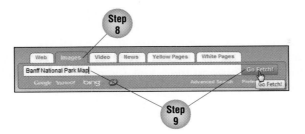

In Brief

Downloading Images from Web Page
1. Display desired web page in Internet Explorer window.
2. Right-click desired image.
3. Click *Save Picture As*.
4. Navigate to desired drive and/or folder.
5. Type file name in *File name* text box.
6. Click Save.

10 Browse the map images that display in the search results, right-click the mouse over one of the maps you want to download, and then click *Save Picture As* at the shortcut menu.

11 At the Save Picture dialog box, with *Desktop* already selected in the Address bar and with the current file name already selected in the *File name* text box, type **BanffMap1** and then click Save or press Enter.

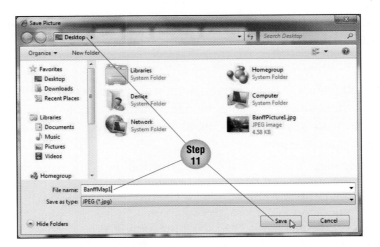

In Addition

Saving an Entire Web Page as a Separate File

You can save as a separate file all of the content that displays on a web page. The web page can be opened like any other file to view or print as needed. To do this, display the web page that you want to save a copy of, click the Page button on the Command bar, and click *Save As* at the drop-down list. At the Save Webpage dialog box, navigate to the drive and/or folder in which you want to save the web page, type a name for the web page in the *File name* text box, and then click Save or press Enter. By default, the web page is saved in the *Web Archive, single file (*.mht)* file format. To open the file at a later date, use Windows Explorer to locate the drive and folder in which you saved the file and then double-click the file name in the Content pane. The web page will open in an Internet Explorer window.

Activity 1.5

Evaluating Content on the Web

The Web is a vast repository of information that is easily accessible and constantly changing. Although there is a wealth of accurate and timely information available at your fingertips, there is also information that may be outdated, inaccurate, or of poor quality that should not be relied upon. Since anyone with an Internet connection and the right software can publish information on the Web, knowing the clues to recognizing accurate and current content is a worthwhile skill.

First, look for an author, publisher, or website owner name and consider if the source is credible. For example, is the author associated with a recognizable company, government, or news organization? Second, look for the date the information was published. Is the content outdated? If yes, consider the impact that more current information might have on the information you are evaluating. Third, look for indications that a bias may exist in the content. For example, is there a sponsor on the site that might indicate the information is one-sided? Can the information be validated by another source?

Project

The development manager at Marquee Productions is working on research for a new documentary about the Apollo space missions. She has asked you to locate information on the Web that she can add to her research. You want to be careful that the information you provide for the project is credible.

1. With the Internet Explorer window active, click in the Address bar, type **www.google.com**, and then press Enter.

2. At the Google home page, type **Apollo lunar missions** in the Search text box and then click the Search button or press Enter.

3. Click a link to a page that interests you.

4. At the web page, try to locate the author or publisher name, the date the article was published, and/or the date the page was last updated. If the web page contains any ads or sponsors, consider if this advertising has an impact on the content you are reading.

   > Some pages put this information at the bottom of the page, while other pages place the author and date at the beginning of the article. If you cannot find an author or date, look for a Contacts link on the website you are viewing to see if you can determine the name of the company that has published the information. Also, look over the web address to see if the address provides a clue to the authorship. For example, a web address with a *.edu* domain is indicating the source is from a page connected with a university.

5. Click the New Tab tab to open a new browsing window.

   Your tab name may vary.

   Step 5

   Exploring the Moon: Apollo Missions

   New Tab (Ctrl+T)

6. Click in the Address bar, type **www.nasa.gov/mission_pages/apollo**, and then press Enter.

7. Scroll to the bottom of the page and read the information in the banner next to the NASA logo that provides information about the date the page was last updated, the page editor, and the NASA Official.

Step 7

8 Click the tab for the first web page that you visited about Apollo lunar missions and click the Back button to return to the search results list.

9 Click the link to another page that interests you and try to locate similar information about the date, author, and publisher that you viewed at NASA's website.

10 Compare the two pages shown side by side in Figure 1.3. Note that one page provides details about dates and authors while the other page does not have the same references.

> The page without the references may not necessarily have inaccurate data or be an otherwise poor quality source of information about the Apollo missions; however, the absence of an author or date of revision means that you would have difficulty citing this source for a research paper or other academic assignment.

11 Close Internet Explorer. Click the Close all tabs button at the Internet Explorer dialog box.

FIGURE 1.3

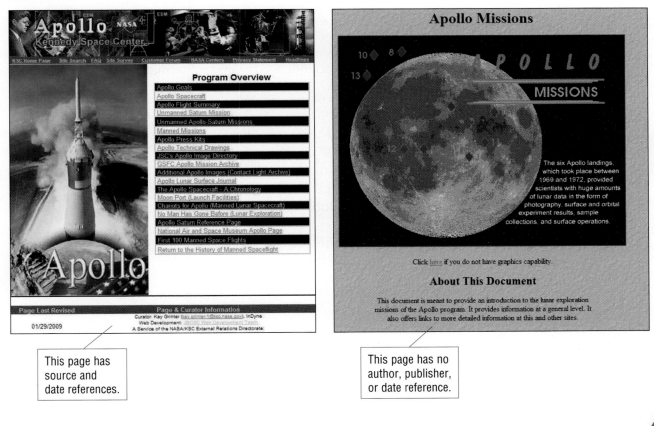

This page has source and date references.

This page has no author, publisher, or date reference.

Features Summary

Feature	Button	Keyboard Shortcut
go back to previous web page	←	Alt + Left Arrow
go forward to next web page	→	Alt + Right Arrow
History pane	Tools ▼	Ctrl + Shift + H
launch Internet Explorer	🅔	
print current web page	🖨 ▼	Ctrl + P
select Address bar	http://www.emcp.com/	Alt + D
select Instant Search box	Bing 🔍 ▼	Ctrl + E

Knowledge Check

Completion: In the space provided at the right, indicate the correct term, command, or option.

1. Type a URL in this bar at the Internet Explorer window. _____
2. The letters *URL* stand for this. _____
3. Click this button on the Internet Explorer toolbar to display the previous web page. _____
4. Click in this box located at the right end of the Internet Explorer Navigation bar to locate web pages using a keyword or phrase. _____
5. Reduce the number of search results by looking for these options at the search engine's website. _____
6. Download an image from a website to a file on your computer by right-clicking the image and selecting this option at the shortcut menu. _____

Skills Review

Note: Check with your instructor before completing the Skills Review activities to find out if you have to print the pages that you visit.

Review 1 Browsing the Internet and Navigating with Hyperlinks

1. Open Internet Explorer.
2. Click in the Address bar, type **www.si.edu**, and then press Enter. (This is the home page for the Smithsonian Institution.)
3. Click a link to a topic that interests you and read the page.
4. Click another link and read the page.
5. Click the Back button until the Smithsonian Institution home page displays.

Review 2 Searching for Specific Sites

1. At the Internet Explorer window, use the Instant Search box to look for websites on mountain climbing.
2. In the search results, click a link to a site that interests you.
3. Display the Yahoo! website and then use advanced options to search for websites with the *.com* domain on mountain climbing in British Columbia, Canada.
4. Visit at least two sites in the search results that interest you.

Review 3 Downloading Content from a Web Page

1. Using your favorite search engine, search for websites on parasailing in Hawaii. Find a site that contains a parasailing image that you like.
2. Download the parasailing image to the desktop, saving it as **ParasailImage1**.
3. Search for maps of Hawaii.
4. Browse the map images and then select one to download to the desktop, saving it as **HawaiiMap1**.
5. Close Internet Explorer.

Skills Assessment

Note: Check with your instructor before completing the Skills Assessment activities to find out if you have to print the pages that you visit.

Assessment 1 Visiting Web Pages for Current News Articles

1. Sam Vestering, a manager at Worldwide Enterprises, likes to keep up-to-date with current events by reading the daily headlines for various newspapers. He has asked you to scan the home pages for two online newspapers—the *New York Times* and *USA Today*—for articles of interest. To begin, open Internet Explorer.
2. Go to the website of the *New York Times* at www.nytimes.com. Scan the headlines for today's publication, click the link to an article that interests you, and then read the article.
3. Visit the website of *USA Today* at www.usatoday.com, click the link to an article that interests you, and then read the article.

Assessment 2 Navigating Websites for Theatre Programs

1. Cal Rubine, the chair of the Theatre Arts Division at Niagara Peninsula College, has asked you to visit the web pages for the theatre and/or drama departments at two universities to compare programs. Visit the home page for York University, Toronto, Canada, at www.yorku.ca.
2. Locate the web page for the Theatre Department and then read about the program.
3. Visit the home page for New York University at www.nyu.edu.
4. Using the NYU A–Z search in the ABOUT NYU section, locate the web page for the Department of Drama (undergraduate) and then read about the program. If necessary, click links to more pages to find program details.

Assessment 3 Downloading Content on Ski Resorts

1. You work for First Choice Travel and are preparing a brochure on snow skiing vacations. You need some information and images for the brochure. Search for information on snow skiing resorts in Utah.
2. Visit a website that interests you and contains an image of the resort or mountains.
3. Download an image from the web page to the desktop, saving it as **UtahResortImage1**.
4. Close Internet Explorer.

Assessment 4 Deleting Downloaded Content on the Desktop

1. At the Windows 7 desktop, right-click the **_UtahResortImage1_** file saved to the desktop and click _Delete_ at the shortcut menu. Click _Yes_ at the Delete File dialog box to move the file to the Recycle Bin.
2. Delete all of the other downloaded files saved to the desktop from this section.

Microsoft® Excel 2010

Nita Rutkosky

Pierce College at Puyallup, Puyallup, Washington

Denise Seguin

Fanshawe College, London, Ontario

Audrey Rutkosky Roggenkamp

Pierce College at Puyallup, Puyallup, Washington

Paradigm
PUBLISHING

St. Paul • Los Angeles • Indianapolis

Managing Editor	Sonja Brown
Developmental Editor	Brenda Palo
Supplements Developmental Editor	Brenda Owens
Production Editor	Donna Mears
Cover and Text Designer	Leslie Anderson
Copy Editors	Susan Capecchi and Laura Nelson
Desktop Production	Ryan Hamner and Jack Ross
Proofreader	Laura Nelson
Testers	Carley Bomstad, Amy McGuire, Rob Neilly, and Lindsay Ryan
Indexers	Ina Gravitz and Sandi Schroeder

Text: ISBN 978-0-76383-780-8
Text & CD: ISBN 978-0-76383-781-5

© 2011 by Paradigm Publishing, Inc.
875 Montreal Way
St. Paul, MN 55102
Email: educate@emcp.com
Website: www.emcp.com

Contents

Introducing
Excel 2010

Microsoft Excel 2010 is a popular choice among individuals and companies to organize, analyze, and present data in columns and rows in a document called a *worksheet*. More than one worksheet can be created and saved in a file called a *workbook*. Entries are placed in a worksheet in a *cell*, which is the intersection of a column with a row. A cell is labeled with the column letter and row number, such as A1. Worksheets can be created to track, analyze, and chart any type of data that can be set up in a column and row format. Expenses, sales, assets, liabilities, grades, statistics, research study data, machine production records, weather records, and gas usage are just a few examples of the type of information that can be stored in an Excel workbook. While working in Excel, you will create and edit worksheets for the following six companies.

First Choice Travel is a travel center offering a full range of traveling services from booking flights, hotel reservations, and rental cars to offering travel seminars.

The Waterfront Bistro offers fine dining for lunch and dinner and also offers banquet facilities, a wine cellar, and catering services.

Worldwide Enterprises is a national and international distributor of products for a variety of companies and is the exclusive movie distribution agent for Marquee Productions.

Marquee Productions is involved in all aspects of creating movies from script writing and development to filming. The company produces documentaries, biographies, as well as historical and action movies.

Performance Threads maintains an inventory of rental costumes and also researches, designs, and sews special-order and custom-made costumes.

The mission of the Niagara Peninsula College Theatre Arts Division is to offer a curriculum designed to provide students with a thorough exposure to all aspects of the theater arts.

In Section 1 you will learn how to
Create Worksheets to Analyze Data

Begin your work in Excel by entering labels in columns or rows to create the worksheet layout. Next, add the values that correspond to the labels. Finally, create formulas to add, subtract, multiply, or divide to calculate the desired results. Once a worksheet has been created, the power and versatility of Excel is put to use by performing what-if analyses. What happens to net profit if sales increase by 4 percent? What happens to monthly cash flow if the wages of all employees are raised 3 percent? To answer these types of questions, you edit a value and then watch Excel's recalculation feature automatically update all other values dependent on the number you changed.

Start a new worksheet by entering labels to create the worksheet layout.

	A	B	C	D	E	F	G	H	I	J	K	L
1						Payroll						
2					Week Ended: September 24, 2011							
3										Total	Pay	Gross
4			Sun	Mon	Tue	Wed	Thu	Fri	Sat	Hours	Rate	Pay
5	Lou	Cortez										
6	Jasmine	Hill										
7	Heather	Kiley										
8	Dayna	McGuire										
9	Carla	Modano										
10	Tyler	Santini										
11	Pat	Soulliere										
12	Moira	Su-Lin										
13	Toni	Williams										
14												
15	Total											
16												
17	Hours Proof											
18	Gross Pay Proof											

Next, add the values to record quantities, rates, or other numeric entries.

	A	B	C	D	E	F	G	H	I	J	K
1						Payroll					
2					Week Ended: September 24, 2011						
3										Total	Pay
4			Sun	Mon	Tue	Wed	Thu	Fri	Sat	Hours	Rate
5	Lou	Cortez	8	0	6	8	0	8	8		8.25
6	Jasmine	Hill	8	0	8	8	0	8	6		8.25
7	Heather	Kiley	0	8	6	8	5	5	8		8.25
8	Dayna	McGuire	6	5	8	8	7	0	6		8.25
9	Carla	Modano	0	0	8	8	7	7	8		8.25
10	Tyler	Santini	8	0	8	8	6	7	0		8.25
11	Pat	Soulliere	8	8	0	8	7	7	0		8.25
12	Moira	Su-Lin	0	8	0	8	7	7	8		8.25
13	Toni	Williams	8	0	0	8	8	7	4		8.25

Create the formulas to add, subtract, multiply, or divide.

	A	B	C	D	E	F	G	H	I	J	K	L
1						Payroll						
2					Week Ended: September 24, 2011							
3										Total	Pay	Gross
4			Sun	Mon	Tue	Wed	Thu	Fri	Sat	Hours	Rate	Pay
5	Lou	Cortez	8	0	6	8	0	8	8	=SUM(C5:I5)	8.25	=J5*K5
6	Jasmine	Hill	8	0	8	8	0	8	6	=SUM(C6:I6)	8.25	=J6*K6
7	Heather	Kiley	0	8	6	8	5	5	8	=SUM(C7:I7)	8.25	=J7*K7
8	Dayna	McGuire	6	5	8	8	7	0	6	=SUM(C8:I8)	8.25	=J8*K8
9	Carla	Modano	0	0	8	8	7	7	8	=SUM(C9:I9)	8.25	=J9*K9
10	Tyler	Santini	8	0	8	8	6	7	0	=SUM(C10:I10)	8.25	=J10*K10
11	Pat	Soulliere	8	8	0	8	7	7	0	=SUM(C11:I11)	8.25	=J11*K11
12	Moira	Su-Lin	0	8	0	8	7	7	8	=SUM(C12:I12)	8.25	=J12*K12
13	Toni	Williams	8	0	0	8	8	7	4	=SUM(C13:I13)	8.25	=J13*K13
14												
15	Total		=SUM(C5:C14)	=SUM(D5:D14)	=SUM(E5:E14)	=SUM(F5:F14)	=SUM(G5:G14)	=SUM(H5:H14)	=SUM(I5:I14)	=SUM(J5:J14)		=SUM(L5:L14)
16												
17	Hours Proof	=SUM(C5:I13)										
18	Gross Pay Proof	=B17*K5										

	A	B	C	D	E	F	G	H	I	J	K	L
1						Payroll						
2					Week Ended: September 24, 2011							
3										Total	Pay	Gross
4			Sun	Mon	Tue	Wed	Thu	Fri	Sat	Hours	Rate	Pay
5	Lou	Cortez	8	0	6	8	0	8	8	38	8.25	$ 313.50
6	Jasmine	Hill	8	0	8	8	0	8	6	38	8.25	$ 313.50
7	Heather	Kiley	0	8	6	8	5	5	8	40	8.25	$ 330.00
8	Dayna	McGuire	6	5	8	8	7	0	6	40	8.25	$ 330.00
9	Carla	Modano	0	0	8	8	7	7	8	38	8.25	$ 313.50
10	Tyler	Santini	8	0	8	8	6	7	0	37	8.25	$ 305.25
11	Pat	Soulliere	8	8	0	8	7	7	0	38	8.25	$ 313.50
12	Moira	Su-Lin	0	8	0	8	7	7	8	38	8.25	$ 313.50
13	Toni	Williams	8	0	0	8	8	7	4	35	8.25	$ 288.75
14												
15	Total		46	29	44	72	47	56	48	342		$2,821.50
16												
17	Hours Proof	342										
18	Gross Pay Proof	$2,821.50										

The desired results are shown in the finished worksheet.

In Section 2 you will learn how to
Edit and Format Worksheets

Excel allows you to apply formatting attributes and add color to enhance the appearance of the worksheet and draw a reader's attention to important titles, totals, or other results. A feature in Excel provides the ability to apply a theme which coordinates colors, fonts, and effects to provide a worksheet with a professional appearance in just a few mouse clicks. A variety of formats, grouped into categories, are available for numbers, dates, and times. Insert images such as clip art or a logo to enhance a worksheet or add a corporate identity.

The Waterfront Bistro
3104 Riverfront Drive
Buffalo, NY 14280
716 555 3166

Quotation

TO: Marquee Productions
955 South Alameda Street
Los Angeles, CA 90037

DATE: 5-Nov-10

ATT: Camille Matsui

RE: Remote Location Filming
July 11 to August 31

Note: All prices include tax.

Item	No of Persons	Price per Person	No of Days	Total
Buffet Lunch	56	8.34	52	$ 24,286.08
Soup and salad				
Vegetable tray with dip				
Seafood hors d'oeuvres				
Hot entrée				
Deli tray and rolls				
Dessert				
Beverages	56	3.91	52	11,385.92
Coffee and tea				
Assorted juice				
Mineral water				
Snacks	56	3.91	52	11,385.92
Muffins				
Donuts				
Fruit tray				
Vegetable tray with dip				
Transport		33.00	52	1,716.00
Total				$ 48,773.92

Terms: Due upon receipt of invoice payable in U.S. funds

Apply formatting enhancements including:

- adding borders
- adding fill color
- adjusting row height
- adjusting column width
- applying a cell style
- applying a theme
- changing text alignment within cells
- changing font, font size, font color
- changing font attributes to bold and/or italic
- indenting text within a cell
- formatting numbers

Niagara Peninsula College

Time	Monday	Tuesday	Wednesday	Thursday	Friday
Room: T1101			**Period Covered: January 1 to April 30**		
8:00 AM	SM100-01 Prasad	AC215-03 McLean (lab)		MG210-01 Spelberger	SM240-03 Prasad
9:00 AM			LE100-03 Das		
10:00 AM	LE253-03 Das			SM355-02 Prasad	SD350-04 Attea
11:00 AM					
12:00 PM	SD451-01 Attea	PD250-02 Kemper	Common Period	PD320-03 Kemper	
1:00 PM					LE310-02 Das
2:00 PM	PD340-02 Kemper	MG410-03 Spelberger	AC478-01 Simmons	AC480-01 Simmons (lab)	
3:00 PM					MG210-01 Spelberger
4:00 PM	MG150-02 Spelberger	SM165-01 Prasad	AC140-01 Chou		
5:00 PM					

Use features such as Format Painter, Cell Styles, and Themes to apply formats quickly and consistently.

In Section 3 you will learn how to
Use Function Formulas and Add Visual Elements

Excel's functions make the task of writing formulas easier. Functions are grouped by category such as statistical, financial, date, and logical. Excel provides over 300 prebuilt formulas to perform calculations. The Insert Function dialog box is available to assist with locating and creating a function. Create charts from data to emphasize trends or compare data sets. Add emphasis to worksheets or charts by drawing arrows and adding text boxes.

The Waterfront Bistro
Quarterly Expense Budget Forecast

| | Last Year's Avg Qtr | Target Factors for Increases by Quarter | | | | |
| | | 1.05 | 1.08 | 1.15 | 1.14 | |
		Qtr1	Qtr2	Qtr3	Qtr4	Total
Advertising	$ 2,150.00	$ 2,257.50	$ 2,322.00	$ 2,472.50	$ 2,451.00	$ 9,503.00
Bank charges	500.00	525.00	$ 540.00	$ 575.00	$ 570.00	$ 2,210.00
Cleaning	650.00	682.50	$ 702.00	$ 747.50	$ 741.00	$ 2,873.00
Linens	1,100.00	1,155.00	$ 1,188.00	$ 1,265.00	$ 1,254.00	$ 4,862.00
Office supplies	175.00	183.75	$ 189.00	$ 201.25	$ 199.50	$ 773.50
Telephone	250.00	262.50	$ 270.00	$ 287.50	$ 285.00	
Utilities	2,050.00	2,152.50	$ 2,214.00	$ 2,357.50	$ 2,337.00	
Total		$ 7,218.75	$ 7,425.00	$ 7,906.25	$ 7,837.50	$
Average expense		$ 1,031.25	$ 1,060.71	$ 1,129.46	$ 1,119.64	$
Maximum expense		$ 2,257.50	$ 2,322.00	$ 2,472.50	$ 2,451.00	$
Minimum expense		$ 183.75	$ 189.00	$ 201.25	$ 199.50	$

Enter formulas using Excel's built-in functions.

The Waterfront Bistro
Patio Expansion Loan Analysis

	Funds Unlimited	Venture Funds Inc.	Details
Interest Rate	7.25%	8.15%	Annual rate
Term	15	12	Years for repayment
Loan Amount	420,000	420,000	Principal borrowed
Monthly Payment	($3,834.02)	($4,580.92)	Includes principal and interest

NOTE:
Both payments are calculated based on a constant interest rate and a constant payment.

Total loan payments	($690,124.34)	($659,651.81)

A Strong Finish!

Avg check per person
NRA Avg check per person

Illustrate trends or comparisons of data sets using charts.

Percent of Moviegoers by Age Group in 2007

60 and older
50 to 59 years old
40 to 49 years old
30 to 39 years old
25 to 29 years old
12 to 24 years old

Younger moviegoers are also the highest percent of frequent moviegoers attending at least one movie per month!

In Section 4 you will learn how to
Work with Multiple Worksheets and Tables

Large amounts of data are managed easily if they are separated into individual worksheets. Worksheets can be copied or moved to rearrange the order and logically organized by renaming and applying a tab color to the sheet tabs. Formulas can be created that reference cells in other worksheets or a cell can be linked to another worksheet to ensure the data flows from one worksheet to another. A list can be formatted as a table, which can be sorted, filtered, and formatted as a separate entity within a worksheet.

Organize large amounts of data in smaller worksheets.

The Waterfront Bistro

Quarterly Sales Report

	October	November	December	Quarter Total
Food - Dining Room	$ 44,875	$ 47,856	$ 55,645	$ 148,376
Food - Patio	$ 1,785	$ -	$ -	$ 1,785
Food - Catering	$ 30,254	$ 33,746	$ 65,245	$ 129,245
Total Food	**$ 76,914**	**$ 81,602**	**$ 120,890**	**$ 279,406**
Beverage - Dining Room	$ 41,623	$ 4,687	$ 5,642	$ 51,952
Beverage - Patio	$ 245	$ -	$ -	$ 245
Beverage - Catering	$ 3,245	$ 3,165	$ 6,452	$ 12,862
Total Beverage	**$ 45,113**	**$ 7,852**	**$ 12,094**	**$ 65,059**

The Waterfront Bistro

Sales Summary

	Total Sales
Food - Dining Room	$ 526,884
Food - Patio	$ 136,825
Food - Catering	$ 364,648
Total Food	**$1,028,357**
Beverage - Dining Room	$ 89,213
Beverage - Patio	$ 13,843
Beverage - Catering	$ 37,274
Total Beverage	**$ 140,330**
Beer & Liquor - Dining Room	$ 56,118
Beer & Liquor - Patio	$ 16,584
Beer & Liquor - Catering	$ 40,121
Total Beer & Liquor	**$ 112,823**
TOTAL SALES	**$ 1,281,510**
Proof Total	$ 1,281,510
Gross Profit Factor	30%
Estimated Gross Profit	$ 384,453

Create formulas and link cells to summarize worksheets.

The Waterfront Bistro

Catering Contracts

First Name	Last Name	Contact Phone	Event	Date	Room	Guests	Special Menu	Price Per Person	Contract Total
Nicole	Griffin	905 555 4166	25th Wedding Anniversary	6/17/2011	Starlake	54	Yes	31.95	$ 1,725.30
Dana	Russell	716 555 4965	Birthday Party	5/30/2011	Starlake	36	No	26.95	$ 970.20
Walter	Szucs	905 555 6998	Birthday Party	6/10/2011	Starlake	42	No	28.95	$ 1,215.90
Sofia	Delgado	716 555 8465	Birthday Party	8/10/2011	Starlake	55	No	21.95	$ 1,207.25
Carlotta	Balducci	716 555 9665	Birthday Party	8/22/2011	Starlake	62	Yes	25.95	$ 1,608.90
Sonora	Yee	716 555 2668	Birthday Party	12/31/2011	Starlake	73	Yes	31.95	$ 2,332.35
Cecily	Hillmore	716 555 6598	Business Meeting	1/13/2011	Starlake	35	No	21.95	$ 768.25
Lane	Gill	416 555 3264	Business Meeting	3/29/2011	Starlake	71	No	21.95	$ 1,558.45
Mei-Yin	Zhang	716 555 2121	Business Meeting	12/1/2011	Starlake	28	Yes	31.95	$ 894.60
Cristian	Martinez	716 555 4331	Business Meeting	12/15/2011	Starlake	18	No	31.95	$ 575.10
Bianca	Vargas	716 555 3884	Engagement Party	10/15/2011	Starlake	40	Yes	31.95	$ 1,278.00
Reed	Pavelich	716 555 2286	Wedding	7/25/2011	Starlake	110	Yes	31.95	$ 3,514.50
Total						624		28.28	$ 17,648.80

Format a list as a table to filter and format the list as a separate entity.

Excel SECTION 1

Analyzing Data Using Excel

Skills

- Start Excel and identify features in the Excel window
- Save a workbook using Save and Save As
- Enter labels and values
- Use the fill handle to enter a series
- Enter formulas
- Create a formula using SUM
- Copy a formula
- Test a worksheet for accuracy
- Apply the Accounting Number format to values
- Right-align labels
- Sort a selection
- Use the Help feature
- Center a label across multiple columns
- Change the page orientation to landscape
- Preview and print a worksheet
- Display cell formulas in a worksheet
- Navigate a large worksheet using the mouse and the keyboard
- Jump to a specific cell using Go To

Student Resources

Before beginning the activities in Excel, copy to your storage medium the Excel folder on the Student Resources CD. This folder contains the data files you need to complete the projects in each Excel section.

Projects Overview

Edit a weekly sales report, create a payroll worksheet, create a condensed quarterly income statement, and sort a standard inventory list.

Create a projected distribution revenue schedule for a new movie release.

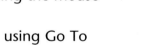

Complete an estimated travel costs worksheet.

Create an international student registration report and a target enrollment report.

Prepare a price quotation for costume alterations and rental.

Model Answers for Projects

These model answers for the projects that you complete in Section 1 provide a preview of the finished projects before you begin working and also allow you to compare your own results with these models to ensure you have created the materials accurately.

ES1-WBWeeklySales.xlsx is the project in Activity 1.1.

Weekly Sales Report

For the week ended:	24-Sep							
	Sunday	**Monday**	**Tuesday**	**Wednesday**	**Thursday**	**Friday**	**Saturday**	**Total**
Food - Dining Room	2,585.00	1,006.00	1,255.00	1,345.00	1,488.00	1,596.00	2,137.00	11,412.00
Food - Patio	1,154.00	312.00	488.00	578.00	1,065.00	1,147.00	1,549.00	6,293.00
Food - Catering	2,477.00	-	-	1,865.00	1,855.00	4,266.00	3,157.00	13,620.00
Total Food	**6,216.00**	**1,318.00**	**1,743.00**	**3,788.00**	**4,408.00**	**7,009.00**	**6,843.00**	**31,325.00**
Beverage - Dining Room	341.00	88.00	195.00	229.00	214.00	198.00	235.00	1,500.00
Beverage - Patio	244.00	49.00	88.00	97.00	96.00	84.00	128.00	786.00
Beverage - Catering	652.00	-	-	314.00	247.00	394.00	214.00	1,821.00
Total Beverage	**1,237.00**	**137.00**	**283.00**	**640.00**	**557.00**	**676.00**	**577.00**	**4,107.00**
Beer & Liquor - Dining Room	1,577.00	175.00	269.00	492.00	323.00	224.00	485.00	3,545.00
Beer & Liquor - Patio	652.00	56.00	96.00	78.00	184.00	168.00	227.00	1,461.00
Beer & Liquor - Catering	984.00	-	-	344.00	411.00	884.00	774.00	3,397.00
Total Beer & Liquor	**3,213.00**	**231.00**	**365.00**	**914.00**	**918.00**	**1,276.00**	**1,486.00**	**8,403.00**
TOTAL SALES	**10,666.00**	**1,686.00**	**2,391.00**	**5,342.00**	**5,883.00**	**8,961.00**	**8,906.00**	**43,835.00**
Gross Profit Factor	**32%**							
Estimated Gross Profit	**3,413.12**	**539.52**	**765.12**	**1,709.44**	**1,882.56**	**2,867.52**	**2,849.92**	**14,027.20**

ES1-WBPayroll.xlsx is the project in Activities 1.2 to 1.8.

Payroll
Week Ended: September 24, 2011

		Sun	Mon	Tue	Wed	Thu	Fri	Sat	Total Hours	Pay Rate	Gross Pay
Lou	Cortez	8	0	6	8	0	8	8	38	8.25	$ 313.50
Jasmine	Hill	8	0	8	8	0	8	6	38	8.25	$ 313.50
Heather	Kiley	0	8	6	8	5	5	8	40	8.25	$ 330.00
Dayna	McGuire	6	5	8	8	7	0	6	40	8.25	$ 330.00
Carla	Modano	0	0	8	8	7	7	8	38	8.25	$ 313.50
Tyler	Santini	8	0	8	8	6	7	0	37	8.25	$ 305.25
Pat	Soulliere	8	8	0	8	7	7	0	38	8.25	$ 313.50
Moira	Su-Lin	0	8	0	8	7	7	8	38	8.25	$ 313.50
Toni	Williams	8	0	0	8	8	7	4	35	8.25	$ 288.75
Total		46	29	44	72	47	56	48	342		$ 2,821.50

Hours
Proof   342

Gross
Pay Proof $ 2,821.50

Student Name

ES1-WBPayroll.xlsx is the project in Activity 1.9.

			Sun	Mon	Tue	Wed
						Payroll
					Week Ended: September 24, 2011	
Lou	Cortez	8	0	6	8	0
Jasmine	Hill	8	0	8	8	0
Heather	Kiley	0	8	6	8	5
Dayna	McGuire	6	5	8	8	7
Carla	Modano	0	0	8	8	7
Tyler	Santini	8	0	8	8	6
Pat	Soulliere	8	8	0	8	7
Moira	Su-Lin	0	8	0	8	7
Toni	Williams	8	0	0	8	8
Total		=SUM(C5:C14)	=SUM(D5:D14)	=SUM(E5:E14)	=SUM(F5:F14)	=SUM(G5:G14)
Hours Proof	=SUM(C5:I13)					
Gross Pay Proof	=B17*K5					
Student Name						

Thu	Fri	Sat	Total Hours	Pay Rate	Gross Pay
8	8	=SUM(C5:I5)	8.25	=J5*K5	
8	6	=SUM(C6:I6)	8.25	=J6*K6	
5	8	=SUM(C7:I7)	8.25	=J7*K7	
0	6	=SUM(C8:I8)	8.25	=J8*K8	
7	8	=SUM(C9:I9)	8.25	=J9*K9	
7	0	=SUM(C10:I10)	8.25	=J10*K10	
7	0	=SUM(C11:I11)	8.25	=J11*K11	
7	8	=SUM(C12:I12)	8.25	=J12*K12	
7	4	=SUM(C13:I13)	8.25	=J13*K13	
=SUM(H5:H14)	=SUM(I5:I14)	=SUM(J5:J14)		=SUM(L5:L14)	

Activity 1.1

Completing the Excel Worksheet Cycle

Information is created in Excel in a *worksheet* and is saved in a file called a *workbook*. A workbook can contain several worksheets. Imagine a worksheet as a page with horizontal and vertical lines drawn in a grid representing columns and rows. Data is entered into a *cell*, which is the intersection of a column with a row. Columns are lettered A to Z, AA to AZ, BA to BZ, and so on. The last column in the worksheet is labeled *XFD*. Rows are numbered 1, 2, 3, and so on. A column letter and a row number identify each cell. For example, A1 is the cell address for the intersection of column A with row 1. Each worksheet in Excel contains 16,384 columns and 1,048,576 rows. By default, an Excel workbook contains three worksheets labeled *Sheet1, Sheet2,* and *Sheet3*. Additional sheets can be inserted as needed.

Project

Tutorial 1.1
Creating and Saving a Worksheet

You have been asked to update a weekly sales report for The Waterfront Bistro by adding data and viewing the impact of changing a cell used to calculate gross margin.

1. At the Windows desktop, click the Start button on the Taskbar.

2. Point to *All Programs*.

3. Click *Microsoft Office*.

4. Click *Microsoft Excel 2010*.

   Depending on your operating system and/or system configuration, the steps you complete to open Excel may vary.

5. At the Excel screen, identify the various features by comparing your screen with the one shown in Figure 1.1. If necessary, maximize the Excel window. Depending on your screen resolution, your screen may vary slightly. Refer to Table 1.1 for a description of the screen features.

FIGURE 1.1 The Excel Screen

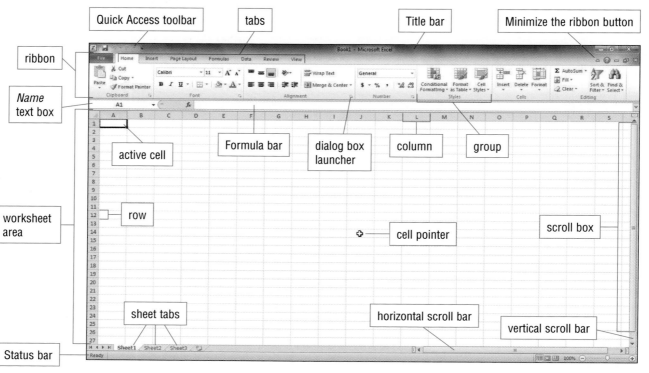

TABLE 1.1 Excel Screen Features

Feature	Description
active cell	location in the worksheet that will display typed data or that will be affected by a command
cell pointer	select cells when you see this icon by clicking or dragging the mouse
dialog box launcher	click the downward-pointing diagonal arrow at the bottom right in a group to open the dialog box with more options for that group
File tab	displays the Backstage view with document management actions, such as save or print, and a list of recently opened workbooks
Formula bar	displays the contents stored in the active cell
Minimize the ribbon button	click to show or hide the ribbon
Name text box	displays the active cell address or name assigned to active cell
Quick Access toolbar	contains buttons for commonly used commands which can be executed with a single mouse click
ribbon	area from which commands and features for performing actions on a cell or worksheet are accessed; begin by selecting a tab and then choosing the command or feature
sheet tabs	identifies the worksheets in the workbook; use these tabs to change the active worksheet
Status bar	displays current mode, action messages, View buttons, and Zoom slider
tabs	commands and features in the ribbon are organized into related groups which are accessed by clicking a tab name
Title bar	displays workbook name followed by Microsoft Excel
vertical and horizontal scroll bars	used to view various parts of the worksheet beyond the current screen
worksheet area	contains cells used to create the worksheet

6 Click the File tab and then click the Open button in the Backstage view.

> The Backstage view organizes document management tasks into tabs. Quick Command buttons such as Save, Save As, Open, and Close are located at the top of the left pane in Backstage view. Below the Quick Command buttons the view is organized into tabs. You will learn more about these tabs in later activities. You can also open a workbook by clicking the Open button on the Quick Access toolbar. If the Open button does not display on the Quick Access toolbar, click the Customize Quick Access Toolbar button that displays at the right side of the toolbar and then click *Open* at the drop-down list.

7 At the Open dialog box, navigate to the ExcelS1 folder on your storage medium.

> To change to a different drive, click the drive letter in the *Computer* section in the Navigation pane. (You may need to scroll down the Navigation pane to see the *Computer* section.) Change to a different folder by double-clicking the folder name in the Content pane.

8 Double-click *WBWeeklySales.xlsx*.

> This workbook contains one worksheet with sales for The Waterfront Bistro for the week ended September 24, 2011. The formulas to sum the sales have already been created. Notice some of the cells in the column labeled *Saturday* are empty. You will enter these values in Steps 11 through 14.

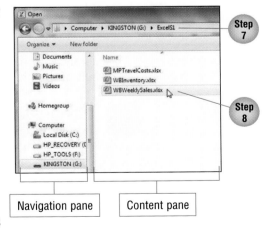

Navigation pane   Content pane

continues

9 Click the File tab and then click the Save As button in the Backstage view.

> Use the *Save* option to save a file using the same name. If you want to keep the original workbook and save the workbook with the changes under a new name, use *Save As*.

10 At the Save As dialog box, with ExcelS1 the active folder on your storage medium, press the Home key, type **ES1-** at the beginning of the current file name in the *File name* text box, and then press Enter or click Save.

> Excel files have the file extension .xlsx at the end of a workbook name. When naming a file do not change or delete this file extension because the operating system recognizes files ending with *.xlsx* are Microsoft Excel workbooks. If you change or delete the extension, the operating system will not know which program is associated with the data.

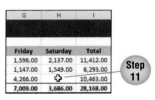

11 Move the cell pointer over the intersection of column H with row 6 (H6) and then click to make H6 the active cell.

G	H	I
Friday	Saturday	Total
1,596.00	2,137.00	11,412.00
1,147.00	1,549.00	6,293.00
4,266.00	✛	10,463.00
7,009.00	3,686.00	28,168.00

Step 11

12 Type **3157** and then press Enter.

> Notice that the entry in H7 has changed. This is because the formula created in H7 was dependent on H6. As soon as you enter a value in H6, any other dependent cells are automatically updated. Can you identify other cells that changed as a result of the new value in H6?

Need Help?

Typing mistake? Make corrections as you type by pressing the Backspace key to delete characters to the left of the insertion point; or, if you notice the mistake after you have left the cell, make the cell active and double-click the cell to open the cell for editing.

(13) Click H10 to make the cell active and then type **214**.

(14) Click H14 to make the cell active, type **774**, and then press Enter.

(15) Look at the entry in B19. This percentage is used to calculate the Estimated Gross Profit in row 20 (Total Sales times the Gross Profit Factor). Next, you will change the entry in B19 to see the effect on the estimated gross profit values.

(16) Click B19 to make the cell active, type **32%**, and then press Enter.

Notice the new estimated gross profit values in cells B20 through I20.

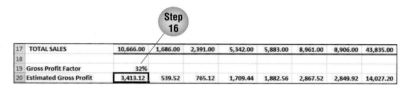

Step 12
Step 13
Step 14
Step 16

	Friday	Saturday	Total
	1,596.00	2,137.00	11,412.00
	1,147.00	1,549.00	6,293.00
	4,266.00	3,157.00	13,620.00
	7,009.00	6,843.00	31,325.00
	198.00	235.00	1,500.00
	84.00	128.00	786.00
	394.00	214.00	1,821.00
	676.00	577.00	4,107.00
	224.00	485.00	3,545.00
	168.00	227.00	1,461.00
	884.00	774.00	3,397.00
	1,276.00	1,486.00	8,403.00
	8,961.00	8,906.00	43,835.00

17	TOTAL SALES	10,666.00	1,686.00	2,391.00	5,342.00	5,883.00	8,961.00	8,906.00	43,835.00
18									
19	Gross Profit Factor	32%							
20	Estimated Gross Profit	3,413.12	539.52	765.12	1,709.44	1,882.56	2,867.52	2,849.92	14,027.20

(17) Click the File tab and then click the Save button, or click the Save button 🖫 on the Quick Access toolbar.

(18) Click the File tab, click the Print tab in the left pane of Backstage view, and then click the Print button, or click the Quick Print button 🖶 on the Quick Access toolbar.

If the Quick Print button does not display on the Quick Access toolbar, click the Customize Quick Access Toolbar button that displays at the right side of the toolbar and then click *Quick Print* at the drop-down list. The worksheet's page layout options have been set to print the worksheet in landscape orientation and centered horizontally between the left and right margins. You will learn how to set these options in a later activity.

(19) Click the File tab and then click the Close button in the Backstage view.

When no workbooks are currently open, Excel displays a blank grey screen.

In Brief

Start Excel
1. Click Start.
2. Point to *All Programs*.
3. Point to *Microsoft Office*.
4. Click *Microsoft Excel 2010*.

Open Workbook
1. Click File tab.
2. Click Open button.
3. Navigate to storage medium and folder.
4. Double-click workbook name.

Save Workbook with New Name
1. Click File tab.
2. Click Save As button.
3. Type new workbook name.
4. Click Save or press Enter.

In Addition

AutoComplete

The AutoComplete feature in Excel will complete text entries for you as you start to type a new entry in a cell. If the first few letters that you type match another entry in the column, Excel automatically fills in the remaining text. Press Tab, Enter, or one of the arrow keys to accept the text Excel suggests, or continue typing the correct text. You can turn off AutoComplete by clicking the File tab and then clicking the Options button near the bottom of the left pane in the Backstage view. Click *Advanced* in the left pane of the Excel Options dialog box, click the *Enable AutoComplete for cell values* check box to clear the box, and then click OK.

Activity 1.2

Entering Labels and Values; Using Fill Options

A *label* is an entry in a cell that helps the reader relate to the values in the corresponding column or row. Labels are generally entered first when creating a new worksheet since they define the layout of the data in the columns and rows. By default, Excel aligns labels at the left edge of the column. A *value* is a number, formula, or function that can be used to perform calculations in the worksheet. By default, Excel aligns values at the right edge of the column. Take a few moments to plan or sketch out the layout of a new worksheet before entering labels and values. Decide the calculations you will need to execute and how to display the data so that it will be easily understood and interpreted.

Project You need to calculate gross pay in a new payroll worksheet for the hourly paid staff at The Waterfront Bistro. Begin by entering labels and values.

The Waterfront
B·I·S·T·R·O

SNAP

Tutorial 1.2
Writing a Formula

1 At the blank Excel screen, click the File tab, click the New tab in the Backstage view, and then click the Create button with Blank Workbook already selected in the *Available Templates* section of the view.

> You can also start a new blank workbook by clicking the New button on the Quick Access toolbar. If the New button does not display on the Quick Access toolbar, click the Customize Quick Access Toolbar button that displays at the right side of the toolbar and then click *New* at the drop-down list. Also consider using the shortcut key Ctrl + N to begin a new blank workbook.

2 Type **Payroll** as the title for the new worksheet in A1.

> When you type a new entry in a cell, the entry appears in the Formula bar as well as within the active cell in the worksheet area. To end a cell entry, press Enter, move to another cell in the worksheet, or click the Enter button on the Formula bar.

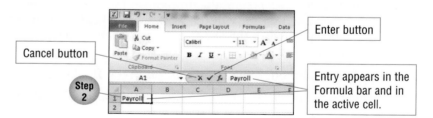

Cancel button

Enter button

Step 2

Entry appears in the Formula bar and in the active cell.

3 Press Enter.

4 With A2 the active cell, type **Week Ended: September 24, 2011** and then press Enter.

> Notice the entry in A2 is overflowing into columns B, C, and D. You can allow a label to spill over into adjacent columns as long as you do not plan to enter other data in the overflow cells. In a later section, you will learn how to adjust column widths.

5 Enter the remaining labels as shown on the next page by making the appropriate cell active, typing the label, and then pressing Enter or clicking another cell. (Do not complete the labels for the days of the week beyond *Sun*, as this will be done in Steps 6–8.)

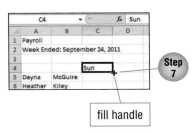

Step 4

Step 5

	A	B	C	D	E	F	G	H	I	J	K	L
1	Payroll											
2	Week Ended: September 24, 2011											
3										Total	Pay	Gross
4			Sun							Hours	Rate	Pay
5	Dayna	McGuire										
6	Heather	Kiley										
7	Pat	Soulliere										
8	Jasmine	Hill										
9	Moira	Su-Lin										
10	Carla	Modano										
11	Toni	Williams										
12	Tyler	Santini										
13	Lou	Cortez										
14												
15	Total											

6 Click C4 to make the cell active.

> A thick black border surrounds the active cell. A small black square displays at the bottom right corner of the active cell. This black square is called the ***fill handle***. The fill handle is used to fill adjacent cells with the same data or consecutive data. The entries that are automatically inserted in the adjacent cells are dependent on the contents of the active cell. You will use the fill handle in C4 to automatically enter the remaining days of the week in D4 through I4.

7 Point at the fill handle in C4. The cell pointer changes from the large white cross ✚ to a thin black cross ✛.

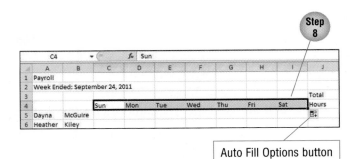

Step 7

8 Hold down the left mouse button, drag the pointer to I4, and then release the mouse.

fill handle

> The entries *Mon* through *Sat* appear in D4 to I4. As you drag the pointer to the right, a gray border surrounds the selected cells and a ScreenTip appears below the pointer indicating the label or value that will be inserted. When you release the left mouse button, the cells remain selected and the Auto Fill Options button 🔲 appears. Clicking the Auto Fill Options button causes a drop-down list to appear with various alternative actions for filling text or data into the cells.

Step 8

C4			fₓ	Sun					
	A	B	C	D	E	F	G	H	I	J
1	Payroll									
2	Week Ended: September 24, 2011									
3										Total
4			Sun	Mon	Tue	Wed	Thu	Fri	Sat	Hours
5	Dayna	McGuire								
6	Heather	Kiley								

Auto Fill Options button

Need Help?

Mon through Sat does not appear? You probably dragged the mouse using the cell pointer instead of the fill handle. This action selects cells instead of filling them. Go back to Step 6 and try again, making sure you drag when you see the thin black cross.

continues

9 Click C5 to make the cell active.

10 Type **6** and then press the Right Arrow key.

11 Type **5** in D5 and then press the Right Arrow key.

12 Type the following values in the cells indicated:

    E5   **8**
    F5   **8**
    G5   **7**
    H5   **0**
    I5   **6**

13 Make F5 the active cell.

14 Point at the fill handle in F5 and then drag the pointer down to F13.

> This time the active cell contained a value. The value *8* is copied to the adjacent cells.

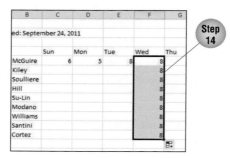

Step 14

15 Enter the remaining values for employee hours as shown below. Use the fill handle where there are duplicate values in adjacent cells to enter the data as efficiently as possible.

	A	B	C	D	E	F	G	H	I	J
1	Payroll									
2	Week Ended: September 24, 2011									
3										Total
4			Sun	Mon	Tue	Wed	Thu	Fri	Sat	Hours
5	Dayna	McGuire	6	5	8	8	7	0	6	
6	Heather	Kiley	0	8	6	8	5	5	8	
7	Pat	Soulliere	8	8	0	8	7	7	0	
8	Jasmine	Hill	8	0	8	8	0	8	6	
9	Moira	Su-Lin	0	8	0	8	7	7	8	
10	Carla	Modano	0	0	8	8	7	7	8	
11	Toni	Williams	8	0	0	8	8	7	4	
12	Tyler	Santini	8	0	8	8	6	7	0	
13	Lou	Cortez	8	0	6	8	0	8	8	

Step 15

16 Click K5 to make the cell active, type **8.25**, and then press Enter.

17 Position the cell pointer over cell K5, hold down the left mouse button, drag down to K13, and then release the mouse.

> A group of adjacent cells is referred to as a *range* (**a range is two or more cells**). Select a range of cells when you want to perform an action on a group of cells.

18 With Home the active tab in the ribbon, click the Fill button in the Editing group and then click *Down* at the drop-down list.

19 Click in any cell in the worksheet to deselect the range of cells in column K.

20 Click the Save button on the Quick Access toolbar.

21 At the Save As dialog box with ExcelS1 the active folder, type **ES1-WBPayroll** in the *File name* text box and then press Enter.

In Addition

More about the Fill Command

The fill handle is versatile and can be used to enter a series of values, dates, times, or other labels as a pattern. The pattern is established based on the cells you select before dragging the fill handle. In the worksheet shown below, the cells in columns C through J were all populated using the fill handle. In each row, the first two cells in columns A and B were selected and then the fill handle dragged right to column J. Notice the variety of patterns used to extend a series.

Use the Auto Fill Options button drop-down list to control how the series is entered. After dragging the fill handle, the Auto Fill Options button is displayed at the end of the series. Pointing at the button causes the button to expand and display a down-pointing arrow. Click the down-pointing arrow and then select the desired fill action from the options in the drop-down list. By default, *Fill Series* is active.

	A	B	C	D	E	F	G	H	I	J	K	L	M
1	Examples using the fill handle to continue a series in adjacent cells												
2	In each row below, the first two cells were selected and then the fill handle dragged right.												
3	1	2	3	4	5	6	7	8	9	10			
4	10	20	30	40	50	60	70	80	90	100			
5	9:00	10:00	11:00	12:00	13:00	14:00	15:00	16:00	17:00	18:00			
6	2011	2012	2013	2014	2015	2016	2017	2018	2019	2020			
7	Quarter 1	Quarter 2	Quarter 3	Quarter 4	Quarter 1	Quarter 2	Quarter 3	Quarter 4	Quarter 1	Quarter 2			
8	Period 1	Period 2	Period 3	Period 4	Period 5	Period 6	Period 7	Period 8	Period 9	Period 10			
9	Year 1	Year 2	Year 3	Year 4	Year 5	Year 6	Year 7	Year 8	Year 9	Year 10			
10													
11											○ Copy Cells		
12											◉ Fill Series		
13											○ Fill Formatting Only		
14											○ Fill Without Formatting		
15													

Activity 1.3

Performing Calculations Using Formulas

A *formula* is entered into a cell to perform mathematical calculations in a worksheet. All formulas in Excel begin with the equals sign (=) as the first character. After the equals sign, the cell addresses that contain the values you want to calculate are entered between mathematical operators. The mathematical operators are + (addition), − (subtraction), * (multiplication), / (division), and ^ (exponentiation). An example of a valid formula is =A3*B3. The value in A3 is multiplied by the value in B3 and the result is placed in the formula cell. By including the cell address in the formula rather than typing the actual value, you can utilize the powerful recalculation feature in Excel. If you change a cell's content, the worksheet is automatically recalculated so that all values are current.

Project

You will use two methods to enter formulas to calculate total hours and gross pay for the first two employees listed in the Payroll worksheet for The Waterfront Bistro.

The Waterfront
B·I·S·T·R·O

SNAP

Tutorial 1.3
Copying and Testing
a Formula

1 With **ES1-WBPayroll.xlsx** open, make J5 the active cell.

Begin a formula by activating the cell in which you want the result placed.

2 Type **=c5+d5+e5+f5+g5+h5+i5** and then press Enter.

The values in C5 through I5 are added and the result, *40*, is displayed in J5.

	A	B	C	D	E	F	G	H	I	J	K	L
1	Payroll											
2	Week Ended: September 24, 2011											
3												
4			Sun	Mon	Tue	Wed	Thu	Fri	Sat	Total Hours	Pay Rate	Gross Pay
5	Dayna	McGuire	6	5	8	8	7	0	6	=c5+d5+e5+f5+g5+h5+i5		
6	Heather	Kiley	0	8	6	8	5	5	8		8.25	

Step 2

Cell references are color-coded to the originating cell for quick reference and error checking.

3 Press the Up Arrow key to move the active cell back to J5.

Notice that the result of the formula is displayed in the worksheet area and the formula used to calculate the result is shown in the Formula bar. Notice also that the column letters in cell addresses are automatically converted to uppercase.

4 Make J6 the active cell, type the formula **=c6+d6+e6+f6+g6+h6+i6**, and then press Enter.

Seem like too much typing? A more efficient way to add a series of cells is available. This method will be introduced in the next activity after you learn the pointing method for entering formulas.

5 Make L5 the active cell.

To calculate gross pay, you need to multiply the total hours times the pay rate. In Steps 6–10, you will enter this formula using the pointing method.

6 Type the equals sign (=).

7 Click J5.

A moving dashed border (called a *marquee*) displays around J5, indicating it is the cell included in the formula, and the cell address is added to the formula cell (J5) with a blinking insertion point after the reference. Notice also that the Status bar displays the action *Point*.

Need Help?

Click the wrong cell by mistake? Simply click the correct cell, or press Esc to start the formula over again.

In Brief

Enter Formula
1. Activate formula cell.
2. Type =.
3. Type first cell address.
4. Type operator symbol.
5. Type second cell address.
6. Continue Steps 3–5 until finished.
7. Press Enter or click Enter button.

Enter a Formula Using Pointing Method
1. Activate formula cell.
2. Type =.
3. Click first cell.
4. Type operator symbol.
5. Click second cell.
6. Repeat Steps 3–5 until finished.
7. Press Enter or click Enter button.

8 Type an asterisk (*), which is the multiplication symbol.

The marquee surrounding cell J5 disappears and J5 is color-coded with the cell reference J5 within the formula cell.

9 Click K5.

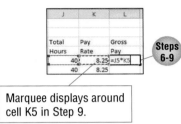

Steps 6–9

Marquee displays around cell K5 in Step 9.

10 Click the Enter button ✔ on the Formula bar.

The result *330* is displayed in L5. In Activity 1.6 you will learn how to display two decimal places for cells containing dollar values.

11 Use the pointing method or type the formula **=j6*k6** to calculate the gross pay for Heather Kiley in L6.

J	K	L	
Total Hours	Pay Rate	Gross Pay	
40	8.25	330	Step 11
40	8.25	330	

12 Click the Save button on the Quick Access toolbar.

In Addition

Order of Operations

If you include several operators in a formula, Excel calculates the result using the order of operations as follows: negations (e.g., –1) first, then percents (%), then exponentiations (^), then multiplication and division (* and /), and finally addition and subtraction (+ and –). If a formula contains more than one operator at the same level of precedence—for example, both an addition and a subtraction operation—Excel calculates the equation from left to right. To change the order of operations, use parentheses around the part of the formula you want calculated first.

Formula	Calculation
=B5*C5/D5	Both operators are at the same level of precedence—Excel would multiply the value in B5 times the value in C5 and then divide the result by the value in D5.
=B5+B6+B7*C10	Multiplication takes precedence over addition, so Excel would first multiply the value in B7 times the value in C10. Excel would then take the value in B5, add to it the value in B6, and then add the result of the multiplication.
=(B5+B6+B7)*C10	Because of the parentheses, Excel would first add the values in B5 through B7, then multiply this sum times the value in C10.

Activity 1.4

Using the SUM Function

The formulas to calculate the hours worked by the first two employees were lengthy. A more efficient way to calculate the total hours for Dayna McGuire in J5 would be to enter the formula =SUM(C5:I5). This formula includes one of Excel's built-in functions called SUM. A *function* is a preprogrammed formula. The structure of a formula utilizing a function begins with the equals sign (=), followed by the name of the func-tion, and then the *argument*. Argument is the term given to the values identified within parentheses. In the example provided, the argument C5:I5 contains the starting cell and the ending cell separated by a colon (:). The colon is used to indicate a range is to be summed; a *range* is a rectangular-shaped block of cells. Since the SUM function is used frequently, an AutoSum button is available in the Home tab.

Project

You decide to use a more efficient method of payroll calculation, so you will use the SUM function to complete the hours worked for the Payroll worksheet.

SNAP

Tutorial 1.3
Copying and Testing a Formula

1 With **ES1-WBPayroll.xlsx** open, make J5 the active cell and then press the Delete key.

> This deletes the cell contents. There was nothing wrong with the formula already entered in J5. You are deleting it so that the formulas in the completed worksheet will be consistent.

2 Click the AutoSum button Σ in the Editing group in the Home tab. (Do not click the down-pointing arrow to the right of the AutoSum button.)

> A moving marquee surrounds cells C5 through I5 and a ScreenTip appears below the formula cell indicating the correct format for the SUM function. Excel enters the formula =SUM(C5:I5) in J5. The suggested range C5:I5 is selected within the formula so that you can highlight a different range with the mouse if the suggested range is not correct.

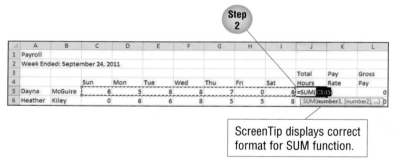

ScreenTip displays correct format for SUM function.

3 Press Enter.

> Since the range Excel suggests is the correct range, you can finish the formula by pressing Enter or by clicking the Enter button on the Formula bar.

4 With J6 the active cell, press the Delete key to delete the existing formula in the cell.

5 Click the AutoSum button. When Excel displays the formula =SUM(C6:I6), click the Enter button in the Formula bar.

6 Make J7 the active cell and then click the AutoSum button.

> Notice this time the range of cells Excel is suggesting to add (J5:J6) is the wrong range. When you click the AutoSum button, Excel looks for multiple values in the cells immediately above the active cell. In this case, there are multiple values above J7 so Excel inserts J5:J6 as the range in the SUM formula. You need to correct the range of cells that you want to add.

7 Position the cell pointer over C7, hold down the left mouse button, drag the pointer to the right to I7, and then release the mouse button.

In Brief

Enter SUM Function
1. Activate formula cell.
2. Click AutoSum button.
3. Press Enter, or drag to select correct range and press Enter.

OR
1. Drag to select range of cells to be summed including result cell.
2. Click AutoSum button.

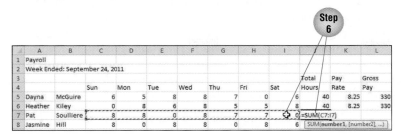

Step 6

8 Press Enter.

Now that you have seen how the AutoSum button operates, you already know that the suggested range for the next employee's total hours will be incorrect. In Step 9, you will select the range of cells *first* to avoid the incorrect suggestion.

9 Position the cell pointer over C8, hold down the left mouse button, drag the pointer right to J8, and then release the mouse button.

Notice you are including J8, the cell that will display the result, in the range of cells.

10 Click the AutoSum button.

The result, *38*, appears in cell J8.

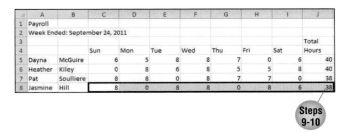

Steps 9-10

11 Click J8 and look in the Formula bar at the formula the SUM function created: *=SUM(C8:I8)*.

Since Excel created the correct SUM formula from a range of selected cells, you decide to try calculating total hours for more than one employee in one step using the method employed in Steps 9 and 10 but with an expanded range.

12 Position the cell pointer over C9, hold down the left mouse button, drag the pointer down and right to J13, and then release the mouse button.

13 Click the AutoSum button.

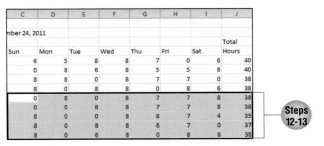

Steps 12-13

14 Click cells J9, J10, J11, J12, and J13 to confirm that the correct formulas appear in the Formula bar.

15 Click the Save button on the Quick Access toolbar.

Activity 1.5

Copying Formulas

Many times you may create a worksheet in which several formulas are basically the same. For example, in the payroll worksheet, the formula to total the hours for Dayna McGuire is =*SUM(C5:I5)*, for Heather Kiley =*SUM(C6:I6)*, and so on. The only difference between the two formulas is the row number. Whenever formulas are this similar, you can use the Copy and Paste feature to copy the formula from one cell to another. The cell containing the original formula is called the **source**, and the cell(s) to which the formula is copied is called the **destination**. When the formula is pasted, Excel automatically changes column letters or row numbers to reflect the destination location. By default, Excel assumes **relative addressing**—cell addresses update relative to the destination.

Project

To simplify your completion of the Payroll worksheet, you will copy formulas using two methods: Copy and Paste and the fill handle.

1 With **ES1-WBPayroll.xlsx** open, make L6 the active cell.

> This cell contains the formula =*I6*K6* to calculate the gross pay for Heather Kiley. You will copy this formula to the remaining cells in column L to finish the Gross Pay column.

2 Click the Copy button 📋 in the Clipboard group in the Home tab. (Do not click the down-pointing arrow to the right of the Copy button.)

> A moving marquee surrounds the active cell indicating the source contents are copied to the Clipboard, which is a temporary storage location. The source being copied is the formula =*I6*K6*, not the value *330*.

3 Select the range L7:L13. To do this, position the cell pointer over L7, hold down the left mouse button, drag the pointer down to L13, and then release the mouse button.

marquee indicating source range

Step 3

4 Click the Paste button 📋 in the Clipboard group in the Home tab. (Do not click the down-pointing arrow on the button.)

> Excel copies the formula to the selected cells, displays the results, and the Paste Options (Ctrl) button appears. Clicking the Paste Options (Ctrl) button will display a drop-down list with various alternatives for pasting the data. The moving marquee remains around the source cell and the destination cells remain highlighted. The moving marquee disappears as soon as you start another activity or press the Esc key.

Step 4

Paste Options button

5 Press the Esc key to remove the marquee and the Paste Options (Ctrl) button, click L7, and then look at the entry in the Formula bar: =*J7*K7*.

> The row number in the source formula was increased by one to reflect the destination. The actions you completed in Steps 1 through 4 are called **relative copying**.

6 Use the Down Arrow key to check the remaining formulas in column L.

7 Make C15 the active cell.

8 Click the AutoSum button and then click the Enter button in the Formula bar.

> The SUM function inserts the formula *=SUM(C5:C14)*. Next, you will copy the formula using the fill handle.

9 Drag the fill handle in C15 right to L15.

> When the active cell contains a formula, dragging the fill handle causes Excel to copy the formula and change cell references relative to each destination location.

In Brief

Copy Formula
1. Activate source cell.
2. Click Copy button.
3. Select destination cell(s).
4. Click Paste button.

	A	B	C	D	E	F	G	H	I	J	K	L
1	Payroll											
2	Week Ended: September 24, 2011											
3										Total	Pay	Gross
4			Sun	Mon	Tue	Wed	Thu	Fri	Sat	Hours	Rate	Pay
5	Dayna	McGuire	6	5	8	8	7	0	6	40	8.25	330
6	Heather	Kiley	0	8	6	8	5	5	8	40	8.25	330
7	Pat	Soulliere	8	8	0	8	7	7	0	38	8.25	313.5
8	Jasmine	Hill	8	0	8	8	0	8	6	38	8.25	313.5
9	Moira	Su-Lin	0	8	0	8	7	7	8	38	8.25	313.5
10	Carla	Modano	0	0	8	8	7	7	8	38	8.25	313.5
11	Toni	Williams	8	0	0	8	8	7	4	35	8.25	288.75
12	Tyler	Santini	8	0	8	8	6	7	0	37	8.25	305.25
13	Lou	Cortez	8	0	6	8	0	8	8	38	8.25	313.5
14												
15	Total		46	29	44	72	47	56	48	342	74.25	2821.5

Step 9

Need Help?

If the results do not appear in D15 through L15, you probably dragged the cell pointer instead of the fill handle. Click C15 and try again, making sure you drag using the thin black cross.

10 Make K15 the active cell and then press the Delete key.

> The sum of the *Pay Rate* column is not useful information.

11 Make D15 the active cell and look at the entry in the Formula bar: *=SUM(D5:D14)*.

> The column letter in the source formula was changed to reflect the destination.

12 Use the Right Arrow key to check the formulas in the remaining columns.

13 Click the Save button on the Quick Access toolbar.

In Addition

Copy and Paste versus Fill

What is the difference between Copy and Paste and the fill handle? When you use Copy, the contents of the source cell(s) are placed in the Clipboard. The data will remain in the Clipboard and can be pasted several times in the current worksheet, into any other worksheet that is open, or into an open document in another program. Use Copy and Paste when the formula is to be inserted more than once or into nonadjacent cells. Use the fill handle when the formula is only being copied to adjacent cells.

Activity 1.6

Testing the Worksheet; Improving the Worksheet Appearance; Sorting

When you have finished building the worksheet, verifying that the formulas you entered are accurate is a good idea. The worksheet could contain formulas that are correct in structure but not mathematically correct for the situation. For example, the wrong range may be included in a SUM formula, or parentheses missing from a multioperator formula may cause an incorrect result. Various methods can be employed to verify a worksheet's accuracy. One method is to create a proof formula in a cell beside or below the worksheet that will verify the totals. For example, in the payroll worksheet the *Total Hours* column can be verified by creating a formula that adds all of the hours for all of the employees.

Data in Excel can be rearranged by sorting rows in either ascending order or descending order. You can select a single column or define a custom sort to specify multiple columns that determine the sort order.

Project

To confirm the accuracy of your calculations in the Payroll worksheet, you will enter proof formulas to test the worksheet and then use two formatting options to improve the worksheet's appearance.

1 With **ES1-WBPayroll.xlsx** open, make A17 the active cell.

2 Type **Hours**, press Alt + Enter, type **Proof**, and then press Enter.

Alt + Enter is the command to insert a line break in a cell. This command is used when you want multiple lines within the same cell. The height of the row is automatically expanded to accommodate the multiple lines.

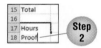

Tutorial 1.3
Copying and Testing a Formula

Tutorial 1.4
Sorting Data and Using Help

3 Make B17 the active cell.

4 Click in the Formula bar, type **=sum(c5:i13)**, and then click the Enter button or press Enter. (Alternatively, you could click the AutoSum button and then drag the pointer across the range C5 through I13.)

Excel displays the result, *342*, which verifies that your total hours in J15 is correct. Can you think of another formula that would have accomplished the same objective? *Hint: Think of the direction you added to arrive at the total hours in J15.*

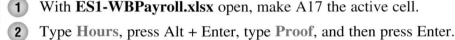

Typed range is color-coded for easy referencing and error checking.

	A	B	C	D	E	F	G	H	I	J
1	Payroll									
2	Week Ended: September 24, 2011									
3										Total
4			Sun	Mon	Tue	Wed	Thu	Fri	Sat	Hours
5	Dayna	McGuire	6	5	8	8	7	0	6	40
6	Heather	Kiley	0	8	6	8	5	5	8	40
7	Pat	Soulliere	8	8	0	8	7	7	0	38
8	Jasmine	Hill	8	0	8	8	0	8	6	38
9	Moira	Su-Lin	0	8	0	8	7	7	8	38
10	Carla	Modano	0	0	8	8	7	7	8	38
11	Toni	Williams	8	0	0	8	8	7	4	35
12	Tyler	Santini	8	0	8	8	6	7	0	37
13	Lou	Cortez	8	0	6	8	0	8	8	38
14										
15	Total		46	29	44	72	47	56	48	342
16										
17	Hours Proof	m(c5:i13)								

Need Help?

Didn't get 342? Then one of the cell entries is incorrect. Look through previous pages to see if the difference between 342 and your result equals a cell entry that you missed.

5 Make A18 the active cell.

6 Type **Gross**, press Alt + Enter, type **Pay Proof**, and then press Enter.

7 Make B18 the active cell.

> Since all of the employees are paid the same rate of pay, you can verify the *Gross Pay* column by multiplying the total hours times the pay rate.

8 Type **=b17*k5** and then press the Right Arrow key.

> The result, *2821.5,* confirms that the value in L15 is correct. The importance of testing a worksheet cannot be emphasized enough. Worksheets often contain important financial or statistical data that can form the basis for strategic business decisions.

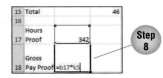

9 Look at the completed worksheet shown below. Notice that some of the values in column L show no decimals, while others show 1 or 2 decimal places. Also notice the labels do not align directly over the values below them.

Labels do not align directly over values.

	A	B	C	D	E	F	G	H	I	J	K	L
1	Payroll											
2	Week Ended: September 24, 2011											
3										Total	Pay	Gross
4			Sun	Mon	Tue	Wed	Thu	Fri	Sat	Hours	Rate	Pay
5	Dayna	McGuire	6	5	8	8	7	0	6	40	8.25	330
6	Heather	Kiley	0	8	6	8	5	5	8	40	8.25	330
7	Pat	Soulliere	8	8	0	8	7	7	0	38	8.25	313.5
8	Jasmine	Hill	8	0	8	8	0	8	6	38	8.25	313.5
9	Moira	Su-Lin	0	8	0	8	7	7	8	38	8.25	313.5
10	Carla	Modano	0	0	8	8	7	7	8	38	8.25	313.5
11	Toni	Williams	8	0	0	8	8	7	4	35	8.25	288.75
12	Tyler	Santini	8	0	8	8	6	7	0	37	8.25	305.25
13	Lou	Cortez	8	0	6	8	0	8	8	38	8.25	313.5
14												
15	Total		46	29	44	72	47	56	48	342		2821.5
16												
17	Hours Proof	342										
18	Gross Pay Proof	2821.5										

Decimal places are not consistent.

continues

10 Select the range L5:L15.

These final steps in building a worksheet are meant to improve the appearance of cells. In column L, Excel uses up to 15 decimal places for precision when calculating values. Since the *Gross Pay* column represents a sum of money, you will format these cells to display a dollar sign and show two decimal places.

11 Click the Accounting Number Format button $ in the Number group in the Home tab. (Do not click the down-pointing arrow to the right of the button.)

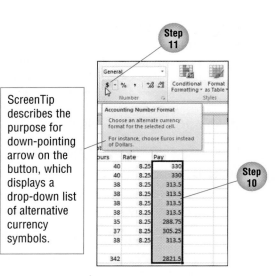

ScreenTip describes the purpose for down-pointing arrow on the button, which displays a drop-down list of alternative currency symbols.

The Accounting Number format adds a dollar sign, a comma in the thousands place, and two decimal places to each value in the selection.

12 Make B18 the active cell and then click the Accounting Number Format button.

13 Select the range C3:L4.

As previously mentioned, labels are aligned at the left edge of a column while values are aligned at the right edge. In the next step, you will align the labels at the right edge of the column so they appear directly over the values they represent.

14 Click the Align Text Right button in the Alignment group in the Home tab.

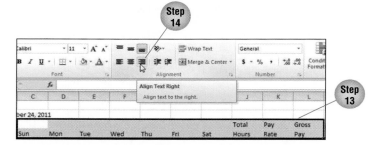

15 Click in any cell to deselect the range.

In the next steps, you will rearrange the names in the payroll worksheet so that they are in alphabetical order by last name. Since the last name is not the first column in the worksheet, you will need to define a custom sort.

16 Select the range A5:L13.

You are selecting the range before executing the sort command since you do not want to include the cells above and below the list of names in the sort action.

17 Click the Sort & Filter button in the Editing group in the Home tab.

18 Click *Custom Sort* at the drop-down list.

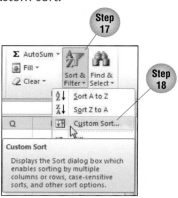

19 At the Sort dialog box, click the down-pointing arrow at the right of *Sort by* in the *Column* section and then click *Column B* at the drop-down list.

> The default entries of *Values* for *Sort On* and *A to Z* for *Order* are correct since you want the cells sorted by the text entries in column B in ascending order.

20 Click OK.

21 Click in any cell to deselect the range. Compare your sorted worksheet to the one shown below.

	A	B	C	D	E	F	G	H	I	J	K	L
1	Payroll											
2	Week Ended: September 24, 2011											
3										Total	Pay	Gross
4			Sun	Mon	Tue	Wed	Thu	Fri	Sat	Hours	Rate	Pay
5	Lou	Cortez	8	0	6	8	0	8	8	38	8.25	$ 313.50
6	Jasmine	Hill	8	0	8	8	0	8	6	38	8.25	$ 313.50
7	Heather	Kiley	0	8	6	8	5	5	8	40	8.25	$ 330.00
8	Dayna	McGuire	6	5	8	8	7	0	6	40	8.25	$ 330.00
9	Carla	Modano	0	0	8	8	7	7	8	38	8.25	$ 313.50
10	Tyler	Santini	8	0	8	8	6	7	0	37	8.25	$ 305.25
11	Pat	Soulliere	8	8	0	8	7	7	0	38	8.25	$ 313.50
12	Moira	Su-Lin	0	8	0	8	7	7	8	38	8.25	$ 313.50
13	Toni	Williams	8	0	0	8	8	7	4	35	8.25	$ 288.75
14												
15	Total		46	29	44	72	47	56	48	342		$2,821.50
16												
17	Hours Proof	342										
18	Gross Pay Proof	$2,821.50										

22 Click the Save button on the Quick Access toolbar.

In Addition

Rotating Text in Cells

The Alignment group in the Home tab contains an Orientation button, which can be used to rotate text within cells. Text can be rotated counterclockwise, clockwise, changed to a vertical alignment, rotated up vertically, or rotated down vertically. Often, text set in narrow columns is angled to improve the label appearance. In the screen shown at the right, the cells containing the days of the week in the payroll worksheet are angled counterclockwise.

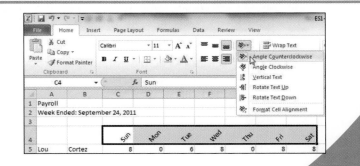

Activity 1.7

An extensive online Help resource is available that contains information on Excel features and commands. Click the Microsoft Excel Help button located near the upper right corner of the screen (below the Minimize button on the Title bar) to open the Excel Help window. By default, the Help feature searches for an Internet connection. A message at the bottom right corner of the window will indicate whether Help will display information in Excel resources at Office Online or in the Offline Help file.

Another method to use Help resources is to point to a button in the tab and then press function key F1.

Project

Tutorial 1.4
Sorting Data and Using Help

After reviewing the Payroll worksheet, you think the first two title rows would look better if the text was centered over the columns in the worksheet. You will use the Help feature to look up the steps to do this.

1 With **ES1-WBPayroll.xlsx** open, make A1 the active cell.

To center the title rows above the columns in the worksheet, you decide to browse the buttons in the Alignment group in the Home tab. The Merge & Center button in the group seems appropriate but you are not sure of the steps to work with this feature.

2 Point to the Merge & Center button in the Alignment group in the Home tab and read the information that displays in the ScreenTip.

3 With the pointer still resting on the Merge & Center button, press function key F1 and then read the paragraphs below the title *Merge cells or split merged cells* in the Excel Help window.

4 Scroll down the Help window, click <u>Merge and center adjacent cells</u> below the subtitle *What do you want to do?* and then read the information describing the steps to merge cells.

5 Close the Excel Help window.

6 Select the range A1:L1 and then click the Merge & Center button in the Alignment group in the Home tab.

A1 is merged across columns A through L and the text *Payroll* is automatically centered within the merged cell.

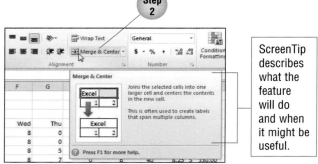

ScreenTip describes what the feature will do and when it might be useful.

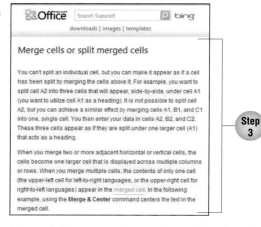

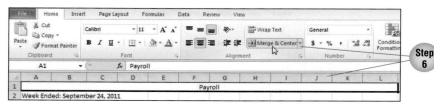

7 Select the range A2:L2 and then click the Merge & Center button.

> The two titles in the payroll worksheet are now centered over the cells below them.

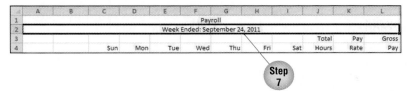

Step 7

8 Click the Microsoft Office Excel Help button 🔘 located near the upper right corner of the screen (below the Minimize button on the Title bar).

> You can also access Help resources by typing a search phrase and browsing related topics in the Help window.

9 Type **preview worksheet** in the Search text box and then click the Search button or press Enter.

Step 9

10 Click the <u>Preview worksheet pages before printing</u> hyperlink and then read the information that displays in the window.

Search results for: preview worksheet

Preview worksheet pages before printing

Step 10

Since Microsoft Office Online is updated frequently, your search results list may vary for this hyperlink, including its title or position in the list.

11 Close the Excel Help window.

12 Click the Save button on the Quick Access toolbar.

In Addition

Using Offline Help

By default Excel checks for a live Internet connection when the Help feature is activated. If no connection is found, Excel displays the Help window shown at the right. Office Online provides additional resources such as online training and templates along with the most up-to-date information. You can disable online Help searches if you want to turn off the online access for reasons similar to the following:
- You are currently experiencing a slow Internet connection.
- You are in a location where you have to pay hourly for Internet access.
- You are away from your normal site and are concerned about privacy.

Click the down-pointing arrow to the right of the Search button and then click *Excel Help in the Content from this computer* section at the drop-down list to temporarily suspend online searches.

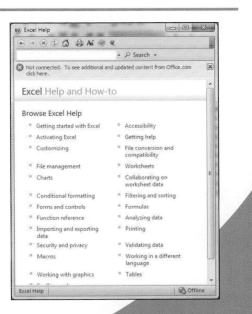

Activity 1.8

Previewing; Changing Page Orientation; Printing a Worksheet

Many times a worksheet is printed to have a paper copy, or **hard copy**, to file or to attach to a report. Large, complex worksheets are often easier to proofread and check from a paper copy. The Quick Print button on the Quick Access toolbar will print the active worksheet using default print options. Display the Print tab in Backstage view to preview the worksheet and modify print options. For example, to change the page orientation while previewing how the worksheet will print, click the File tab and then click the Print tab in Backstage view. A preview of how the worksheet will look when printed displays at the right side of Backstage view. The center of Backstage view is divided into three categories: *Print, Printer,* and *Settings.* Use the galleries available in each category to modify print options. Use Backstage view to preview the worksheet before printing to avoid wasted paper by checking in advance whether the entire worksheet will fit on one page, or to preview and/or change other print options.

Project The Payroll worksheet is finished. You want to preview the worksheet and then print a copy for the office manager.

1. With **ES1-WBPayroll.xlsx** open, make A20 the active cell and then type the student information your instructor has directed for printouts. For example, type your first and last names and then press Enter.

   Make sure you have checked if other identifying information such as your program or class number should be included.

Tutorial 1.5
Formatting and Printing Options

Tutorial 1.6
Previewing and Printing a Workbook

2. Click the File tab and then click the Print tab to display the worksheet in Backstage view as shown in Figure 1.2.

FIGURE 1.2 Print Preview Window

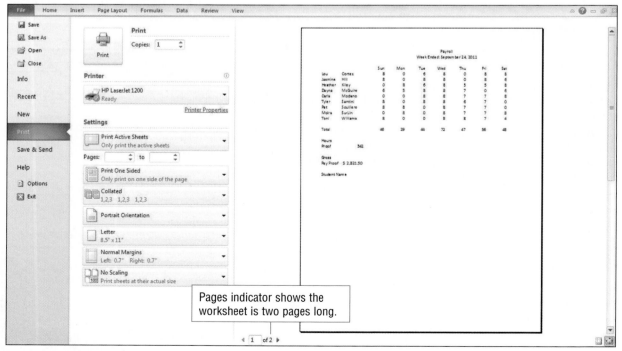

Pages indicator shows the worksheet is two pages long.

3 The right side of the view displays the first page of the worksheet as it will print with the current print options. Notice the pages indicator at the bottom left of the preview shows that you are viewing page *1 of 2* pages. Click the Next Page button ▶ located at the right of the current page number to display page 2.

4 The second page of the printout appears showing the columns that could not fit on page 1.

5 Click the *Page Orientation* gallery (currently displays *Portrait Orientation*) in the *Settings* category of the Print tab.

> One method to reduce the printout to one page is to change the orientation of the paper from portrait to landscape. In **portrait** orientation, the page is printed on paper taller than it is wide. In **landscape** orientation, the data is rotated to print on paper that is wider than it is tall.

6 Click *Landscape Orientation* at the drop-down list.

> The preview updates to show the worksheet in landscape orientation. Notice that all of the columns now fit on one page.

In Brief

Preview Worksheet
1. Click File tab.
2. Click Print tab.

Change to Landscape Orientation
1. Click File tab.
2. Click Print tab.
3. Click *Page Orientation* gallery.
4. Click *Landscape Orientation*.

7 Click the Print button located at the top left of the Print tab in the *Print* category.

> Backstage view closes and the worksheet prints on the default printer. The default settings in the Print tab of Backstage view are to print one copy of all pages in the active worksheet. You will learn how to adjust page layout and print settings in a later section.

Your printer name will vary.

8 At the worksheet, scroll right if necessary until you see the vertical dashed line between columns located to the right of the *Gross Pay* column.

> The dashed vertical line is a page break. Page breaks appear after you have previewed or printed a worksheet. A worksheet that spans many rows will display a horizontal dashed line below the last row that can fit on the page. The dashed lines do not print.

9 Click the Save button on the Quick Access toolbar.

Activity 1.9

Displaying Formulas; Navigating a Worksheet

Sometimes you may want to print a worksheet with the cell formulas displayed rather than the formula results. Printing a second copy of a worksheet with the cell formulas is a good idea when complicated formulas that would take you a long time to redo exist in the worksheet. To display cell formulas, open the Excel Options dialog box from the Backstage view, click the Advanced tab and click the *Show formulas in cells instead of their calculated results* check box in the *Display options for this worksheet* section.

Once a worksheet becomes larger, you will need to scroll to the right or scroll down to locate cells with which you need to work. The horizontal and vertical scroll bars are used to scroll with the mouse. Scrolling using the scroll bars does not move the position of the active cell. You can also scroll using the arrow keys or with keyboard commands. Scrolling using the keyboard moves the active cell.

Project You will print a second copy of the payroll worksheet with the cell formulas displayed and practice navigating the worksheet using the scroll bars and keyboard shortcuts.

The Waterfront
B·I·S·T·R·O

1. With **ES1-WBPayroll.xlsx** open, click the File tab to open Backstage view.

2. Click the Options button [Options] located near the bottom of the left pane just above the Exit button.

3. At the Excel Options dialog box, click *Advanced* in the left pane.

4. Scroll down the Advanced options for working with Excel pane until you see the section titled *Display options for this worksheet*.

5. Click the *Show formulas in cells instead of their calculated results* check box to insert a check mark and then click OK.

   The cells in the worksheet are automatically expanded and cells that contain formulas now display the formula in the worksheet area.

6 Click the File tab, click the Print tab, and then click the Print button to print the worksheet with the cell formulas, or click the Quick Print button on the Quick Access toolbar.

> The worksheet will print on two pages in the expanded cell formulas view. In a later section you will learn how to adjust column widths and scale a worksheet to reduce the number of pages for a wide printout.

7 Position the mouse pointer on the right scroll arrow at the right edge of the horizontal scroll bar and then click the left mouse button a few times to scroll to the right edge of the worksheet.

8 Position the mouse pointer on the horizontal scroll box, hold down the left mouse button, drag the scroll box to the left edge of the horizontal scroll bar, and then release the mouse button.

> The width or height of the scroll box indicates the proportional amount of the used cells in the worksheet that is visible in the current window. The position of the scroll box within the scroll bar indicates the relative location of the visible cells within the remainder of the worksheet.

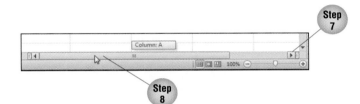

Step 7

Step 8

9 Press Ctrl + Home.

> Ctrl + Home makes A1 the active cell.

10 Press the Page Down key once.

> Each time you press the Page Down key you move the active cell down one screen.

11 Press the Page Up key once.

> Each time you press the Page Up key, you move the active cell up one screen.

12 Click the Find & Select button 🔍 in the Editing group in the Home tab and click *Go To* at the drop-down list.

Step 12

continues

In Brief

Go to Specific Cell
1. Click Find & Select button.
2. Click *Go To*.
3. Type cell address.
4. Click OK.

13 At the Go To dialog box, type **L15** in the *Reference* text box and then click OK or press Enter.

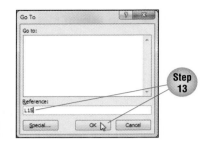

Step 13

> The active cell is positioned in L15. Notice that using Go To moved the position of the active cell.

14 Use the Up, Down, Left, and Right Arrow keys to practice moving around the worksheet.

> Holding down a directional arrow key causes the screen to scroll very quickly. Table 1.2 illustrates more keyboard scrolling techniques.

15 Click the Save button on the Quick Access toolbar.

16 Click the File tab and then click the Close button in the Backstage view.

TABLE 1.2 Keyboard Movement Commands

Press	To move to
Arrow keys	one cell up, down, left, or right
Ctrl + Home	A1
Ctrl + End	last cell in worksheet
Home	beginning of row
Page Down	down one screen
Page Up	up one screen
Alt + Page Down	one screen to the right
Alt + Page Up	one screen to the left

In Addition

Viewing a Large Worksheet by Splitting the Window

You can split a worksheet into more than one window to facilitate viewing different sections of a large worksheet at the same time. For example, to view the employee names at the left edge of the window and see the formulas to calculate each person's gross pay in column L while the worksheet is displayed with the wide columns in cell formulas, you could split the window vertically as shown below. Each window contains a set of scroll bars to allow you to scroll to different areas within each split section of the worksheet. To split a worksheet into two vertical windows, drag the split box located at the bottom right of the Excel window immediately right of the right scroll arrow in the horizontal scroll bar to the position you want the split to occur. When you rest the pointer on the split box, the pointer changes to a double vertical line with a left- and right-pointing arrow. Drag the split bar back to the right edge of the screen to remove the split. The split box at the top of the vertical scroll bar can be used to create a horizontal split in a worksheet.

	A	B	C	D	E		I	J	K	L
1										
2					Split bar					
3								Total	Pay	Gross
4			Sun	Mon	Tue		Sat	Hours	Rate	Pay
5	Lou	Cortez	8	0	6		8	=SUM(C5:I5)	8.25	=J5*K5
6	Jasmine	Hill	8	0	8		6	=SUM(C6:I6)	8.25	=J6*K6
7	Heather	Kiley	0	8	6		8	=SUM(C7:I7)	8.25	=J7*K7
8	Dayna	McGuire	6	5	8		6	=SUM(C8:I8)	8.25	=J8*K8
9	Carla	Modano	0	0	8		8	=SUM(C9:I9)	8.25	=J9*K9
10	Tyler	Santini	8	0	8		0	=SUM(C10:I10)	8.25	=J10*K10
11	Pat	Soulliere	8	8	0		0	=SUM(C11:I11)	8.25	=J11*K11
12	Moira	Su-Lin	0	8	0		8	=SUM(C12:I12)	8.25	=J12*K12
13	Toni	Williams	8	0	0		4	=SUM(C13:I13)	8.25	=J13*K13
14										
15	Total		=SUM(C5:C14)	=SUM(D5:D14)	=SUM(E5:E14)		=SUM(I5:I14)	=SUM(J5:J14)		=SUM(L5:L14)

Features Summary

Feature	Ribbon Tab, Group	Button	Quick Access Toolbar	File tab	Keyboard Shortcut
Accounting Number format	Home, Number	$			
align text right	Home, Alignment				
cell formulas		Options		Options	Ctrl + ~
close a workbook				Close	Ctrl + F4
copy	Home, Clipboard				Ctrl + C
custom sort	Home, Editing				
fill down	Home, Editing	Fill ▾			Ctrl + D
fill left	Home, Editing	Fill ▾			
fill right	Home, Editing	Fill ▾			Ctrl + R
fill up	Home, Editing	Fill ▾			
Go To	Home, Editing				Ctrl + G
Help		?			F1
merge and center	Home, Alignment				
new workbook				New	Ctrl + N
open				Open	Ctrl + O
paste	Home, Clipboard				Ctrl + V
Print Preview				Print	Ctrl + P
print				Print	Ctrl + P or Ctrl + F2
save			💾	Save	Ctrl + S
save with a new name				Save As	F12
SUM function	Home, Editing	Σ			Alt + =

Knowledge Check

Completion: In the space provided at the right, indicate the correct term, command, or option.

1. This area contains commands and features for performing actions divided into tabs and groups. _____

2. This area displays the formula stored within the cell (not the result). _____

3. The cell pointer changes to this when pointing at the small black square at the bottom right corner of the active cell. _____

4. This would be the formula entry to divide the contents of cell C6 by the contents in cell C12. _____

5. This is the term for the method used to create a formula by typing the equals sign and operator symbols while clicking reference cells between the typed symbols. _____

6. This term is used to refer to the values identified within parentheses in the SUM function. _____

7. The AutoSum button is located in this group in the Home tab. _____

8. Do this action if Excel suggests the wrong range after clicking the AutoSum button. _____

9. This button appears after copied cells are pasted into the destination range. _____

10. This is the term for the formulas entered beside or below a worksheet that are designed to verify the worksheet's accuracy. _____

11. This format adds a dollar sign, a comma in the thousands place, and two decimal places to each value in the selected range. _____

12. Click the Sort & Filter button in the Editing group in the Home tab and then click this option at the drop-down list to display the Sort dialog box. _____

13. This keyboard shortcut will open the Excel Help window when pointing to a button. _____

14. Display this tab in Backstage view to change the page orientation. _____

15. Open this dialog box to type a cell reference to which you want to move the active cell. _____

Skills Review

Note: If you submit your work in hard copy, check with your instructor before completing these reviews to find out if you need to print two copies of each worksheet, with one of the copies showing the cell formulas instead of the calculated results.

Review 1 Creating Labels, Values, and Formulas

1. Create a new folder on your storage medium and name it **ExcelEOS**.
2. Create the worksheet shown in Figure 1.3. Use the fill handle whenever possible to facilitate data entry. In rows 8, 13, and 17, press the spacebar twice before typing the cell entry to indent the text.
3. Format E6:H17 to the Accounting Number format.
4. Create the following formulas by typing the entry, using the pointing method, or using the AutoSum button:
   a. In cell E8, subtract Cost of Goods Sold from Sales by entering =e6-e7.
   b. In cell E13, add the three expenses by entering =sum(e10:e12).
   c. In cell E15, subtract Total Expenses from Gross Margin by entering =e8-e13.
   d. In cell E16, multiply Net Income Before Taxes by 22% by entering =e15*22%.
   e. In cell E17, subtract Taxes from Net Income Before Taxes by entering =e15-e16.
5. Copy and paste formulas in column E to columns F and G as follows:
   a. Copy the formula in E8 and then paste the formula to the range F8:G8.
   b. Copy the formula in E13 and then paste the formula to the range F13:G13.
   c. Select and copy the range E15:E17 and then paste the formulas to the range F15:G17.
6. Click in cell H6 and then use the AutoSum button to enter the formula to add E6:G6.
7. Copy the formula in H6 to the remaining cells in column H.
8. Save the workbook in the ExcelEOS folder and name it **ES1-R1-WBQtrlyIncome.xlsx**.

FIGURE 1.3 Review 1 Worksheet

	A	B	C	D	E	F	G	H
1	The Waterfront Bistro							
2	Condensed Quarterly Statement of Income							
3	For the Quarter Ended September 30, 2011							
4	In Thousands							
5					Jul	Aug	Sep	Total
6	Sales				51.2	53.7	55.6	
7	Cost of Goods Sold				35.2	44.8	45.7	
8	Gross Margin							
9								
10	Advertising Expense				2.1	2.1	2.1	
11	Wages and Benefits Expense				10.2	9.4	10.6	
12	Miscellaneous and Overhead Expense				1.3	1.3	1.3	
13	Total Expenses							
14								
15	Net Income Before Taxes							
16	Taxes							
17	Net Income After Taxes							

Review 2 Improving the Appearance of the Worksheet; Previewing and Printing

1. With **ES1-R1-WBQtrlyIncome.xlsx** open, merge and center the title in row 1 across columns A through H.
2. Merge and center A2, A3, and A4 across columns A through H.
3. Change the alignment of the range E5:H5 to Align Text Right.
4. Use the Help feature to find out how to display fewer decimal places.
5. Select the range E6:H17 and then decrease the number of decimal places to one decimal place.
6. Deselect the range E6:H17 and then display the worksheet in Backstage view to preview how the worksheet will look when printed.
7. Print the worksheet.
8. Display the worksheet with cell formulas displayed and then print another copy of the worksheet.
9. Clear the option to show formulas in cells.
10. Save and then close **ES1-R1-WBQtrlyIncome.xlsx**.

Skills Assessment

Note: If you submit your work in hard copy, check with your instructor before completing these Assessments to find out if you need to print two copies of each worksheet with one of the copies showing the cell formulas instead of the calculated results.

Assessment 1 Adding Values and Formulas to a Worksheet

1. Open **MPTravelCosts.xlsx** and then save the workbook in the ExcelEOS folder and name it **ES1-A1-MPTravelCosts**.
2. This worksheet was started to calculate the travel costs for a remote location film shoot for July 11 to August 31, 2011. Melissa Gehring of First Choice Travel has just confirmed the following costs that you were waiting for to finish the worksheet. All costs are tax included.
   - Airfare to the location and back to Los Angeles airport is $588.15 per person.
   - The hotel is booked for two people per room and will cost $76.20 per room per night.
   - Each person travelling to the location will receive a daily expense allowance of $27.
3. Enter the appropriate values provided above in the *Unit Cost* column in the worksheet.
4. Enter formulas in the required cells in column G to calculate the extended cost. For example, the airfare formula is the quantity times the unit cost, the hotel and daily expense allowance formulas are the quantity times the unit cost times the number of days.
5. Enter the formula in G10 to add the three expense results.
6. Apply alignment and formatting options you learned in this section to any cells that you consider would improve the appearance of the worksheet.
7. Save, print, and then close **ES1-A1-MPTravelCosts.xlsx**.

Assessment 2 Creating a New Workbook

1. You work with Bobbie Sinclair, business manager at Performance Threads. You are preparing a contract quotation for costume rental and alteration fees for costumes needed by Marquee Productions for its remote location film shoot July 11 to August 31, 2011. Create a new workbook that will calculate the contract price using the following information.
   - Seventeen Renaissance period costumes will be provided at a rental cost of $88.50 per day, tax included, for a total of 50 days.
   - A fee of $110.00 per costume, tax included, is charged for alterations provided on site.
2. Make sure the total contract price is summed below the rental and alteration fee calculations.
3. Apply alignment and formatting options you learned in this section to any cells that you consider would improve the appearance of the worksheet.
4. Save the workbook in the ExcelEOS folder and name it **ES1-A2-PTCostumeCont**.
5. Print and then close **ES1-A2-PTCostumeCont.xlsx**.

Assessment 3 Creating a New Workbook

1. You work with Sam Vestering, manager of North American Distribution for Worldwide Enterprises. You are preparing a projected distribution revenue schedule for Marquee Productions' latest film *Going Global*, to be released September 2, 2011. Create a new workbook that will estimate Worldwide's projected revenue using the following information (see Table 1.3 on the next page):
   - Preview cities receive the film on the Friday before the general release date and pay Worldwide Enterprises 15% of projected box office revenues.
   - General release cities pay Worldwide Enterprises 10% of projected box office revenues.
   - All distribution fees and projected revenues are in U.S. dollars.
   - Include a total of the projected revenue for Worldwide Enterprises. ***Hint: Consider creating this worksheet by grouping the preview cities and the general release cities separately.***
2. Apply alignment and formatting options you learned in this section to any cells that you consider would improve the appearance of the worksheet.
3. Use the Sort feature to rearrange the order of the cities in ascending order.
4. Save the workbook in the ExcelEOS folder and name it **ES1-A3-WEGGProjRev**.
5. Print and then close **ES1-A3-WEGGProjRev.xlsx**.

TABLE 1.3 Assessment 3

City	Release Category	Projected Box Office Sales in Thousands
New York	Preview	41.9
Tucson	General	15.3
Los Angeles	Preview	47.1
Denver	Preview	19.6
Orlando	General	29.6
Des Moines	General	10.4
Wichita	Preview	11.2
Boston	General	26.9
Philadelphia	General	21.4
Dallas	General	18.7
Milwaukee	General	12.6
Atlanta	Preview	33.1
Vancouver	General	31.7
Calgary	General	15.8
Toronto	Preview	29.2
Montreal	Preview	17.3

Assessment 4 Finding Information on Sorting

1. In Activity 1.6 you learned how to sort the employee names in the payroll worksheet using the Sort dialog box. There are other methods with which you can sort a worksheet. Use Excel Help to find out more ways you can sort data in Excel.
2. Open **WBInventory.xlsx** and then save the workbook with Save As in the ExcelEOS folder and name it **ES1-A4-WBInventory**.
3. Sort the worksheet in ascending order by the *Item* column.
4. Print the worksheet.
5. Sort the worksheet in ascending order by the *Supplier Name* column.
6. Print the worksheet.
7. Save and then close **ES1-A4-WBInventory.xlsx**.

Assessment 5 Individual Challenge
Creating a School Budget

1. Create a worksheet to calculate the estimated total cost of completing your diploma or certificate. You determine the items that need to be included in the worksheet such as tuition, fees, textbooks, supplies, accommodation costs, transportation, telephone, food, and entertainment. If necessary, use the Internet to find reasonable cost estimates if you want to include an item such as cell phone charges and want to research competitive rates for your area. Arrange the labels and values by quarter, semester, or academic year according to your preference. Make sure to include a total that shows the total cost of your education.
2. Save the worksheet in the ExcelEOS folder and name it **ES1-A5-SchoolBudget**.

3. Apply alignment and formatting options you learned in this section to any cells that you consider would improve the appearance of the worksheet.
4. If necessary, change the page orientation to landscape and then print the worksheet.
5. Save and then close **ES1-A5-SchoolBudget.xlsx**.

Marquee Challenge

Challenge 1 Preparing an International Student Registration Report

1. You work at Niagara Peninsula College in the Registrar's Office. The Registrar has asked you to create the annual report for international student registrations. Create the worksheet shown in Figure 1.4.
2. Calculate the tuition fees in column I by multiplying the credit hours times the fee per hour and then use the SUM function to calculate the total international student fees.
3. Apply format options as shown and format the values in column I to an appropriate number format.
4. Add the current date and your name in rows 4 and 19, respectively.
5. Change the page orientation to landscape.
6. Save the workbook in the ExcelEOS folder and name it **ES1-C1-NPCIntlRegRpt**.
7. Print and then close **ES1-C1-NPCIntlRegRpt.xlsx**.

FIGURE 1.4 Challenge 1

	A	B	C	D	E	F	G	H	I
1				Niagara Peninsula College					
2				International Student Registrations					
3				for the 2011/2012 Academic Year					
4				Report Date: (Current Date)					
5		Last	First	Home			Credit	Fee per	Tuition
6	ID #	Name	Name	Country	Program	Semester	Hours	Hour	Fee
7	241588	Cano	Sergio	Spain	BIS11	1	45	432	
8	241578	Flannigan	Maren	Ireland	BIS11	1	60	432	
9	241856	Chou	Terry	China	BMK12	1	45	432	
10	286953	Zhang	Joseph	China	BIN32	2	45	432	
11	274586	Alivero	Maria	Mexico	CMP12	2	45	432	
12	268451	Torres	Phillip	Ecuador	CTN14	2	60	432	
13	234851	Davis	Caitlyn	Australia	OAM24	3	60	432	
14	299635	Muir	Christa	Australia	GRD13	4	30	432	
15	247523	North	Marlo	Bahamas	HTC24	2	30	432	
16	277458	Cervinka	Mary	Croatia	TTM14	4	30	432	
17									
18					TOTAL INTERNATIONAL STUDENT FEES:				
19	Prepared by: (Student Name)								

Challenge 2 Preparing a Theatre Arts Target Enrollment Report

1. You work with Cal Rubine, chair of the Theatre Arts division at Niagara Peninsula College. Cal needs the target student enrollment report to assist with the revenue projections for the upcoming budget. Cal has asked you to create the worksheet shown in Figure 1.5.

2. Cal uses the actual enrollments from the prior year (2010/2011) to calculate the target for the next year. In some programs, Cal expects that enrollment will be higher than the previous year due to new registrants, transfers from other programs, and students returning to pick up missed credits. In other programs, Cal expects that enrollment will decline from the previous year due to students dropping the program, transfers to other colleges, and students failing to meet the minimum GPA for progression. Cal has provided the percentages in Table 1.4 for you to use to create the formulas in the *Target* column.

3. Use the SUM function to calculate the total target estimated enrollments.

4. Apply alignment options as shown and add the current date and your name in rows 8 and 9, respectively.

5. If necessary, format the values in the *Target* column to zero decimal places and then change the page orientation to landscape.

6. Save the workbook in the ExcelEOS folder and name it **ES1-C2-NPCTargetEnrolRpt**.

7. Print and then close **ES1-C2-NPCTargetEnrolRpt.xlsx**.

FIGURE 1.5 Challenge 2

	A	B	C	D	E	F	G	H	I	J
1					Niagara Peninsula College					
2					Target Student Enrollments					
3					For the 2012/2013 Academic Year					
4					Theatre Arts Division					
5										
6	Academic chair: Cal Rubine									
7										
8	Report date: (current date)									
9	Prepared by: (student name)						Actual			
10					Program	Semester		Enrollment		
11	Program Name				Code	Offering		2010/2011		Target
12	Theatre Arts: Acting				TAA12	1 2 3 4		210		
13	Theatre Arts: Stage Management				TAM23	1 2		55		
14	Theatre Arts: Lighting & Effects				TAL42	1 2		67		
15	Theatre Arts: Production				TAP32	1 2 3 4		221		
16	Theatre Arts: Sound				TAS14	1 2		38		
17	Theatre Arts: Business Management				TAB25	1 2 3 4		64		
18										
19					ESTIMATED ENROLLMENTS FOR 2012/2013:					

TABLE 1.4 Challenge 2

Program Name	Target Percent
Theatre Arts: Acting	95%
Theatre Arts: Stage Management	106%
Theatre Arts: Lighting & Effects	112%
Theatre Arts: Production	85%
Theatre Arts: Sound	103%
Theatre Arts: Business Management	75%

Excel SECTION 2

Editing and Formatting Worksheets

Skills

- Edit the content of cells
- Clear cells and cell formats
- Use proofing tools
- Insert and delete columns and rows
- Move and copy cells
- Use Paste Options to link cells
- Adjust column width and row height
- Change the font, size, style, and color of cells
- Apply numeric formats and adjust the number of decimal places
- Use Undo, Redo, and Repeat
- Change cell alignment and indentation
- Add borders and shading
- Copy formats using Format Painter
- Apply cell styles
- Apply a theme
- Find and replace cell entries and formats
- Freeze and unfreeze panes
- Change the zoom percentage
- Insert, move, and resize pictures and clip art

Projects Overview

Edit and format a quotation and invoice for catering services. View and edit a special events booking worksheet.

Create a direct wages budget for a remote film shoot.

Complete and format a costume cost report and an invoice for costume production.

Create a room timetable.

Edit and format a revenue summary report for movie distribution.

Model Answers for Projects

These model answers for the projects that you complete in Section 2 provide a preview of the finished projects before you begin working and also allow you to compare your own results with these models to ensure you have created the materials accurately.

ES2-WBQuoteToMP.xlsx is the project in Activities 2.1 to 2.9.

The Waterfront Bistro

3104 Rivermist Drive
Buffalo, NY 14280
716 555 3166

Quotation

TO: Marquee Productions
955 South Alameda Street
Los Angeles, CA 90037

DATE: 5-Nov-10

ATT: Camille Matsui

RE: Remote Location Filming
July 11 to August 31

Note: All prices include tax.

Item	No. of Persons	Price per Person	No. of Days	Total
Buffet Lunch	56	8.34	52	$ 24,286.08
Soup and salad				
Vegetable tray with dip				
Seafood hors d'oeuvres				
Hot entrée				
Deli tray and rolls				
Dessert				
Beverages	56	3.91	52	11,385.92
Coffee and tea				
Assorted juice				
Mineral water				
Snacks	56	3.91	52	11,385.92
Muffins				
Donuts				
Fruit tray				
Vegetable tray with dip				
Transport		33.00	52	1,716.00
Total				$ 48,773.92

Terms: Due upon receipt of invoice payable in U.S. funds

ES2-WBSpecEvents.xlsx is the project in Activities 2.10 to 2.12.

The Waterfront Bistro
2011 Special Event Bookings

Contact Name	Contact Phone	Event	Date	Room	Guests	Special Menu	Price Per Person
Cecily Hillmore	716 555 6598	Business Meeting	1/15/2011	Starlake	42	No	23.95
Frances Corriveau	716 555 3256	Birthday Party	1/23/2011	Westview	82	Yes	29.95
Orlando Fagan	716 555 3694	25th Wedding Anniversary	3/10/2011	Westview	95	Yes	29.95
Kim Pockovic	905 555 3698	Birthday Party	3/18/2011	Westview	65	Yes	36.95
Lane Gill	416 555 3264	Business Meeting	3/29/2011	Starlake	55	No	22.95
Percy Bresque	716 555 1248	50th Wedding Anniversary	4/12/2011	Westview	102	Yes	35.95
Max Santore	905 555 3264	Wedding	4/28/2011	Sunset	188	Yes	27.95
Omar Hamid	716 555 8796	Engagement Party	5/8/2011	Sunset	67	Yes	29.95
Jack Torrance	716 555 1469	Business Meeting	5/15/2011	Westview	34	No	24.95
Dana Russell	716 555 4965	Birthday Party	5/30/2011	Starlake	54	No	28.95
Walter Szucs	905 555 6998	Birthday Party	6/10/2011	Starlake	84	No	34.95
Nicole Griffin	905 555 4166	25th Wedding Anniversary	6/17/2011	Starlake	78	Yes	34.95
Zack Doucet	716 555 3488	Wedding	6/20/2011	Sunset	215	Yes	29.95
Jesse Golinsky	716 555 4218	Business Meeting	6/26/2011	Westview	60	No	25.95
Cora Jin Ping	716 555 7774	Baby Shower	7/10/2011	Sunset	75	Yes	22.95
Elizabeth McMaster	716 555 9442	Engagement Party	7/11/2011	Sunset	94	Yes	28.95
Reed Pavelich	716 555 2286	Wedding	7/25/2011	Starlake	145	Yes	34.95
Alfredo Juanitez	716 555 4668	Business Meeting	7/31/2011	Westview	37	No	24.95
Yanfang Guo	716 555 4856	50th Wedding Anniversary	8/10/2011	Starlake	62	No	34.95
Jelena Boskovic	716 555 3456	Business Meeting	8/18/2011	Westview	27	Yes	29.95
Priscilla Melo	716 555 3145	Business Meeting	8/25/2011	Westview	34	Yes	25.95
Tracie McIntyre	716 555 3496	Birthday Party	9/2/2011	Sunset	26	No	22.95
Krista Pressey	716 555 7469	50th Wedding Anniversary	9/5/2011	Sunset	95	No	28.95
Langford Hill	716 555 8798	Wedding	9/25/2011	Starlake	185	No	34.95
Naomi Sayers	905 555 3486	Wedding	10/15/2011	Starlake	245	Yes	24.95
Lesley Reedman	716 555 4123	Wedding	10/22/2011	Westview	110	Yes	34.95
Mitchell Langley	905 555 4637	Wedding	11/19/2011	Sunset	85	Yes	29.95
Sally Ramirez	716 555 9648	Engagement Party	12/5/2011	Starlake	34	No	25.95
Paulina Ordonez	905 555 1435	25th Wedding Anniversary	12/10/2011	Westview	45	No	22.95
Arietta Teneqja	905 555 1345	Business Meeting	12/15/2011	Sunset	67	Yes	28.95
Subrein El-Keri	416 555 9765	Engagement Party	12/18/2011	Westview	47	Yes	34.95
Edwina Blakely	716 555 3477	Birthday Party	12/20/2011	Westview	65	No	24.95
Laura Fernandez	416 555 1345	Shareholders Meeting	12/28/2011	Westview	194	No	39.95

Activity 2.1

Editing and Clearing Cells; Using Proofing Tools

The contents of a cell can be edited directly within the cell or in the Formula bar. Clearing a cell can involve removing the cell contents, format, or both. The Spelling feature is a useful tool to assist with correcting typing errors within a worksheet. After completing a spelling check, you will still need to proofread the worksheet since the spelling checker will not highlight all errors and cannot check the accuracy of values. Other Proofing tools available include a Research feature to search for external information, a Thesaurus to find a word with similar meaning, and a Translate tool to translate a selected word into a different language.

Project

SNAP

Tutorial 2.1
Editing Data in a
Worksheet

Dana Hirsch, manager of The Waterfront Bistro, has begun a catering services quotation for Marquee Productions. Dana has asked you to finish the quotation by correcting spelling, following up on costs, and improving the appearance. You will be working on this quotation through most of this section.

1 Open **WBQuoteToMP.xlsx**. *Note: This worksheet contains intentional spelling errors that will be corrected in this activity.*

2 Save the workbook with Save As in the ExcelS2 folder and name it **ES2-WBQuoteToMP**.

3 Double-click D18.

> Double-clicking a cell inserts a blinking insertion point in the cell; Edit appears in the Status bar. The insertion point position varies depending on the location of the cell pointer when Edit mode is activated.

4 Press the Right or Left Arrow key as needed to move the insertion point between the decimal point and *7* and then press the Delete key.

5 Type **3** and then press Enter.

Step 5

6 Make D30 the active cell.

7 Move the pointer after *7* in the Formula bar and then click the left mouse button.

> The cell pointer changes to an I-beam pointer I when positioned in the Formula bar.

8 Press Backspace to delete *7*, type **4**, and then click the Enter button on the Formula bar.

Step 8

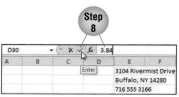

9 Make A7 the active cell and then press Delete.

> Delete or Backspace clears only the contents of the cell; formats or comments applied to the cell remain in effect.

10 Make A1 the active cell and then press Delete.

> Notice the text is deleted from the cell but the color in the background of the cell remains.

11 Select the range A1:C1. Click the Clear button in the Editing group in the Home tab and then click *Clear All* at the drop-down list.

Step 11

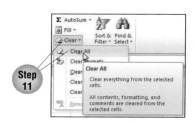

> Clear All removes everything from a cell, including formats or comments.

12 Click A1, click the Review tab, and then click the Spelling button 🔲.

> Spell check begins at the active cell. Words within the worksheet that are not found in the dictionary are highlighted as potential errors. Use buttons in the Spelling dialog box to skip the word (Ignore Once or Ignore All), replace the word with the highlighted word in the *Suggestions* list box (Change), or add the word to the dictionary (Add to Dictionary) if spelled correctly.

13 Click the Ignore All button in the Spelling dialog box to skip all occurrences of *Rivermist* in the worksheet since the street name is spelled correctly.

14 Click the Change button in the Spelling dialog box to replace *Remoat* with *Remote*.

15 Click the Change button in the Spelling dialog box to replace *Persns* with *Persons*.

16 Complete the spell check, changing words as required. Click OK at the message that the spelling check is complete for the entire sheet.

> Double-click the correct spelling in the *Suggestions* list box if the correct word is not initially selected. Click in the *Not in Dictionary* text box if the correct spelling is not in the list, edit as required, and then click Change. You can drag the Spelling dialog box out of the way if you need to see the selected word within the worksheet.

17 Make A36 the active cell.

18 Click the Thesaurus button 📖 in the Proofing group in the Review tab.

> Use the Thesaurus to replace a word in the worksheet with another word of similar meaning. Thesaurus is a feature within the Research task pane.

19 Point to the word *Transport* in the task pane word list, click the down-pointing arrow that appears, and then click *Insert* at the drop-down list.

> The word *Delivery* is replaced with *Transport* in A36.

20 Click the Close button at the top right of the Research task pane.

21 Save **ES2-WBQuoteToMP.xlsx**.

Step 13

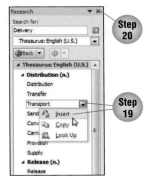

Step 20

Step 19

In Brief

Edit Cell
1. Double-click cell.
2. Insert and/or delete text.
3. Press Enter or click another cell.

Clear Cell
1. Click Clear button in Home tab.
2. Click *Clear All*, *Clear Formats*, *Clear Contents*, or *Clear Comments*.

Spell Check
1. Click Review tab.
2. Click Spelling button.
3. Click Ignore Once, Ignore All, Change, or Add to Dictionary as required.

In Addition

Research Task Pane

You can use the Research task pane to search for information online without leaving the worksheet. For example, you can conduct an Internet search, look up information in online encyclopedias or business reference sites, or find a current stock quote using MSN Money Stock Quote. Choose the online source by clicking the down-pointing arrow at the right of the *Resources* list box (located below the *Search for* text box).

Activity 2.2

Inserting and Deleting Columns and Rows

Insert rows or columns using options from the Insert button in the Home tab or from the context-sensitive shortcut menu that displays when you right-click a selected area. Inserted rows are placed above the active cell or selected rows and existing rows are shifted down. Columns are inserted left of the active cell or selected columns and existing columns are shifted right. When rows or columns are deleted, data automatically is shifted up or left to fill space and relative references in formulas are updated.

Project You will add items to and delete items from the quotation by inserting and deleting rows and columns.

Tutorial 2.2
Inserting, Adjusting, and Deleting Rows and Columns

① With **ES2-WBQuoteToMP.xlsx** open, position the cell pointer (displays as a right-pointing black arrow ➡) over row indicator *21*, hold down the left mouse button, drag the mouse down over *22*, and then release the mouse.

This selects rows 21 and 22. Inserted rows are placed *above* the selected rows and columns are inserted to the *left*.

② Click the Home tab, click the Insert button arrow in the Cells group, and then click *Insert Sheet Rows* at the drop-down list.

Two blank rows are inserted. All rows below the inserted rows are shifted down.

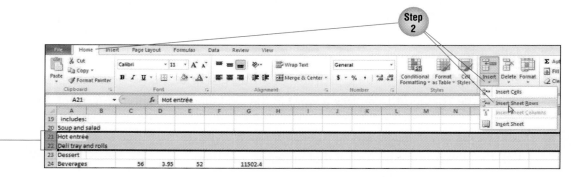

③ Click A21, type **Vegetable tray with dip**, and then press Enter.

④ Type **Seafood hors d'oeuvres** and then press Enter.

⑤ Make active any cell in row 29.

⑥ Click the Delete button arrow in the Cells group and then click *Delete Sheet Rows* at the drop-down list.

The data in row 29 is removed from the worksheet. All rows below the deleted row shift up to fill in the space.

⑦ Right-click row 19 to display the shortcut menu and Mini toolbar and then click *Delete*.

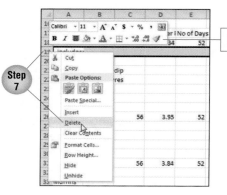

Mini toolbar

8 Right-click row 26 to display the shortcut menu and Mini toolbar and then click *Delete*.

9 Delete row 30 from the worksheet.

10 Position the cell pointer over column indicator letter *F* (displays as a down-pointing black arrow ↓), right-click the mouse, and then click *Delete* at the shortcut menu.

> Data in columns to the right of the deleted column are shifted left to fill in the space.

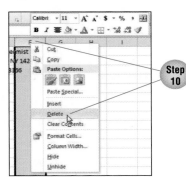

Step 10

In Brief

Insert Rows or Columns
1. Select required number of rows or columns.
2. Click Insert button arrow.
3. Click *Insert Sheet Rows* or *Insert Sheet Columns*.

Delete Rows or Columns
1. Select rows or columns to be deleted.
2. Click Delete button arrow.
3. Click *Delete Sheet Rows* or *Delete Sheet Columns*.

11 Click in any cell to deselect the column.

12 Make F8 the active cell, type **November 5, 2010**, and then press Enter.

> By default, Excel displays dates in the format *dd-mmm-yy* (5-Nov-10).

13 Save **ES2-WBQuoteToMP.xlsx**.

	A	B	C	D	E	F
1					3104 Rivermist Drive	
2					Buffalo, NY 14280	
3					716 555 3166	
4						
5	Quotation					
6						
7						
8	TO:	Marquee Productions			DATE:	5-Nov-10
9		955 South Alameda Street				
10		Los Angeles, CA 90037				

Step 12

In Addition

Inserting and Deleting Cells

In this activity, you selected entire rows and columns before inserting or deleting. This practice is the more common method when you need to add to or delete data from a worksheet. Another method used less frequently is to insert new blank cells or delete a range of cells within the worksheet area. To insert new blank cells, select the range of cells you need to add and then click the Insert button in the Cells group, or click the Insert button arrow and then click *Insert Cells* at the drop-down list to display the dialog box shown at the right. Using the dialog box, you can choose to shift existing cells right or down. Click the Delete button in the Cells group to delete a selected range of cells and shift up the cells below the deleted range. Click the Delete button arrow and then click *Delete Cells* to open the Delete dialog box with options similar to those for Insert.

Moving and Copying Cells

You learned how to use copy and paste to copy formulas in the payroll worksheet for The Waterfront Bistro. You can also use cut and paste to move the contents of a cell or range of cells to another location in the worksheet. The selected cells being cut or copied are called the *source*. The cell or range of cells that is receiving the source data is called the *destination*. If data already exists in the destination cells, Excel replaces the contents. Cells cut or copied to the Clipboard can be pasted more than once in the active workbook, in another workbook, or in another Office application.

Project Continue to work on the catering quotation by moving text in the quotation, duplicating a price, linking cells containing prices, and by copying a food item description.

Tutorial 2.3
Moving, Copying, and Pasting Data in a Workbook

1 With **ES2-WBQuoteToMP.xlsx** open, make A38 the active cell.

2 Click the Cut button ✂ in the Clipboard group in the Home tab.

> A moving marquee surrounds the source after you use Cut or Copy, indicating the cell contents have been placed in the Clipboard.

3 Make E15 the active cell and then click the Paste button 📋 in the Clipboard group. (Do not click the down-pointing arrow on the Paste button because this displays a drop-down list of Paste options.)

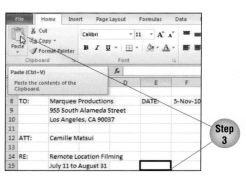

> The text *Note: All prices include tax.* is removed from A38 and placed in E15. In the next step, you will move a range of cells using a method called *drag and drop*.

4 Select the range A14:B15.

> You are only selecting to column B since the entries *Remote Location Filming* and *July 11 to August 31* are stored in B14 and B15, respectively.

5 Point at any one of the four borders surrounding the selected range.

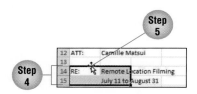

> When you point at a border, the pointer changes from the thick white cross to a white arrow with the move icon attached to it (four-headed arrow).

6 Hold down the left mouse button, drag the top left corner of the range to E12, and then release the mouse.

> A gray border will appear as you drag, indicating the placement of the range when you release the mouse. The destination range displays in a ScreenTip below the gray border.

7 Make D25 the active cell.

8 Click the Copy button  in the Clipboard group.

9 Make D29 the active cell, click the Paste button arrow in the Clipboard group, and then click the Paste Link button in the *Other Paste Options* section of the Paste gallery.

> The existing data in D29 is replaced with the value copied from D25 and the source and destination cells are now linked.
>
> Linking the cells means that any change made to the source cell (D25) will automatically be applied to the destination cell (D29). A Paste Options button appears next to the destination cell (D29). Click the button to return to the Paste Options gallery if you want to choose another paste option. See the In Addition section at the bottom of the page for more information on paste options.

10 Press Esc to remove the moving marquee from D25 and the Paste Options button near D29.

11 Make D25 the active cell and edit the value to *3.91*.

> Notice the value in D29 is also changed to 3.91 automatically.

> D29 changes automatically since the two cells are linked.

12 Make A20 the active cell. Point at any one of the four borders surrounding A20 until the pointer displays as a white arrow with the move icon attached to it, hold down the Ctrl key, and then drag the mouse to A33.

13 Release the mouse button first and then release the Ctrl key.

> A plus sign attached to the pointer indicates the source contents are being *copied* when you drag and drop using the Ctrl key.

14 Save **ES2-WBQuoteToMP.xlsx**.

In Brief

Move or Copy Cells
1. Select source cells.
2. Click Cut or Copy button.
3. Select starting destination cell.
4. Click Paste button.

Copy and Link Cells
1. Select source cells.
2. Click Copy button.
3. Select destination cell.
4. Click Paste button arrow.
5. Click Paste Link button.

In Addition

Paste Options Gallery

The Paste Options gallery (shown at the right) appears in three places: the Paste button arrow in the Clipboard group, the Paste Options button that appears after an entry has been pasted into a cell, or the right-click shortcut menu. The gallery is divided into three sections: *Paste, Paste Values,* and *Other Paste Options*. Within each section buttons are included for various paste options. Hover the mouse over a button in the gallery to view a ScreenTip that describes the button's purpose as well as to see a preview of the paste option applied to the cell in the worksheet. The Paste Options gallery is context sensitive, meaning the buttons that appear are dependent on the type of content that has been copied and the location in which the content is being pasted.

Activity 2.4

Adjusting Column Width and Row Height; Using AutoFit

By default, columns are all the same width and rows are all the same height with columns set by default to a width of 8.43 characters (64 pixels) and rows to a height of 15 points (20 pixels). In some cases you do not have to increase the width when the text is too wide for the column, since labels "spill over" into the next cell if it is empty. Some column headings in the quotation are truncated because an entry exists in the column immediately to the right. Excel automatically adjusts the height of rows to accommodate the size of the text within the cells. Manually increasing the row height adds more space between rows, which can be used to improve readability or as a design technique to draw attention to a series of cells.

Project

Tutorial 2.2
Inserting, Adjusting, and Deleting Rows and Columns

You will widen the columns in which labels are truncated to make sure each entry is entirely visible to readers and increase the height of the row containing the column headings to make them stand out from the text below.

1. With **ES2-WBQuoteToMP.xlsx** open, make any cell in column A the active cell.

2. Click the Format button in the Cells group in the Home tab and then click *Column Width* at the drop-down list.

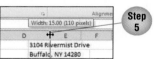

3. At the Column Width dialog box, type **14** and then click OK or press Enter.

   In the next step, you will adjust the width of column D using the mouse.

4. Position the mouse pointer on the boundary line in the column indicator row between columns D and E until the pointer changes to a vertical line with a left- and right-pointing arrow ↔.

5. Hold down the left mouse button, drag the boundary line to the right until *Width: 15.00 (110 pixels)* displays in the ScreenTip, and then release the mouse button.

   As you drag the boundary line to the right or left, a dotted line appears in the column in the worksheet area, indicating the new width. If, after decreasing a column's width, cells that previously had values in them now display as a series of pound symbols (######), the column is now too narrow. Widen the column to redisplay the values.

6. Position the mouse pointer on the boundary line in the column indicator row between columns C and D until the pointer changes to a vertical line with a left- and right-pointing arrow and then double-click the left mouse button.

   Double-clicking the boundary line sets the width to fit the length of the longest entry within the column, referred to as *AutoFit*.

7. Make E17 the active cell, click the Format button in the Cells group, and then click *AutoFit Column Width* at the drop-down list.

   AutoFit Column Width adjusts the width of the column to accommodate the amount of text in the active cell. After reviewing the worksheet, you decide all of the columns with numeric values should be the same width. In the next steps, you will learn how to set the width of multiple columns in one operation.

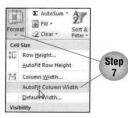

8 Position the mouse pointer on column indicator letter *C*, hold down the left mouse button, and then drag the mouse right to column F.

> This selects columns C through F.

9 Position the mouse pointer on the right boundary line for column E within the selected range of columns until the pointer changes to a vertical line with a left- and right-pointing arrow.

> Any changes made to the width of one column boundary will affect all of the selected columns.

10 Drag the boundary line right until *Width: 15.00 (110 pixels)* displays in the ScreenTip and then release the mouse button.

Step 10

11 Click in any cell to deselect the columns.

> Do not be concerned that the columns are now too wide after this step—you have many formatting tasks to complete that will improve the layout as you work through the next few activities.

12 Move E12:F13 to A14:B15 and then click in any cell to deselect the range. Refer to Activity 2.3 if you need assistance with this step.

> In the next steps, you will adjust row height using the mouse.

13 Position the mouse pointer on the boundary line below row 17 until the pointer changes to a horizontal line with an up- and down-pointing arrow ⬍ .

14 Drag the boundary line down until *Height: 21.00 (28 pixels)* displays in the ScreenTip and then release the mouse button.

Step 14

15 Save **ES2-WBQuoteToMP.xlsx**.

In Addition

Row Height Dialog Box

A sequence of steps similar to the one used for adjusting column width using the Column Width dialog box can be used to increase or decrease the height of a row with the Row Height dialog box, shown at the right. Click any cell within the row, click the Format button in the Cells group in the Home tab, and then click *Row Height* at the drop-down list. Type the desired height and press Enter or click OK.

In Brief

Increase or Decrease Column Width
1. Select column(s).
2. Click Format button in Cells group.
3. Click *Column Width*.
4. Type desired width.
5. Click OK.

Increase or Decrease Row Height
1. Select row(s).
2. Click Format button in Cells group.
3. Click *Row Height*.
4. Type desired height.
5. Click OK.

Adjust Width or Height Using Mouse
Drag boundary to right of column or below row, or double-click boundary to AutoFit.

Activity
2.5

The *font* is the typeface used to display and print data. The default font in Excel is Calibri, but several other fonts are available. The size of the font is measured in units called *points*. A point is approximately 1/72 of an inch measured vertically. The default font size used by Excel is 11-point. The larger the point size, the larger the type. Each font's style can be enhanced to **bold**, *italic*, or ***bold italic***. Cell entries display in black with a white background. Changing the color of the font and/or the color of the background (called *fill*) adds interest or emphasis to the cell entry.

Project To add to the visual appeal of the quotation, you will change the font and font size and apply attributes such as font and fill color to the title *Quotation*.

SNAP

Tutorial 2.4
Applying Formatting to Cell Contents; Using Undo and Redo; Changing Alignment

① With **ES2-WBQuoteToMP.xlsx** open, make A5 the active cell.

② Click the Font button arrow in the Font group in the Home tab, scroll down the list of fonts, and then point to *Book Antiqua* at the drop-down gallery. Notice that Excel applies the font you are pointing at to the active cell so that you can preview the result. This feature is called *Live Preview*. Click *Book Antiqua* at the drop-down gallery.

Live Preview shows you how the cell will look before you choose the font so you can try different font options before making your selection.

Your list of fonts may vary.

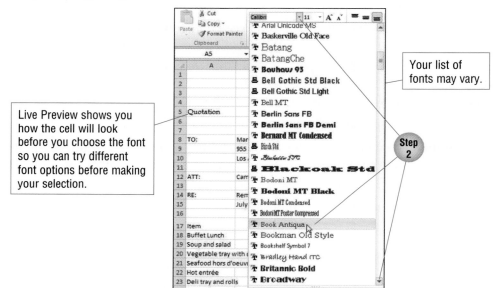

Step 2

③ Click the Font Size button arrow in the Font group and then click *18* at the drop-down list.

The row height is automatically increased to accommodate the larger type size.

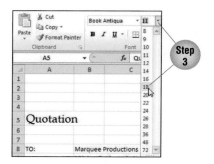

Step 3

(4) With A5 still the active cell, click the Font Color button arrow in the Font group and then click the Blue color box (third from right) in the *Standard Colors* section of the color gallery.

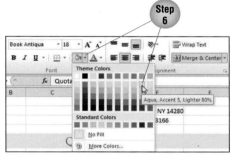

(5) Select A5:F5 and then click the Merge & Center button in the Alignment group.

> The cells in the range A5:F5 have now been merged into one large cell that spans across the six columns. The text within A5, *Quotation*, is now centered within this large cell. As you learned in Section 1, Merge & Center centers titles over multiple columns.

(6) With merged cell A5 still selected, click the Fill Color button arrow in the Font group and then click the *Aqua, Accent 5, Lighter 80%* color box (second from right in second row) in the *Theme Colors* section of the color gallery.

> *Fill* is the color of the background in the cell. Changing the fill color is sometimes referred to as *shading* a cell.

(7) Make F36 the active cell.

(8) Click the Bold button **B** and the Italic button *I* in the Font group.

(9) Save **ES2-WBQuoteToMP.xlsx**.

In Brief

Change Font
1. Select cells.
2. Click Font button arrow.
3. Click desired font.
4. Deselect cells.

Change Font Size
1. Select cells.
2. Click Font Size button arrow.
3. Click desired size.
4. Deselect cells.

Change Font Attributes
1. Select cells.
2. Click desired attribute button.
3. Deselect cells.

In Addition

Format Cells Dialog Box

You can use the Format Cells dialog box with the Font tab selected (shown at the right) to change the font, font size, font style, and color of text. Additional Underline style options such as *Single, Double, Single Accounting*, and *Double Accounting* are available, as well as special effects options *Strikethrough, Superscript*, and *Subscript*. Select the cells you want to change and then click the Font group dialog box launcher button  to open the Format Cells dialog box with the Font tab active.

Formatting Numeric Cells;
Adjusting Decimal Places; Using Undo and Redo

In the payroll worksheet for The Waterfront Bistro, you learned how to format numeric cells to the Accounting Number Format which adds a dollar symbol ($), comma in the thousands, and two decimal places and displays negative values in brackets. Other numeric formats include Comma, Percent, and Currency. By default, cells are initially set to the General format which has no specific numeric style. The number of decimal places in a selected range of cells can be increased or decreased using the Increase Decimal and Decrease Decimal buttons in the Number group of the Home tab.

Use the Undo button on the Quick Access toolbar to reverse the last action. Excel stores up to 100 actions that can be undone or redone and you can repeat actions as many times as you need. Some actions (such as Save) cannot be reversed with Undo.

Project

To display a consistent number of characters for the numeric values, you will apply the Accounting Number and Comma formats to selected ranges within the quotation.

The Waterfront B·I·S·T·R·O

SNAP

Tutorial 2.4
Applying Formatting to Cell Contents; Using Undo and Redo; Changing Alignment

1. With **ES2-WBQuoteToMP.xlsx** open, make F18 the active cell.

2. Hold down the Ctrl key and click F36.

3. Click the Accounting Number Format button $ in the Number group in the Home tab.

4. Click in any cell to deselect the cells.

5. Select F25:F34.

6. Click the Comma Style button in the Number group.

   Comma Style formats cells the same as the Accounting Number format with the exception of the dollar or alternative currency symbol.

7. Click in any cell to deselect the range and review the numeric values in the worksheet. Notice that column D could be improved by applying a format option to the cell that is not showing the same number of decimal places as other values in the column.

8 Make D34 the active cell.

9 Click the Increase Decimal button in the Number group.

> One decimal place is added to or removed from the cells in the selected range each time you click Increase Decimal or Decrease Decimal.

10 With D34 still selected, click the Increase Decimal button again.

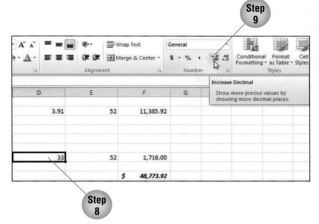

> The value now displays as *33.00* which is consistent with the number of decimal places for the other values in column D.

11 Select F18:F36 and then click the Decrease Decimal button twice in the Number group.

12 Click in any cell to deselect the range.

13 Click the Undo button on the Quick Access toolbar.

> Excel reselects the range and restores one decimal place.

14 Click the Undo button a second time.

> Both decimal places are now restored. With the Undo button arrow, you can display a drop-down list of actions from which you can undo multiple actions in one step.

15 Click the Redo button on the Quick Access toolbar two times.

> Both decimal places are removed again from the selected range.

16 Restore the two decimal places by either clicking the Undo button twice or clicking the Increase Decimal button twice.

17 Click in any cell to deselect the range.

18 Save **ES2-WBQuoteToMP.xlsx**.

In Brief

Change Numeric Format
1. Select cells.
2. Click desired format style button in Number group.
3. Deselect cells.

Undo Action
Click Undo button on Quick Access toolbar or press Ctrl + Z.

Redo Action
Click Redo button on Quick Access toolbar or press Ctrl + Y.

In Addition

Additional Number Format Options

Click the Number Format button arrow in the Number group to display a drop-down list (shown at the right) with additional numeric format options including date, time, fraction, and scientific options. Click *More Number Formats* at the bottom of the list to open the Format Cells dialog box with the Number tab selected. Using this dialog box, you can access further customization options for a format, such as displaying negative values in red, or create your own custom format code.

Activity 2.7

Changing the Alignment and Indentation of Cells; Using Repeat

Data in a cell can be left-aligned, right-aligned, or centered within the column. Cells that have had Merge & Center applied can be formatted to align the text in the merged cell at the left or right. Use the Increase Indent and Decrease Indent buttons to indent text from the left edge of the cell approximately one character width each time the button is clicked. Using buttons along the top row in the Alignment group in the Home tab you can change vertical alignment, rotate text, or wrap text. Use the Repeat keyboard shortcut Ctrl + Y to replicate the last action on another cell. This is useful if you need to perform the same action several times in a row.

Project To improve the appearance of the quotation, you will change the alignment of column headings and values and indent labels from the left edge of column A.

Tutorial 2.4
Applying Formatting to Cell Contents; Using Undo and Redo; Changing Alignment

1. With **ES2-WBQuotetoMP.xlsx** open, edit the column headings in C17 and E17 to include a period (.) after the abbreviation for number. For example, the edited column heading in C17 will be *No. of Persons*.

2. Select C17:F17.

3. Click the Center button ☰ in the Alignment group in the Home tab.

4. Select C18:C29 and then change the alignment to center.

5. Center the entries in E18:E34.

6. Select A19:A24.

7. Click the Increase Indent button ☷ in the Alignment group.

   Each time you click Increase Indent, the contents of the selected cells are indented by approximately one character width. If you click Increase Indent one too many times, click the Decrease Indent button ☷ to return the text to the previous indent position.

8. Select A26:A28 and then click the Increase Indent button.

9. Select A30:A33 and then click the Increase Indent button.

10. Select A17:F17 and then bold the cells.

11. Make F8 the active cell and then click the Align Text Left button ☰ in the Alignment group.

    By default, Excel aligns date entries at the right edge of a column since dates are converted to a serial number and treated in a similar manner to values. You will learn more about using dates in Excel in Section 3.

12 Select A17:F17.

In Activity 2.4, you increased the height of row 17 to 21.00. The Alignment group contains buttons that also allow you to control the alignment of the text between the top and bottom of the cell boundaries. In the next step, you will center the text vertically within the cells.

13 Click the Middle Align button ☰ in the Alignment group.

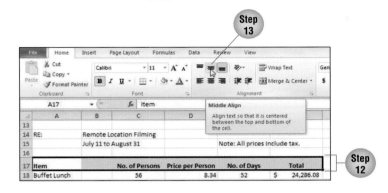

14 Deselect the range.

15 Select E1:F1 and then click *Merge & Center* in the Alignment group.

16 Select E2:F2 and then press Ctrl + Y (the Repeat command).

You can add a Repeat button to the Quick Access toolbar. To do this, click the Customize Quick Access Toolbar button ⊽ that displays at the right side of the toolbar and then click *More Commands* at the drop-down list. At the Excel Options dialog box with Quick Access Toolbar selected in the left pane, scroll down the left list box, click Repeat, click the Add button, and then click OK.

17 Select E3:F3 and then press Ctrl + Y.

You can merge and center in only one row at a time in this situation because data already exists in all three rows.

18 Select E1:E3 and then click the Align Text Right button ☰ in the Alignment group.

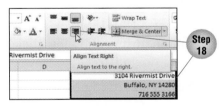

19 Deselect the range.

20 Save **ES2-WBQuoteToMP.xlsx**.

In Addition

Wrapping Text within a Cell

A Wrap Text button 🗐 is available in the Alignment group which you can use to wrap text within a cell if you do not want to widen the column width. Text too wide for the column is displayed on multiple lines and the height of the row is automatically increased. In the example shown at the right, the original cells are shown on the left and the wrapped cells in column A (which has also been made wider) displayed on the right.

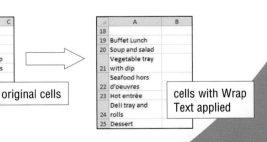

Activity 2.8

Adding Borders and Shading; Copying Formats with Format Painter

Borders in various styles and colors can be applied to display and print in selected cells within the worksheet. Borders can be added to the top, left, bottom, or right edge of a cell. Use borders to underscore headings or totals or to emphasize other cells. Shading adds color and/or a pattern to the background of a cell. Format Painter copies formats from a selected cell to another cell. Use this feature to apply multiple format options from one cell to another cell.

Project As you near completion of the quotation, you will spend time improving the presentation of the worksheet by adding borders and shading.

Tutorial 2.5
Adding Borders and Shading to Cells and Using Format Painter

1. With **ES2-WBQuoteToMP.xlsx** open, select A17:F17.

   In the next steps, you will add a border to the top and bottom of the column headings using the Bottom Border button in the Font group of the Home tab.

2. Click the Bottom Border button arrow in the Font group in the Home tab.

   A drop-down list of border style options displays. The *More Borders* option at the bottom of the list opens the Format Cells dialog box with the Border tab selected in which you can create a custom border.

3. Click *Top and Bottom Border* at the drop-down list.

4. Click in any cell to deselect the range and view the border.

5. Select A18:B18, click the Top and Bottom Border button arrow, and then click *Outside Borders* at the drop-down list.

6. Select A25:B25 and then click the Outside Borders button. (Do not click the arrow.)

   Since the Borders button updates to the most recently selected border style, you can apply the *Outside Borders* option to the active cell without displaying the drop-down list.

7. Select A29:B29 and then click the Outside Borders button.

8. Deselect the range.

9. Make F36 the active cell, click the Outside Borders button arrow, and then click *Top and Double Bottom Border* at the drop-down list.

10. Make A8 the active cell, apply bold, and right-align the cell.

    In the next steps, you will copy the formats from A8 to two other cells.

11 With A8 still the active cell, double-click the Format Painter button ![paintbrush icon] in the Clipboard group.

> A moving marquee surrounds the source cell and a paintbrush displays attached to the cell pointer. This icon means that the formats are copied from the source cell and can be pasted to multiple cells or ranges. Single-clicking Format Painter allows you to copy formats to the next cell or range that you click. Double-click the Format Painter button to toggle the feature on until you turn it off by clicking Format Painter again.

12 Click A12.

13 Click A14.

14 Click E8 and then click the Format Painter button to turn off the feature.

15 Save **ES2-WBQuoteToMP.xlsx**.

Moving marquee in A8 indicates cell formats are being copied from this cell.

Step 12   Step 13   Step 14

In Addition

Creating a Custom Border

If none of the borders available in the drop-down list suit your needs, you can create a custom border. Click the *More Borders* option at the bottom of the Borders list to open the Format Cells dialog box with the Border tab selected shown below. At this dialog box, you can change to a different line style by clicking another line option in the *Style* box, and/or change the line color by clicking the *Color* box arrow and then choosing the desired color at the drop-down gallery. Next, specify the outside and/or inside border you want by clicking one of the buttons in the *Presets* section, clicking one or more of the Border buttons along the perimeter of the preview box, or by clicking inside the preview box at the edge of the cell along which you want the border to appear. When you are finished creating the border, click OK.

Choose the border line style here.

Change the border line color here.

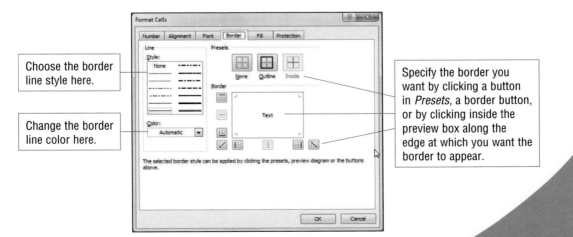

Specify the border you want by clicking a button in *Presets*, a border button, or by clicking inside the preview box along the edge at which you want the border to appear.

Activity 2.9

Using Cell Styles and Themes

Cell Styles contain a group of pre-defined formatting options stored in a name. Styles are an efficient method to consistently apply formats, creating a professional, consistent worksheet appearance. Excel includes several predefined styles which you can apply or modify; you also can choose to create your own cell style. A theme is a set of formatting choices that include a set of colors, a set of heading and body text fonts, and a set of lines and fill effects. Excel provides a variety of themes you can use to format text and cells in a worksheet.

Project Your final steps in improving the presentation of the worksheet will involve applying cell styles and a theme.

Tutorial 2.6
Formatting a Worksheet Using Table Formatting and Themes

1. With **ES2-WBQuoteToMP.xlsx** open, make A5 the active cell.

   You decide to change the formatting of the *Quotation* title to one of the predefined cell styles that Excel provides.

2. Click the Cell Styles button in the Styles group in the Home tab.

   A drop-down gallery appears with the predefined cell styles grouped into five sections: *Good, Bad and Neutral, Data and Model, Titles and Headings, Themed Cell Styles*, and *Number Format*.

3. Move the mouse over several of the cell style designs in the drop-down gallery and watch Live Preview show you the style applied to the title in A5.

4. Click the *Title* style in the *Titles and Headings* section of the gallery.

Live Preview of Title style applied to A5

5 Select A17:F17, click the Cell Styles button in the Styles group, and then click the *Accent2* style in the *Themed Cell Styles* section.

6 Select A18:B18, hold down Ctrl, select A25:B25 and A29:B29, and then release the Ctrl key.

7 Click the Cell Styles button and then click the *Accent1* style in the *Themed Cell Styles* section at the drop-down gallery.

> In the next steps you will apply a theme to the quotation. Changing the theme will cause the fonts, colors, and effects to change for the cells. As with styles, you will be able to view a live preview of the changes before you choose a theme.

8 Deselect the cells.

continues

⑨ Click the Page Layout tab.

⑩ Click the Themes button 🅰 in the Themes group.

⑪ Move the mouse over several of the themes in the drop-down gallery and watch Live Preview show you the changes that will take place in the worksheet.

> Notice that a theme affects the entire worksheet. You did not select a cell or range of cells before you applied a theme.

⑫ Click *Black Tie* at the drop-down gallery.

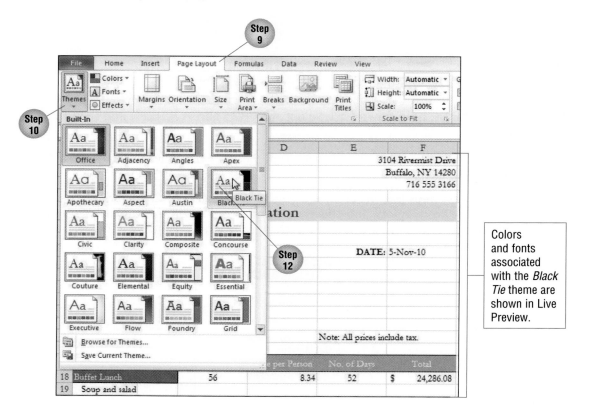

Colors and fonts associated with the *Black Tie* theme are shown in Live Preview.

Need Help?

Apply the wrong theme? Since themes are applied to the entire worksheet, go back to the Themes gallery and select the correct theme. The existing theme will be replaced.

13 Make A1 the active cell, type **The Waterfront Bistro** and press Enter.

14 Select A1:D3, click the Home tab, click the Merge and Center button and the Middle Align button in the Alignment group.

15 With A1 still the active cell, click the Cell Styles button and then click *Accent2* in the *Themed Cell Styles* section of the drop-down gallery.

16 With A1 still the active cell, change the font size to *28*.

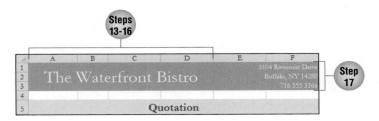

17 Select E1:E3 and apply the *Accent2* cell style.

18 Click in any cell to deselect the range.

19 Click the File tab, click the Print tab, and then click the Print button to print the finished quotation.

20 Save and then close **ES2-WBQuoteToMP.xlsx**.

In Brief

Apply Cell Styles
1. Select cells.
2. Click Cell Styles button.
3. Click desired style in drop-down gallery.

Apply Theme
1. Click Page Layout tab.
2. Click Themes button.
3. Click desired theme in drop-down gallery.

In Addition

Creating a New Style

You can create your own style using the *New Cell Style* option at the bottom of the Cell Styles drop-down gallery. First, select a cell in the current worksheet and apply all of the formatting to the cell that you want saved in the style. Second, with the cell active to which you have applied the desired formats, click the Cell Styles button and then click *New Cell Style* at the drop-down gallery. At the Style dialog box shown at the right, type a name for the style in the *Style name* text box and then click OK. The new style will appear at the top of the Cell Styles gallery in a new section titled *Custom*. Custom styles are saved in the workbook in which they are created. You will not see the new style when you open a new workbook; however, you can copy styles from one workbook to another.

Activity 2.10

Using Find and Replace

Use the Find command to search for specific labels or values that you want to verify or edit. The Find command will move to each cell containing the text you specify. The Replace command will search for a label, value, or format and automatically replace it with another label, value, or format. Use Find and Replace to ensure that all occurrences of the specified label or value are verified or edited.

Project

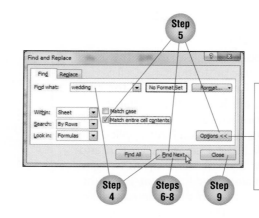

Tutorial 2.7
Finding and Replacing Data and Formatting

Dana Hirsch wants to know how many weddings are booked in 2011. You will use Find to review the wedding bookings in the special events workbook. Dana has also advised you that the prices that were input at 32.95 should be 34.95. You will use the Replace command to correct these errors.

1. Open **WBSpecEvents.xlsx**. Save the workbook with Save As in the ExcelS2 folder and name it **ES2-WBSpecEvents**.

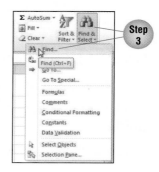

Step 3

2. Press Ctrl + Home to make A1 the active cell.

3. Click the Find & Select button 🔍 in the Editing group in the Home tab and then click *Find* at the drop-down list.

4. Type **wedding** in the *Find what* text box and then click the Find Next button.

> Notice that Excel has moved to C6 which has the entry *25th Wedding Anniversary*. This cell contains the search text *wedding* but you do not want to review wedding anniversary events. In the next step you will specify that you want only cells that match the search text exactly.

5. Click the Options>> button in the Find and Replace dialog box, click the *Match entire cell contents* check box to insert a check mark and then click the Find Next button.

> The dialog box expands when you click the Options>> button to reveal find and replace options. Notice this time, Excel bypassed the entry *50th Wedding Anniversary* in C9 and moved directly to C10 which contains the text *Wedding*.

6. Click Find Next.

> Excel moves the active cell to C16.

7. Click Find Next.

> Excel moves the active cell to C20.

8. Continue clicking Find Next until the active cell returns to C10 near the top of the worksheet.

The Options >> button changes to Options << when the dialog box has been expanded to reveal the additional find and replace settings.

> Your review has determined seven weddings are booked in 2011. Although in this small worksheet you could easily have done this calculation by quickly scanning the contents of column C, in a large worksheet with many rows and columns, the Find command is an efficient method of moving to a specific cell. Typing a specific value into the *Find what* text box could move you to a section title or label very quickly.

9 Click the Close button to close the Find and Replace dialog box.

10 Click the Find & Select button in the Editing group and then click *Replace* at the drop-down list.

11 With *Match entire cell contents* still selected in the Find and Replace dialog box with the Replace tab selected, drag to select *wedding* in the *Find what* text box and then type **32.95**.

12 Press Tab to move the insertion point to the *Replace with* text box and then type **34.95**.

13 Click the Replace All button.

> Excel searches through the entire worksheet and automatically changes all occurrences of *32.95* to *34.95*.

14 Click OK at the message that Excel has completed the search and has made four replacements.

15 Click the *Match entire cell contents* check box to clear the check mark, click the Options<< button to remove the expanded find and replace options, and then click the Close button to close the Find and Replace dialog box.

16 Review the entries in column H and note that no prices exist at 32.95.

17 Save **ES2-WBSpecEvents.xlsx**.

In Brief

Find Label or Value
1. Click Find & Select button in Editing group.
2. Click *Find*.
3. Type label or value in *Find what* text box.
4. Click Find Next.

Replace Label or Value
1. Click Find & Select button.
2. Click *Replace*.
3. Type label or value in *Find what* text box.
4. Type replacement label or value in *Replace with* text box.
5. Click Find Next or Replace All.

In Addition

Replacing Formats

You can use the Replace feature to find formats and replace them with other formats or no formatting. For example, you could use Excel to find all occurrences of bold and blue font color applied to a cell and replace with bold and green font color. At the Find and Replace dialog box with the Replace tab selected, click the Options>> button to expand the dialog box and display Format buttons to the right of the *Find what* and *Replace with* text boxes (shown at the right). Use these buttons to specify the required format options. The Preview box to the left (initially displays *No Format Set*) displays the formats Excel will find and replace.

Activity 2.11

Freezing Panes; Changing the Zoom

When you scroll to the right or down to view parts of a worksheet that do not fit in the current window, some column or row headings may scroll off the screen making it difficult to relate text or values. The Freeze Panes option causes rows and columns to remain fixed when scrolling. Magnify or reduce the worksheet display by dragging the Zoom slider bar button, clicking the Zoom In or Zoom Out buttons, or by specifying a percentage to zoom to at the Zoom dialog box. Changing the magnification does not affect printing since worksheets print at 100% unless scaling options are changed.

Project

You will freeze column and row headings in the special events worksheet to facilitate scrolling and practice with various Zoom settings to view more cells within the current window.

SNAP

Tutorial 2.8
Freezing Panes, Splitting Windows, and Changing the Zoom

1 With **ES2-WBSpecEvents.xlsx** open, make A4 the active cell.

2 Click the View tab.

3 Click the Freeze Panes button 📇 in the Window group.

4 Click *Freeze Panes* at the drop-down list.

The position of the active cell before you freeze panes is important since all rows above and all columns left of the active cell are frozen. Notice you made the active cell A4 so that rows 1 to 3 are now frozen. A horizontal black line appears indicating which rows remain fixed when scrolling.

5 Press the Page Down key a few times to scroll down the worksheet.

Notice rows 1 through 3 do not scroll off the screen.

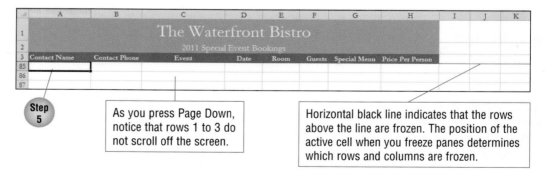

As you press Page Down, notice that rows 1 to 3 do not scroll off the screen.

Horizontal black line indicates that the rows above the line are frozen. The position of the active cell when you freeze panes determines which rows and columns are frozen.

6 Press Ctrl + Home. Notice that Excel returns to A4 instead of A1 since A1 is frozen.

7 Click the Freeze Panes button in the Window group and then click *Unfreeze Panes*.

> The Freeze Panes option changes to Unfreeze Panes when rows or columns have been frozen.

In Brief

Freeze Panes
1. Make cell active below and right of row or column headings you want to freeze.
2. Click View tab.
3. Click Freeze Panes button.
4. Click *Freeze Panes*.

Change Zoom Setting
Drag Zoom slider bar.
OR
Click Zoom In or Zoom Out buttons.
OR
Click zoom percentage value and choose magnification option at Zoom dialog box.

8 Practice dragging the button on the Zoom slider bar (located at the right end of the Status bar above the system time) and watch the cells magnify and shrink as you drag right and left.

9 Drag the slider bar button to the halfway mark on the slider bar to redisplay the worksheet at 100%.

10 Click over *100%* at the left edge of the slider bar to open the Zoom dialog box.

11 At the Zoom dialog box, click *75%* and then click OK.

12 Click the Zoom In button at the right side of the Zoom slider bar (displays as a plus symbol inside a circle).

13 Continue to click the Zoom In button until the zoom percentage returns to 100%.

> When the worksheet is set to 100% magnification, clicking the Zoom In or Zoom Out buttons at either side of the slider bar magnifies or shrinks the display of the worksheet by 10% each time the button is clicked.

14 Save **ES2-WBSpecEvents.xlsx**.

In Addition

Zoom to Selection

The View tab contains a Zoom group with three buttons to change zoom settings. Click the Zoom button in the Zoom group to open the Zoom dialog box. This is the same dialog box that you displayed in Step 10. Click the 100% button to return the view to 100%. Select a range of cells and then click the Zoom to Selection button to cause Excel to scale the zoom setting so that the selected range fills the worksheet area.

Activity 2.12

Inserting, Moving, and Resizing Pictures and Clip Art

When connected to Office Online, the Microsoft Office suite includes a clip art gallery containing thousands of images. Once a clip art image has been inserted, it can be moved, resized, or deleted. The Clip Art task pane allows you to view images in the gallery and insert them into the worksheet with a single click. By default, Excel searches Office Online if you are connected to the Internet. A company logo or other digital picture can also be inserted into a worksheet using the Picture button in the Illustrations group of the Insert tab.

Project

Before printing the special events list, you decide to add a clip art image to the top right and the bistro's logo to the top left of the worksheet. After inserting the images, you will resize and move them.

Tutorial 2.9
Inserting and Using Clip Art Images and Diagrams

1. With **ES2-WBSpecEvents.xlsx** open, make A1 the active cell.

2. Click the Insert tab and then click the Clip Art button in the Illustrations group.

   The Clip Art task pane opens at the right side of the worksheet area.

3. Click in the *Search for* text box at the top of the Clip Art task pane. Delete existing text if necessary and then type **seafood**.

4. If necessary, click the *Include Office.com content* check box to insert a check mark and then click the Go button.

   Available images associated with the keyword *seafood* display in the *Results* section of the Clip Art task pane. By default, Excel searches all media file types (clip art, photographs, movies, and sounds) in all categories of the Office gallery, in Office Online, and in all favorites, unclassified clips, and downloaded clips that have been added to the computer you are using.

5. Scroll the images in the *Results* section until you see the clip art shown at the right. Position the mouse pointer over the picture and then click the mouse once. ***Note: Substitute a similar image if the one shown is not available.***

   The picture is inserted in the worksheet starting at A1.

6. Position the pointer on the round white sizing handle at the bottom right corner of the image, hold down the left mouse button, and drag the pointer up and left until the image fits within the first two rows as shown.

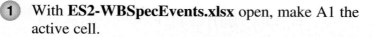

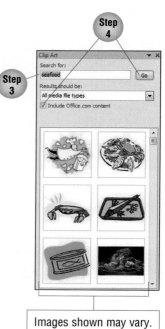

Images shown may vary.

Step 5

Step 6

7 Move the pointer over the image until the four-headed arrow move icon appears attached to the pointer, hold down the left mouse button, and then drag the image until the right edge of the picture is aligned at the right edge of the worksheet.

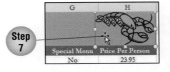
Step 7

8 Click the Close button in the upper right corner of the Clip Art task pane.

9 Click A1, click the Insert tab, and then click the Picture button in the Illustrations group.

10 At the Insert Picture dialog box, navigate to the ExcelS2 folder on your storage medium. If necessary, change the view to *Large Icons* and then double-click the file named **TWBLogo.jpg**.

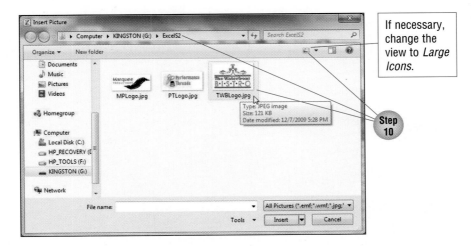

If necessary, change the view to *Large Icons.*

Step 10

11 Use the sizing handles to resize the picture until the logo image fits above the top left edge of the worksheet as shown below.

12 Click in any cell to deselect the logo image.

Steps 11-12

13 Select A1:A2 and add *Outside Borders*. Select A3:H36 and add *All Borders*.

14 Deselect the range, save, print, and then close **ES2-WBSpecEvents.xlsx**.

In Brief

Insert Clip Art
1. Click Insert tab.
2. Click Clip Art button.
3. Search for image by keyword.
4. Click desired image in *Results* section.
5. Move and/or resize as required.
6. Close Clip Art task pane.

Insert Picture from File
1. Click Insert tab.
2. Click Picture button.
3. Navigate to drive and/or folder.
4. Double-click file containing picture.
5. Move and/or size as required.

In Addition

Picture Tools

When a clip art image or picture inserted from a file is selected, the contextual Picture Tools Format tab becomes available. Customize the image using picture tools or picture styles. For example, use the crop button to cut an unwanted area from the image, or set a specific height or width measurement for the image. Buttons in the Arrange group allow you to group multiple images together, control the alignment, rotation, or order of the image within the worksheet. Buttons in the Adjust group allow you to control the brightness, contrast, and color of the image.

Features Summary

Feature	Ribbon Tab, Group	Button	Quick Access Toolbar	Keyboard Shortcut
Accounting Number format	Home, Number	$		
align text left	Home, Alignment			
align text right	Home, Alignment			
bold	Home, Font	B		Ctrl + B
borders	Home, Font			Ctrl + Shift + &
cell styles	Home, Styles			
center	Home, Alignment			
clear cell	Home, Editing			
clip art	Insert, Illustrations			
column width	Home, Cells			
Comma style	Home, Number			
copy	Home, Clipboard			Ctrl + C
cut	Home, Clipboard			Ctrl + X
decrease decimal	Home, Number			
decrease indent	Home, Alignment			
delete cell, column, or row	Home, Cells			
fill color	Home, Font			
find	Home, Editing			Ctrl + F
font	Home, Font	Calibri		Ctrl + 1
font color	Home, Font	A		Ctrl + 1
font size	Home, Font	11		Ctrl + 1
Format Painter	Home, Clipboard			
freeze panes	View, Window			
increase decimal	Home, Number			
increase indent	Home, Alignment			

Feature	Ribbon Tab, Group	Button	Quick Access Toolbar	Keyboard Shortcut
insert cell, column, or row	Home, Cells			
italic	Home, Font			Ctrl + I
merge and center	Home, Alignment			
middle-align	Home, Alignment			
paste	Home, Clipboard			Ctrl + V
picture from file	Insert, Illustrations			
redo an action				Ctrl + Y
repeat				Ctrl + Y
replace	Home, Editing			Ctrl + H
row height	Home, Cells			
Spelling	Review, Proofing			F7
theme	Page Layout, Themes			
Thesaurus	Review, Proofing			Shift + F7
undo an action				Ctrl + Z
zoom	View, Zoom			

Knowledge Check

Completion: In the space provided at the right, indicate the correct term, command, or option.

1. Use this feature to remove everything from a cell including text and formats. _____
2. Make a cell active anywhere in this row to insert a new row between 11 and 12. _____
3. Make a cell active anywhere in this column to insert a new column between E and F. _____
4. This is the term for adjusting a column width to the length of the longest entry. _____
5. This term refers to the feature where Excel shows the results of a format option while pointing to the option in a drop-down list or gallery. _____
6. By default, cells are initially set to this numeric style format. _____
7. Click this button in the Alignment group of the Home tab to center cells vertically between the top and bottom cell boundaries. _____
8. Click this button in the Clipboard group of the Home tab to copy the formats of the active cell. _____
9. This feature stores predefined format options. _____
10. This feature stores a set of colors, fonts, and effects that can be applied to the entire worksheet. _____
11. Make this cell active to freeze rows 1 through 5. _____
12. List two methods for changing the zoom magnification to view more cells in the current window. _____
13. Click this tab and button to search for art on Office Online. _____
14. Click this button in the Illustrations group to insert an image stored in a file. _____

Skills Review

Review 1 Editing, Moving, Copying, and Clearing Cells; Performing a Spell Check; Inserting and Deleting Rows

1. Open **WBInvToNPC.xlsx** and then save the workbook in the ExcelEOS folder and name it **ES2-R1-WBInvToNPC**.
2. Change the amount in D20 from *13.73* to *15.23* and then clear the contents of A8.
3. Change the label in A21 from *Soup* to *French Onion Soup*.
4. Type new data in the cells indicated.

    E14   **PO No.**   F14   **TA-11-643**
5. Delete rows 7, 8, and 9.
6. Complete a spelling check of the worksheet. (All names are spelled correctly.)
7. Move E7:F7 to E10:F10.
8. Copy A24 to A30.

9. Delete those rows that contain the labels *Milk* and *Donuts*.
10. Insert a new row between *Prime Rib* and *Mixed Vegetables* and then type **Seafood Pasta** in column A of the new row.
11. Save **ES2-R1-WBInvToNPC.xlsx**.

Review 2 Adjusting Column Widths; Replacing Data; Moving Cells; Applying Formatting Features; Inserting a Picture

1. With **ES2-R1-WBInvToNPC.xlsx** open, adjust the width of column A to *10.00 (75 pixels)*.
2. Change the width of column C to the length of the longest entry (AutoFit).
3. Change the width of column D to *15.00 (110 pixels)* and column E to *7.00 (54 pixels)*.
4. Use the Replace feature to replace the value *32* with *36* for all occurrences.
5. Create a SUM formula in F33 to total the cells in the column.
6. Apply numeric formats as follows:
   a. Format F17 and F33 to Accounting Number Format.
   b. Format F28 and F31 to Comma Style.
7. Indent once A18:A27 and A29:A30.
8. Select D1:D3 and change the font to 10-point Bookman Old Style bold. (Substitute another font of your choosing if Bookman Old Style is not available.)
9. Move D1:D3 to F1:F3 and then align the text at the right edge of the cells.
10. Merge and center and then apply the Input cell style (*Data and Model* section) to the ranges A17:B17 and A28:B28.
11. Merge and center A5 across columns A–F and then apply the Title cell style to A5.
12. Center the values in columns C and D and the label in F16.
13. Add a top and bottom border to A16:F16 and turn on bold.
14. Add a top and double bottom border to F33 and turn on bold.
15. Add an outside border to A1:F36.
16. Add the fill color Olive Green, Accent 3, Lighter 80% from the Fill Color palette to A5.
17. Add the fill color Olive Green, Accent 3, Lighter 60% from the Fill Color palette to A16:F16.
18. Apply the Clarity theme to the worksheet.
19. Make A1 the active cell, insert the picture file named *TWBLogo.jpg* and resize the picture as necessary so that the logo fits in the first four rows at the top left of the worksheet.
20. Save, print, and then close **ES2-R1-WBInvToNPC.xlsx**. *Note: Check with your Instructor if you submit your work in hard copy to see if you need to print two copies of this worksheet with one of the copies showing the cell formulas instead of the calculated results.*

Skills Assessment

Note: If you submit your work in hard copy, check with your instructor before completing these Assessments to find out if you need to print two copies of each worksheet, with one of the copies showing the cell formulas instead of the calculated results.

Assessment 1 Editing Cells; Inserting Columns; Copying Formulas; Inserting Pictures; Applying Formatting Features

1. Bobbie Sinclair of Performance Threads has started preparing a workbook that tracks the costs of costume research, design, and production for a Marquee Productions project. You have been asked to complete the workbook. Open **PTMarqCost.xlsx** and spend a few moments reviewing the worksheet Bobbie has started.
2. Save the workbook in the ExcelEOS folder and name it **ES2-A1-PTMarqCost.**
3. Complete the worksheet using the following information:
   a. Design costs for all costumes should be *122.50* instead of *22*.
   b. Insert a new column between *Fabric* and *Total Cost* and type the column heading Notions in J9. Type the values in J10:J16 as follows:

Henry II	101.50	John	47.85
Queen Eleanor	88.23	Geoffrey	47.85
Alias	58.40	Philip	47.85
Richard	47.85		

   c. The formula to calculate total cost for each costume is incorrect. Enter the correct formula for the first costume (K10) and then copy the formula to K11:K16. *Hint: The current formula does not include the fabric and notions costs.*
   d. Create a formula in L10 to calculate the costume fee that will multiply the total cost in K10 by *2* and then copy the formula to L11:L16.
   e. Create a formula in M10 to calculate the profit as costume fee minus total cost and then copy the formula to M11:M16.
   f. Format the numeric cells in an appropriate style.
   g. Change the alignment of any headings that could be improved in appearance.
   h. Merge and center the titles in A6 and A7 over the columns.
   i. Insert the picture file named **PTLogo.jpg** and resize it to fit in the five rows at the top left of the worksheet.
   j. Insert a clip art image of your choosing after searching using the word *sewing* and resize the image to fit in the five rows at the top right of the worksheet.
   k. Apply font, border, and color changes to enhance the appearance of the worksheet. Adjust column widths as needed.
4. Change the page layout to landscape orientation and change the *Width* in the Scale to Fit group of the Page Layout tab to *1 page*.
5. Save, print, and then close **ES2-A1-PTMarqCost.xlsx**.

Assessment 2 Completing and Formatting a Worksheet

1. Camille Matsui, production assistant for Marquee Productions, has requested the invoice in advance for the custom-made costumes so that she can make sure the budget funds are allocated. Bobbie Sinclair has started the invoice and has asked you to finish it. Open **PTMarqCostInv.xlsx** and spend a few moments reviewing the invoice Bobbie has started. *Note: Completion of Assessment 1 is required to finish the invoice for this assessment.*

2. Save the workbook in the ExcelEOS folder and name it **ES2-A2-PTMarqCostInv**.

3. Complete the invoice using the following information:
   a. Type the current date in G6.
   b. Refer to your electronic copy or your printout of the costumes in Assessment 1, Step 5. Type the values from the *Costume Fee* column (L10:L16) into the appropriate cells in F15:F21.
   c. Create a formula to total the costume fees in F22. *Hint: Make sure the total agrees with the total costume fee on your printout from Assessment 1.*
   d. A transportation and storage container for each of the seven costumes is *$75.00*. Enter the appropriate formula in F24 that will calculate the fee for seven containers.
   e. Enter in F25 the delivery for all seven costumes as *$250.00*.
   f. Enter in F26 a formula that will add the total for the costume fees with the additional charges.
   g. Enter in F27 a formula that will calculate 13% Canadian Harmonized Sales Tax on the total in F26.
   h. Enter in F28 a formula to calculate the total invoice as the sum of F26 and F27.

4. Insert the picture file named **PTLogo.jpg** in A1 and resize it to fit in the three rows at the top left of the worksheet.

5. Improve the appearance of the worksheet by adjusting column widths, deleting blank rows, moving cells, and/or applying formatting features that you learned in this section.

6. Save, print, and then close **ES2-A2-PTMarqCostInv.xlsx**.

Assessment 3 Performing a Spelling Check; Adjusting Column Width; Using Find and Replace; Inserting Clip Art; Applying Formatting Features

1. Sam Vestering, manager of North American Distribution for Worldwide Enterprises, has created a workbook to summarize revenues from distribution of Marquee Productions' documentary film *The Endangered Monarch Butterfly*. You have been asked to review the worksheet and make enhancements to the appearance. Begin by opening **WEMBRev.xlsx** and reviewing the worksheet's layout, data, and formulas.
2. Save the workbook in the ExcelEOS folder and name it **ES2-A3-WEMBRev**.
3. Make the following corrections:
   a. Perform a spelling check.
   b. Adjust column widths so all data is completely visible.
   c. Change all of the venues named *Cinema House* to *Cinema Magic*.
   d. In A3, type **Date:** and then enter today's date in B3.
   e. Search for a clip art image of a monarch butterfly and then insert the image at the top right of the worksheet.
   f. Improve the appearance of the worksheet by applying formatting features that you learned in this section.
4. Print the worksheet in portrait orientation with the width scaled to fit 1 page.
5. Save and then close **ES2-A3-WEMBRev.xlsx**.

Assessment 4 Finding the Select All Button

1. Use the Help feature to find out where the Select All button is located in the Excel window.
2. Open **WBInventory.xlsx** and save the workbook in the ExcelEOS folder, naming it **ES2-A4-WBInventory**.
3. Click the Select All button and then apply italic formatting.
4. Deselect the cells and then scroll the worksheet to view the change.
5. Save, print, and then close **ES2-A4-WBInventory.xlsx**.

HELP

Assessment 5 Individual Challenge
Locating Information on Theatre Arts Programs

1. You are considering enrolling in a drama/theatre arts program at a college or university. Search the Internet for available programs in postsecondary schools in the United States and Canada. Choose three schools that interest you the most and find out as much as you can about the costs of attending these schools. Try to find information on costs beyond tuition and books, such as transportation and room and board.
2. Create a workbook that compares the costs for each of the three schools. For example, create the cost categories in column A and include three columns next to each cost category where you will enter the costs you found for each school. Total the costs for each of the schools.
3. Apply formatting features that you learned in this section to the worksheet.
4. Save the workbook in the ExcelEOS folder and name it **ES2-A5-TheatreArts**.
5. Print and then close **ES2-A5-TheatreArts.xlsx**.

Marquee Challenge

Challenge 1 Creating a Direct Wages Budget Report for a Film Shoot

1. You work with Chris Greenbaum, production manager at Marquee Productions. Chris has asked you to create the direct wages budget for the company's remote location film shoot. Create the worksheet shown in Figure 2.1. *Note: The logo is a file named MPLogo.jpg*.
2. Link the values in the *Estimated Daily Rates* table (columns I and J) to the *Daily Rate* column (column F) in the budget section.
3. Calculate the extended cost by summing the number of days for site prep, shoot, and cleanup and then multiplying by the daily rate.
4. Calculate the total in G16.
5. Apply formatting options as shown and format the values in column G to an appropriate number format. Use your best judgment to determine the font, font size, column widths, borders, and fill colors.
6. Although not visible in the figure, a border should also be applied along the top (columns A–G) and left edges (rows 1–14) of the budget cells so that when printed, the entire budget has a perimeter border.
7. Print the worksheet in landscape orientation and then save the workbook in the ExcelEOS folder naming it **ES2-C1-MPLocBudg**.
8. Close **ES2-C1-MPLocBudg.xlsx**.

FIGURE 2.1 Challenge 1

Remote Location Film Shoot
July 11 to August 31, 2011

Direct Wages Budget

Personnel	Site Prep Days	Shoot Days	Cleanup Days	Daily Rate	Extended Cost
Crew	9	32	2	1,275	$ 54,825
Cast	0	32	0	13,775	$ 440,800
Actor Assistants	0	32	0	3,250	$ 104,000
Extras	0	19	0	2,800	$ 53,200
Cleaners	9	32	5	875	$ 40,250
Security	7	32	5	3,750	$ 165,000
Administration	9	32	5	1,275	$ 58,650
			Total Direct Wages Budget		$ 916,725

Estimated Daily Rates
Subject to Change

Crew	1,275
Cast	13,775
Actor Assistants	3,250
Extras	2,800
Cleaners	875
Security	3,750
Administration	1,275

Challenge 2 Creating a Room Timetable

1. You are an assistant to the person who schedules classroom space in the Theatre Arts Division at Niagara Peninsula College. You have been given the room schedule for the auditorium for next semester. The division posts a printed copy of the timetable outside the auditorium door so that students know when the room is available to work on projects and rehearse for upcoming plays. You want to use Excel to create and format the timetable so that the printed copy is easy to read and has a more professional appearance.
2. Refer to the data in Figure 2.2 and then create the timetable in a new workbook. Apply formatting features learned in this section to create a colorful, easy-to-read room timetable.
3. Save the workbook in the ExcelEOS folder and name it **ES2-C2-NPCRoomSch**.
4. Print and then close **ES2-C2-NPCRoomSch.xlsx**.

FIGURE 2.2 Challenge 2

Niagara Peninsula College					
Room:	T1101		Period Covered: January 1 to April 30		
Time	Monday	Tuesday	Wednesday	Thursday	Friday
8:00 AM	SM100-01	AC215-03		MG210-01	SM240-03
9:00 AM	Prasad	McLean	LE100-03	Spelberger	Prasad
10:00 AM	LE253-03	(lab)	Das	SM355-02	SD350-04
11:00 AM	Das			Prasad	Attea
12:00 PM	SD451-01	PD250-02	Common	PD320-03	
1:00 PM	Attea	Kemper	Period	Kemper	LE310-02
2:00 PM	PD340-02	MG410-03	AC478-01	AC480-01	Das
3:00 PM	Kemper	Spelberger	Simmons	Simmons	MG210-01
4:00 PM	MG150-02	SM165-01	AC140-01	(lab)	Spelberger
5:00 PM	Spelberger	Prasad	Chou		
Use of this facility is restricted to staff and registered students only of Niagara Peninsula College. Failure to abide by this policy is considered a serious violation of the college's code of conduct.					
Note 1:	Monday through Thursday evenings, room is booked for Continuing Education department.				
Note 2:	Room is booked 8:00 AM to 5:00 PM the second Saturday of each month for the local community theatre group.				

Excel SECTION 3

Using Functions, Setting Print Options, and Adding Visual Elements

Skills

- Create formulas with absolute addresses
- Create AVERAGE, COUNT, MAX, and MIN formulas to perform statistical analysis
- Create TODAY, NOW, and DATE formulas
- Create PMT formulas to calculate loan payments
- Create and use range names
- Create an IF formula to return a result based on a logical test
- Create, edit, and format a column, pie, and line chart
- Draw shapes and text boxes
- Modify and format charts
- Change page layout options for printing such as margins, horizontal and vertical centering, and scaling
- Manipulate a worksheet in Page Layout view
- Insert headers and footers

Projects Overview

Add functions, create charts, and change page layout options for a quarterly expense and revenue budget forecast; finish an invoice by entering dates and changing page layout options; calculate loan payment amounts for a patio expansion loan; calculate year-end bonuses; create charts for performance benchmarks.

Create and format charts for a grades analysis report; create a chart and apply formatting enhancements to an international student registration report.

Calculate and analyze sales commissions; create charts, apply formatting enhancements, and change page layout options to a European Destinations report.

Calculate payments for an office expansion loan for two finance companies.

Create two charts that depict movie attendance statistics for a staff development workshop.

Model Answers for Projects

These model answers for the projects that you complete in Section 3 provide a preview of the finished projects before you begin working and also allow you to compare your own results with these models to ensure you have created the materials accurately.

ES3-WBQtrExpBudg.xlsx is the project in Activities 3.1 and 3.2 and part of the project in Activities 3.7, 3.8, and 3.10.

The Waterfront Bistro

Quarterly Expense Budget Forecast

	Last Year's Avg Qtr	Qtr1 (1.05)		Qtr2 (1.08)		Qtr3 (1.15)		Qtr4 (1.14)		Total	
		Target Factors for Increases by Quarter									
Advertising	$ 2,150.00	$ 2,257.50	$	2,322.00	$	2,472.50	$	2,451.00	$	9,503.00	
Bank charges	500.00	525.00	$	540.00	$	575.00	$	570.00	$	2,210.00	
Cleaning	650.00	682.50	$	702.00	$	747.50	$	741.00	$	2,873.00	
Linens	1,100.00	1,155.00	$	1,188.00	$	1,265.00	$	1,254.00	$	4,862.00	
Office supplies	175.00	183.75	$	189.00	$	201.25	$	199.50	$	773.50	
Telephone	250.00	262.50	$	270.00	$	287.50	$	285.00	$	1,105.00	
Utilities	2,050.00	2,152.50	$	2,214.00	$	2,357.50	$	2,337.00	$	9,061.00	
Total		$ 7,218.75	$	7,425.00	$	7,906.25	$	7,837.50	$	30,387.50	
Average expense		$ 1,031.25	$	1,060.71	$	1,129.46	$	1,119.64	$	4,341.07	
Maximum expense		$ 2,257.50	$	2,322.00	$	2,472.50	$	2,451.00	$	9,503.00	
Minimum expense		$ 183.75	$	189.00	$	201.25	$	199.50	$	773.50	
Count of expense items		7									

Total Operating Expenses Forecast

Pie chart legend:
- Advertising — 31.3%
- Bank charges — 7.3%
- Cleaning — 9.5%
- Linens — 16.0%
- Office supplies — 2.5%
- Telephone — 3.6%
- Utilities — 29.8%

ES3-WBInvPTDirMtg.xlsx is the project in Activity 3.3 and part of the project in Activity 3.11.

The Waterfront Bistro

3104 Rivermist Drive
Buffalo, NY 14280
716 555 3166

Proudly serving you since June-77

Invoice

To: Performance Threads
4011 Bridgewater Street
Niagara Falls, ON L2E 2T6

Date: 3-Jun-2010

Due Date: 3-Jul-2010

Attention: Bobbie Sinclair
Re: Director's Meeting

Item		No. of Persons	Price per Person	Total
1	Appetizer trays	15	5.15	$ 77.25
2	Prime rib dinner	15	32.99	494.85
3	Dessert trays	15	5.95	89.25
4	Coffee and tea	15	1.85	27.75
	Meeting room charge	15	2.50	37.50
	Total			$ 726.60

Note: All prices include tax and gratuity.
Terms: Due upon receipt of invoice payable in U.S. funds

Thank you for your business! Visit us at our website at www.emcp.net/wfbistro

ES3-WBPatioLoan.xlsx is the project in Activity 3.4 and part of the project in Activity 3.11.

The Waterfront Bistro

Patio Expansion Loan Analysis			
	Funds Unlimited	**Venture Funds Inc.**	**Details**
Interest Rate	7.25%	8.15%	Annual rate
Term	15	12	Years for repayment
Loan Amount	420,000	420,000	Principal borrowed
Monthly Payment	($3,834.02)	($4,580.92)	Includes principal and interest

NOTE:
Both payments are calculated based on a constant interest rate and a constant payment.

Total loan payments	($690,124.34)	($659,651.81)	

ES3-WBEmpBonus.xlsx is the project in Activities 3.5, 3.6, and 3.12.

The Waterfront Bistro
Employee Profit Sharing Bonus
January 1, 2011 to December 31, 2011

Employee	Years of Service	Profit Sharing Bonus	Year End Profit	Bonus for 5+ years	Bonus for less than 5 years
Lou Cortez	2	7,177.35	$ 574,188	2.5%	1.25%
Jasmine Hill	5	14,354.70			
Heather Kiley	8	14,354.70			
Dayna McGuire	4	7,177.35			
Carla Modano	5	14,354.70			
Tyler Santini	12	14,354.70			
Pat Soulliere	7	14,354.70			
Moira Su-Lin	1	7,177.35			
Toni Williams	3	7,177.35			
	Total	100,482.90			
Average service	5.2				

ES3-WBQtrExpBudg.xlsx is part of the project in Activities 3.7 and 3.10.

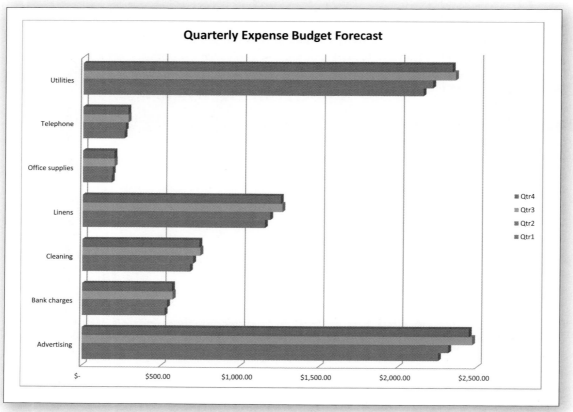

ES3-WBPerfStats.xlsx is the project in Activity 3.9.

The Waterfront Bistro

Quarterly Performance Benchmarks

	Qtr1	Qtr2	Qtr3	Qtr4
Avg check per person	8.25	9.50	15.00	17.25
Avg seat turnover	2.0	1.0	1.5	2.6

National Restaurant Association Statistics

	Qtr1	Qtr2	Qtr3	Qtr4
NRA Avg check per person	10.00	12.50	11.00	14.00
NRA Avg seat turnover	1.3	1.1	1.8	2.0

Activity 3.1

Creating Formulas with Absolute Addressing

In the previous two sections, when you copied and pasted formulas in worksheets, the cell addresses in the destination cells changed automatically *relative* to the destination row or column. The formulas in these worksheets used *relative addressing*. Sometimes you need a cell address to remain fixed when it is copied to another location in the worksheet. To do this, the formulas must include *absolute addressing* for those cell addresses that you do not want changed. Make a cell address absolute by typing a dollar symbol ($) in front of the column letter or row number that cannot be changed. You can also use function key F4 to toggle through variations of the address as relative, absolute, or mixed in which either the row is absolute and the column is relative or vice versa.

Project

Tutorial 3.1
Creating Formulas and Absolute Addresses

Dana has started a worksheet to forecast next year's expenses by quarter. Dana uses a model where next year's expenses are estimated based on last year's average quarter values multiplied by a factor that represents the expected increase for this year. For example, a factor of 1.05 means Dana is expecting the expense to increase by 5%. You will calculate each quarter's expense using the factors in the model Dana has started.

1. Open **WBQtrExpBudg.xlsx** and then save the workbook in the ExcelS3 folder naming it **ES3-WBQtrExpBudg**.

2. Review the layout of the worksheet. Notice the values in D4:G4 are factors that represent the increases by quarter for next year's expenses. For example, *Advertising* in *Qtr1* is expected to increase by a factor of *1.05* (an increase of five percent.)

3. Make D6 the active cell. All of the Qtr1 values in column D will be created by multiplying *Last Year's Avg Qtr* amount by the factor in D4. The formula will include an address that should not change when the formula is copied (D4). To create a formula with an absolute address, type **=b6*d4** and then press function key F4.

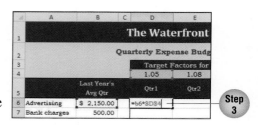

   Pressing F4 causes Excel to insert dollar symbols in front of the row number and column letter immediately left of the insertion point — *d4* becomes $D$4, an absolute address.

4. Press Enter.

   The result *$2,257.50* is entered in D6. In the D6 formula, the first cell reference (B6) is relative and the second cell reference (D4) is absolute. This is an example of *mixed referencing* with some addresses relative and some absolute. When the formula is copied in a later step, only D4 remains the same.

5. With D7 the active cell, type **=b7*d4** and press Enter.

   You can also type the dollar symbol in front of the column letter or row number to make an address absolute.

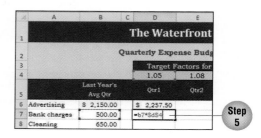

6. Make D7 the active cell and then drag the fill handle down to D12.

7 Click D8 and look at the formula in the Formula bar. Notice that the first cell address (B8) was changed relative to the current row number but the second cell address ($D$4) remained the same as the original when the formula was copied.

8 Make E6 the active cell, type **=b6*e4**, press function key F4, and then press Enter.

9 Make F6 the active cell and then create the formula *=B6*$F$4* by either typing **=b6*f4** and pressing function key F4 or by typing the dollar symbols before *f* and *4*.

10 Make G6 the active cell and then create the formula *=B6*$G$4* by either typing **=b6*g4** and pressing function key F4 or by typing the dollar symbols before *g* and *4*.

11 Select E6:G6 and then drag the fill handle down to row 12.

12 Click a few cells in the copied range and verify that in each case, the cell reference with the dollar symbols remained the same when the formula was copied.

13 Make D14 the active cell and click the AutoSum button to calculate the total for column D. Click the AutoSum button a second time to accept the suggested formula *=SUM(D6:D13)*.

14 Make H6 the active cell, click the AutoSum button, and then press Enter to accept the suggested formula *=SUM(D6:G6)*.

15 Complete the formulas in E14:H14 and H7:H12 by copying the appropriate SUM functions.

16 Save **ES3-WBQtrExpBudg.xlsx**.

In Brief

Make Cell Address Absolute

With insertion point positioned just after cell address or with cell address selected in Formula bar, press F4.

OR

Type dollar symbol immediately preceding column letter and/or row number.

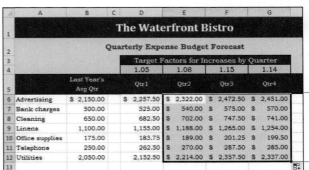

In Addition

More about Mixed Addressing

Excel can be instructed to fix only the row number or the column letter of a cell that is copied and pasted to another location. This table shows more ways that a cell address can use absolute referencing. Pressing F4 repeatedly causes Excel to scroll through each of these variations for the selected cell address.

Example	Action
=$A$12*.01	Neither the column nor the row will change.
=$A12*.01	The column will remain fixed at column A, but the row will change.
=A$12*.01	The column will change, but the row remains fixed at row 12.
=A12*.01	Both the column and row will change.

Activity 3.2

Until now, you have only used the SUM function when you clicked the AutoSum button in the Editing group of the Home tab. Excel includes numerous other built-in formulas that are grouped into function categories. The Statistical category contains several functions that can be used to perform statistical analysis on data, such as calculating medians, variances, frequencies, and so on. The structure of a function formula begins with the equals sign (=), followed by the name of the function, and then the argument within parentheses. *Argument* is the term given to the values to be included in the calculation. The structure of the argument is dependent on the function being used and can include a single range of cells, multiple ranges, single cell references, or a combination thereof.

Project

Dana has asked you to add statistics below the quarterly expenses budget forecast. Specifically, you will calculate the average, maximum, and minimum expenses as well as a count of the number of expense items.

SNAP

Tutorial 3.2
Writing Formulas in Excel

1 With **ES3-WBQtrExpBudg.xlsx** open, type the following labels in the cells indicated.

A17   **Average expense**
A18   **Maximum expense**
A19   **Minimum expense**
A20   **Count of expense items**

2 Make D17 the active cell.

In the next steps, you will insert the AVERAGE function to determine the arithmetic mean of the expenses in column D. If an empty cell or a cell containing text is included in the argument, Excel ignores the cell when determining the result. If, however, the cell contains a zero value, it is included in the average calculation.

3 Click the AutoSum button arrow in the Editing group in the Home tab.

4 Click *Average* at the drop-down list.

Excel inserts the formula *=AVERAGE(D14:D16)* in the active cell with the suggested range highlighted. In the next step, you will drag to select the correct range and then complete the formula.

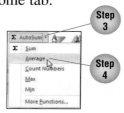

Step 3

Step 4

5 Position the cell pointer over D6, hold down the left mouse button, drag down to D12, and then release the left mouse button.

Excel inserts the range *D6:D12* in the formula and the moving marquee expands to display the selected cells.

	Last Year's Avg Qtr	Qtr1	Qtr2	Q
5				
6 Advertising	$ 2,150.00	$ 2,257.50	$ 2,322.00	$ 2,
7 Bank charges	500.00	525.00	$ 540.00	$
8 Cleaning	650.00	682.50	$ 702.00	$
9 Linens	1,100.00	1,155.00	$ 1,188.00	$ 1,
10 Office supplies	175.00	183.75	$ 189.00	$
11 Telephone	250.00	262.50	$ 270.00	$
12 Utilities	2,050.00	2,152.50	$ 2,214.00	$ 2,
13				
14 **Total**		$ 7,218.75	$ 7,425.00	$ 7,
15				
16				
17 Average expense		=AVERAGE(D6:D12)		
18 Maximum expense		AVERAGE(number1, [number2], ...)		
19 Minimum expense				
20 Count of expense items				

Step 5

Step 1

6 Press Enter or click the Enter button on the Formula bar.

> Excel returns the result *$1,031.25* in D17.

7 Make D18 the active cell, click the AutoSum button arrow, and then click *Max* at the drop-down list.

> The MAX function returns the largest value in the argument.

8 Type **d6:d12** and then press Enter.

> Excel returns the result *$2,257.50* in D18. Typing the range into the formula is sometimes faster if you are sure of the starting and ending cell references.

In Brief

AVERAGE, MAX, MIN, COUNT Functions
1. Make desired cell active.
2. Click AutoSum button arrow.
3. Click desired function.
4. Type or select argument range.
5. Press Enter or click Enter button.

17	Average expense	$ 1,031.25
18	Maximum expense	=MAX(d6:d12)
19	Minimum expense	MAX(**number1**, [number2], ...)
20	Count of expense items	

Steps 7-8

9 With D19 the active cell, type the function **=min(d6:d12)** and then press Enter.

> MIN returns the smallest value in the argument. As soon as you type the letter m after the equals sign, the Formula AutoComplete feature displays a drop-down list of functions that begin with the letter typed. Formula AutoComplete helps you to write formulas by displaying function names, descriptions, and argument syntax. You can scroll the list and point to a function name to display in a ScreenTip the function's purpose. Double-click a function name in the list to enter the function into the cell.

10 With D20 the active cell, type the function **=count(d6:d12)** and then press Enter.

> COUNT returns the number of cells that contain numbers or numbers that have been formatted as text and dates. Empty cells, text labels, or error values in the range are ignored.

11 Select D17:D19 and then drag the fill handle right to column H. (You are not including the Count formula in D20 since the count value (7) does not change.

> This copies the AVERAGE, MAX, and MIN formulas to columns E through H.

5		Last Year's Avg Qtr	Qtr1	Qtr2	Qtr3	Qtr4	Total
6	Advertising	$ 2,150.00	$ 2,257.50	$ 2,322.00	$ 2,472.50	$ 2,451.00	$ 9,503.00
7	Bank charges	500.00	525.00	540.00	575.00	570.00	2,210.00
8	Cleaning	650.00	682.50	702.00	747.50	741.00	2,873.00
9	Linens	1,100.00	1,155.00	1,188.00	1,265.00	1,254.00	4,862.00
10	Office supplies	175.00	183.75	189.00	201.25	199.50	773.50
11	Telephone	250.00	262.50	270.00	287.50	285.00	1,105.00
12	Utilities	2,050.00	2,152.50	2,214.00	2,357.50	2,337.00	9,061.00
13							
14	Total		$ 7,218.75	$ 7,425.00	$ 7,906.25	$ 7,837.50	$ 30,387.50
15							
16							
17	Average expense		$ 1,031.25	$ 1,060.71	$ 1,129.46	$ 1,119.64	$ 4,341.07
18	Maximum expense		$ 2,257.50	$ 2,322.00	$ 2,472.50	$ 2,451.00	$ 9,503.00
19	Minimum expense		$ 183.75	$ 189.00	$ 201.25	$ 199.50	$ 773.50
20	Count of expense items		7				

Step 11

12 Click in any cell to deselect D17:H19.

13 Save and then close **ES3-WBQtrExpBudg.xlsx**.

Activity 3.3

Using Date Functions
TODO, NOW, and DATE

Dates are stored as serial numbers, beginning with the number 1 for January 1, 1900, and increasing sequentially. Times are stored as decimal fractions representing portions of a day. Storing these entries as numbers enables calculations to be performed on cells containing a date or a time. The Date & Time category in the Insert Function dialog box contains functions that can be used to write formulas for cells containing dates. Cells containing dates and times can be formatted using the Number Format drop-down list in the Number group in the Home tab or using the Format Cells dialog box. Various combinations of year, month, day, hour, minutes, and seconds are available for displaying dates and times.

Project

An invoice to Performance Threads needs to be completed by entering the invoice date and the due date. You will open the invoice and experiment with the TODAY and NOW functions to enter the invoice date and then create a formula to calculate the due date. Finally, you will use a DATE function to enter the date The Waterfront Bistro opened in the invoice header.

SNAP

Tutorial 3.2
Writing Formulas in Excel

1. Open **WBInvPTDirMtg.xlsx**.

2. Save the workbook in the ExcelS3 folder and name it **ES3-WBInvPTDirMtg**.

3. Make F6 the active cell, type **=now()**, and then press Enter.

   The current date and time are inserted in F6. In the next step, you will try the TODAY function to see the difference between the two date functions.

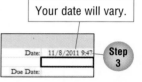

4. Make F6 the active cell, press Delete to clear the cell, type **=today()**, and then press Enter.

   The current date is inserted in the cell with the time displayed as 0:00. Normally, the time does not display when TODAY is used; however, since we first entered the NOW function, Excel retained the time format for the cell. In a later step, you will format the cell to display the month, day, and year only.

5. Make F8 the active cell, type **=f6+30**, and then press Enter to calculate the due date as 30 days from the invoice date.

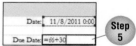

6. Make F4 the active cell.

7. Click the Formulas tab in the ribbon and then click the Date & Time button in the Function Library group.

8. Click *DATE* at the drop-down list of Date & Time functions.

   The Function Arguments dialog box opens with a text box for each section of the function argument.

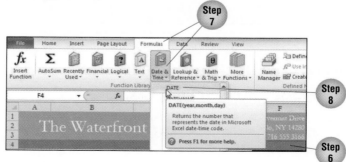

9. Type **1977** in the *Year* text box.

10 Press Tab to move the insertion point to the *Month* text box and then type **06**.

11 Press Tab to move the insertion point to the *Day* text box, type **15**, and then click OK.

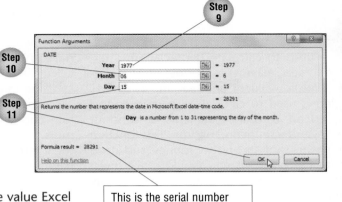

Step 9

Step 10

Step 11

The Function Arguments dialog box displays the serial number for June 15, 1977, as 28291 which is the value Excel stores in the cell. Notice the formula in the Formula bar is *=DATE(1977,6,15)*.

This is the serial number representing June 15, 1977.

12 Right-click F4 and then click *Format Cells* at the shortcut menu.

13 If necessary, click the Number tab in the Format Cells dialog box.

Since the active cell contains a date function, the *Date* category will be automatically selected in the *Category* list box.

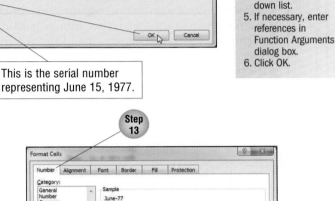

Step 13

Date category is automatically selected.

Step 14

14 Scroll down the list of formats in the *Type* list box; click *March-01*, the format that will display the date as the full month followed by two digits for the year; and then click OK.

15 Format F4 to 10-point Candara italic.

16 Select F6:F8 and then display the Format Cells dialog box with the Number tab selected.

17 Click *Date* in the *Category* list box. Scroll down the *Type* list box; click *14-Mar-2001*, the format that displays the date as dd-mmm-yyyy; and then click OK.

18 Click in any cell to deselect F6:F8.

19 Save and then close **ES3-WBInvPTDirMtg.xlsx**.

Steps 12-15

Steps 16-18

In Brief

Date Functions
1. Make desired cell active.
2. Click Formulas tab.
3. Click Date & Time button.
4. Click desired function at drop-down list.
5. If necessary, enter references in Function Arguments dialog box.
6. Click OK.

In Addition

TIME Function

Time values are stored as decimal numbers that represent the portion of a day starting at 0 (12:00:00 AM) and continuing up to 0.999988426, representing (23:59:59 PM). The format of the TIME function using the 24-hour clock is *=TIME(hour,minute,second)*. In the worksheet shown at the right, the formula *=(C2-B2)*24* is used to calculate how many hours the employee worked.

Activity 3.4

Using the Financial Function PMT

You can use Excel's financial functions to calculate depreciation, interest rates, payments, terms, present values, future values, and so on. The PMT function is used to calculate a payment for a loan based on constant payments, a constant interest rate, and a set period of time. This function is useful if you want to borrow money and need to estimate the payment you would make given a specified interest rate and length of time to pay back the loan. To use the PMT function correctly, the time periods for the interest rate and the term have to be consistent. For example, if you want to calculate the monthly payment on a loan, make sure the interest rate and the number of periods are expressed in months, or convert the interest rate and time period to months within the formula. The PMT function requires three arguments: the interest rate for the loan *(Rate)*, the number of payments to be made *(Nper)*, and the amount of money that is borrowed *(Pv)*.

Project

The Waterfront Bistro is planning a patio expansion next year. Dana Hirsch has received pre-approval from two finance companies and wants you to estimate monthly loan payments for each to help decide from which company to borrow funds.

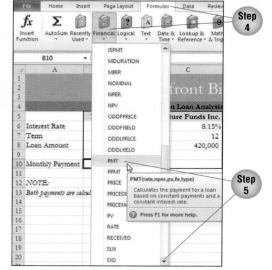

1. Open **WBPatioLoan.xlsx**.

2. Save the workbook in the ExcelS3 folder and name it **ES3-WBPatioLoan**.

3. Make B10 the active cell.

4. Click the Formulas tab and then click the Financial button in the Function Library group.

5. Scroll down the *Financial* drop-down list and then click *PMT*.

6. If necessary, drag the Function Arguments dialog box Title bar to the right of column B.

7. With the insertion point positioned in the *Rate* text box, click the mouse in B6 and then type */12*.

   The interest rate in B6 is 7.25% which is the annual interest rate. Typing */12* divides the annual interest rate by 12 to obtain a monthly interest rate. Since you want to calculate a payment per month you need to ensure the time periods for all input values are the same.

8. Click in the *Nper* text box, click B7, and then type **12*.

   The term in B7 represents the number of years that loan payments will be made. Multiplying this value times 12 payments per year represents the total number of payments to be made for the loan. Note that you have converted both the interest rate and the number of payments within the function arguments to months.

9. Click in the *Pv* text box, click B8, and then click OK.

   Pv stands for ***present value*** and represents the principal amount that is being borrowed. Excel returns the payment amount *$3,834.02* for the Funds Unlimited loan in B10. Payments are displayed as negative values; in this spreadsheet file, negative values are displayed in red and within parentheses. Consider loan payments as money that is subtracted from your cash balance, which helps you relate to the negative value returned in the formula cell. If you prefer, you can enter a negative value in B8 (-420,000) and the calculated payment displays as a positive number.

PMT formula is entered as you complete the Function Argument entries.

Step 7

In Brief

Financial Functions
1. Make desired cell active.
2. Click Formulas tab.
3. Click Financial button.
4. Click desired function name.
5. Enter references in Function Arguments dialog box.
6. Click OK.

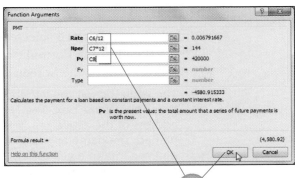

10 Make C10 the active cell.

11 Click the Insert Function button f_x on the Formula bar.

> The Insert Function dialog box can be used to find an Excel function. This is useful if you do not know the category for which a function is associated. You can locate a function by typing a description of the formula and then clicking the Go button.

12 At the Insert Function dialog box, type **loan payments** in the *Search for a function* text box and then click Go.

13 With *PMT* already selected in the *Select a function* list box, click OK.

14 At the Function Arguments dialog box, enter the parameters as indicated and then click OK.

Rate	**C6/12**
Nper	**C7*12**
Pv	**C8**

Step 14

15 Make A15 the active cell, type **Total loan payments**, and press Enter.

16 Make B15 the active cell, type **=b10*12*b7**, and then press Enter.

> This calculates the total amount that will have to be paid back for the loan from Funds Unlimited.

17 Use the fill handle in B15 to copy the formula to C15.

18 Use the Format Painter feature to copy the formats from B10 to B15:C15 and then apply the *All Borders* option to B15:C15.

> Notice that the loan from Venture Funds Inc. is a better choice for The Waterfront Bistro provided the bistro can afford the higher monthly payments. Although the interest rate is higher than Funds Unlimited's loan, the shorter term means the loan is repaid faster with a lower total cost.

10	Monthly Payment	($3,834.02)	($4,580.92)	Includes principal and interest
11				
12	NOTE:			
13	Both payments are calculated based on a constant interest rate and a constant payment.			
14				
15	Total loan payments	($690,124.34)	($659,651.81)	

Steps 15-18

19 Save and then close **ES3-WBPatioLoan.xlsx**.

Activity 3.5

Creating and Using Range Names

Assigning a name to a cell or a range of cells allows you to reference the cell(s) by a descriptive label rather than the cell address or range address when creating formulas, printing, or when navigating a large worksheet. Referencing by name makes a formula easier to understand. For example, a formula such as *=Sales-Expenses* is readily understood. A standard formula such as *=D3-D13* requires the reader to look at the labels next to the values in the formula cells in order to grasp the formula's purpose. A range name can be a combination of letters, numbers, underscore characters, or periods up to 255 characters. The first character in a range name must be a letter, an underscore, or a back-slash (\). Spaces are not valid in a range name. To create a range name, select the desired cells and then type the name in the *Name* text box at the left of the Formula bar.

Project

The profit-sharing bonus for the employees needs to be calculated. Dana has started the worksheet and asked you to finish it. Since the bonus amount varies depending on the employee's years of service, you decide to begin by naming cells so that you can use names in the function to help you build the correct formula.

SNAP

Tutorial 3.4
Naming and Using a Range

1. Open **WBEmpBonus.xlsx**.

2. Save the workbook in the ExcelS3 folder and name it **ES3-WBEmpBonus**.

   To begin, you want to name the cells in column B *Years*. The first step in naming a range is to select the cell or group of cells to which the name will be associated.

3. Select B7:B15.

4. With the range B7:B15 selected, point at the white box at the left end of the Formula bar (currently displays *B7* in the box). Notice the ScreenTip displays *Name Box*.

   The white box at the left end of the Formula bar is called the *Name* box. The *Name* box displays the cell address of the active cell. If the active cell has been named, the name appears in the *Name* box. To assign a new name to a cell or selected range, click in the *Name* box and type the desired name.

5. Click in the *Name* box (white box at left end of Formula bar), type **Years**, and press Enter.

   Notice the range name now appears in the *Name* box. You want to assign a name to each cell that will be referenced when you create the profit-sharing formula in the next project. In the next steps you will assign a range name to individual cells that will be needed to calculate the profit-sharing bonus.

6. Make E7 the active cell.

7. Click in the *Name* box, type **Profit** and press Enter.

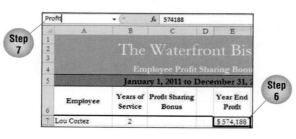

In Brief

Naming a Range
1. Select cell(s).
2. Click in *Name* box.
3. Type desired range name.
4. Press Enter.

8 Make F7 the active cell, click in the *Name* box, type **FiveAndOver**, and then press Enter.

9 Make G7 the active cell, click in the *Name* box, type **LessThanFive**, and then press Enter.

10 Click the down-pointing arrow at the right of the *Name* box.

A drop-down list of range names in the current workbook appears. To move the active cell to a named cell or range, click the range name in the drop-down list.

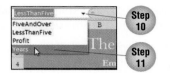

11 Click *Years* at the drop-down list.

The range B7:B15 is selected since this is the group of cells associated with the name *Years*.

12 Make A19 the active cell, type **Average service**, and then press Enter.

13 Make B19 the active cell, type **=average(years)**, and then press Enter.

Notice that range names are not case sensitive when you use the name in a formula. When you type the range name *years* in the formula, notice that Excel color-codes B7:B15 to show you the cells that are being referenced in the formula.

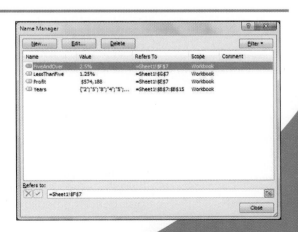

14 Format B19 to display only one decimal place.

15 Save **ES3-WBEmpBonus.xlsx**.

In Addition

Managing Range Names

To edit or delete a range name, display the Name Manager dialog box shown at the right. To do this, click the Formulas tab and then click the Name Manager button in the Defined Names group. The Name Manager dialog box displays the range names in the active workbook and provides buttons to edit or delete the name.

Activity 3.6

Using the Logical IF Function

The IF function returns one of two values in a cell based on a true or false answer to a question called a logical test. The format of an IF function is =IF(logical_test,value_if_true,value_if_false). For example, assume a salesperson earns a 3 percent commission if sales are greater than or equal to $100,000, or a 2 percent commission for sales less than $100,000. Assume the sales value resides in B4. The logical_test in this example would be B4>=100000. Excel can only return a true or false answer when this test is performed. The commission will be calculated at either B4*3% (value_if_true) or B4*2% (value_if_false). In this example, the IF function formula would be =IF(B4>=100000,B4*3%,B4*2%).

Project

The catering staff participate in a profit-sharing bonus at the end of a year. The bonus amount is based on the year-end profit and the employee's years of service—2.5% for those with 5 years of service and more, and 1.25% for those employees with less than 5 years of service. Since the percentage bonus can be either one of two values, you need an IF function to calculate the bonus.

The Waterfront
B·I·S·T·R·O

SNAP

Tutorial 3.5
Using the Logical IF
Function

1. With **ES3-WBEmpBonus.xlsx** open, make C7 the active cell.

2. Click the Formulas tab.

3. Click the Logical button in the Function Library group.

4. Click *IF* at the drop-down list.

The Function Arguments dialog box for the IF statement opens. Notice the three arguments: *Logical_test, Value_if_true,* and *Value_if_false.* To begin, you want Excel to test whether the value in the years of service column (column B) is less than 5. This test determines whether Excel calculates the bonus using the lower percent paid to employees with fewer than five years of service or the higher percent paid to employees with five or more years of service. Recall that in the last project you created range names. In the next steps, you will see how using range names will make the IF statement much easier to create and understand.

5. With the insertion point positioned in the *Logical_test* text box, type **years<5**, and then press Tab.

Watch the entries that appear at the right of each argument text box as you build the formula. Excel updates these entries to show you how the formula is working as you build each argument. Notice that next to the *Logical_test* text box you now see the TRUE and FALSE results Excel is calculating for each entry in the Years range.

6. With the insertion point positioned in the *Value_if_true* text box, type **profit*lessthanfive** and then press Tab.

If the value in B7 is less than 5, Excel calculates the bonus as the profit (E7) times 1.25% (G7). Another advantage to using range names is that by default, range names refer to the named cell using absolute references. Since the formula will be copied to rows 8–15, absolute references are required for those cells that reference the profit and the percents.

90   EXCEL Section 3

7 With the insertion point positioned in the *Value_if_false* text box, type **profit*fiveandover**.

> If the value in B7 is greater than or equal to 5, the formula calculates the profit (E7) times 2.5% (F7). Notice that below the text boxes, Excel shows the result that will be placed in the active cell *Formula result = 7177.35*. Looking at B7 you will note that Lou Cortez has 2 years of service so Excel is calculating Lou's bonus as $574,188 times 1.25%.

In Brief

IF Function
1. Make desired cell active.
2. Click Formulas tab.
3. Click Logical button.
4. Click *IF*.
5. Type formula in *Logical_test* text box.
6. Type value or formula in *Value_if_true* text box.
7. Type value or formula in *Value_if_false* text box.
8. Click OK.

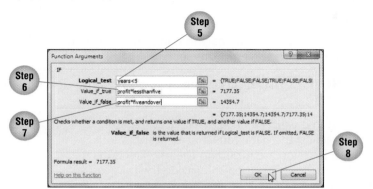

8 Click OK.

9 Drag the fill handle in C7 down to row 15 and then click in any cell to deselect the range.

10 Make C17 the active cell, click the AutoSum button in the Function Library group, and then press Enter to calculate the total bonuses to be paid.

11 Format the values in column C to Comma Style.

12 Click C7 and review the formula in the Formula bar that was created using the IF Function Arguments dialog box *=IF(Years<5, Profit*LessThanFive,Profit*FiveAndOver)*.

> The formula may be easier to comprehend if you include the range names when reading it to yourself.

13 Save and then close **ES3-WBEmpBonus.xlsx**.

> values in column C formatted to Comma Style in Step 11

In Addition

More about IF Function Arguments

One advantage to creating an IF function using the Function Arguments dialog box is that the correct syntax is added automatically to the formula. For example, you did not need to worry about typing commas between arguments or the opening and closing brackets in this project. These elements are automatically added to the formula. Notice also that the range names in the completed formula are displayed in the case used when the range name is created. For example, you typed profit*lessthanfive but the formula you reviewed at Step 12 displayed this entry as Profit*LessThanFive. When creating your range names consider the readability of the formula and use upper- and lowercase letters to facilitate comprehension. Another alternative is to use underscores between words in a range name.

Activity 3.7

Creating a Column Chart

Numerical values are often more easily understood when presented visually in a chart. Excel includes several chart types such as column, line, pie, bar, area, scatter, and others with which you can graphically portray data. The chart can be placed in the same worksheet as the data or it can be inserted into its own sheet. To create a chart, first select the cells containing the data you want to graph and then choose the chart type. Excel graphs the data in a separate object which can be moved, resized, and formatted.

Project Dana Hirsch has asked you to create a chart to compare the quarterly expenses in the budget forecast you completed earlier in this section.

Tutorial 3.6
Creating Charts in Excel

1. Open **ES3-WBQtrExpBudg.xlsx**, select A5:A12, hold down the Ctrl key, and then select D5:G12.

   The first step in creating a chart is to select the range of cells containing the data you want to graph. Notice in the range that you are including the row labels in column A. Labels are included to provide the frame of reference for each bar, column, or other chart series. If you select multiple ranges, ensure that the data in each range has a consistent number of cells in the range.

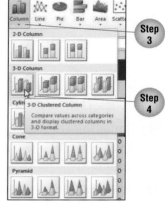

Step 3

Step 4

2. Click the Insert tab.

3. Click the Column button in the Charts group.

4. Click *3-D Clustered Column* at the drop-down list (first from left in *3-D Column* section).

   Excel graphs the data in a 3-D column chart and places the chart inside an object box in the center of the worksheet.

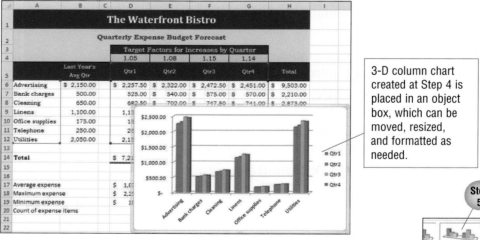

3-D column chart created at Step 4 is placed in an object box, which can be moved, resized, and formatted as needed.

Step 5

5. Click the Move Chart button in the Location group in the Chart Tools Design tab.

Need Help?

Can't see the Chart Tools Design tab? You probably clicked outside the chart to deselect the object and the contextual tab disappeared. Click over the chart to select the object and the contextual Chart Tools Design tab reappears.

6 At the Move Chart dialog box, click *New sheet*.

7 With *Chart1* selected in the *New sheet* text box, type **ColumnChart** and then click OK.

> The chart object is moved to a new sheet in the workbook with a tab labeled *ColumnChart*. The chart is automatically scaled to fill the entire page in landscape orientation.

8 Click *Layout 3* in the Chart Layouts group.

> This layout adds a title to the top center of the chart and moves the legend to the bottom center.

9 Click once over *Chart Title* to select the title object, click a second time at the beginning of the text to place an insertion point inside the chart title box, delete *Chart Title*, and then type **Quarterly Expense Budget Forecast**.

Quarterly Expense Budget Forecast

10 Click inside the chart area to deselect the title text.

11 Click the More arrow button ▼ in the Chart Styles group in the Chart Tools Design tab.

More
Change the overall visual style of the chart.

12 Click *Style 26* in the drop-down gallery (second option in the fourth row).

Step 12

Style 26

13 Save **ES3-WBQtrExpBudg.xlsx**.

In Brief

Create Column Chart
1. Select cells.
2. Click Insert tab.
3. Click Column button.
4. Click desired chart type.
5. Move and/or resize chart as required.
6. Apply design options.

In Addition

Changing the Data in a Chart

Click the Select Data button in the Data group in the Chart Tools Design tab to add cells to, or delete cells from, the source range that was selected to generate the chart. At the Select Data Source dialog box shown at the right, you can add, edit, or delete a data series or edit the category axis labels.

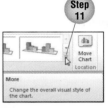

Activity 3.8

Creating a Pie Chart

Pie charts illustrate each data point's size in proportion to the total of all items in the data source range. Each slice in the pie chart is displayed as a percentage of the whole pie. You can choose to display the percent values, the actual values used to gener-ate the chart, or both values as data labels inside or outside the pie slices. Use a pie chart when you have only one data series you want to graph and there are no negative or zero values within the data range.

Project

Dana Hirsch has requested a second chart from the quarterly expense budget forecast worksheet that displays each expense as a proportion of the total expenses.

Tutorial 3.6
Creating Charts in Excel

1 With **ES3-WBQtrExpBudg.xlsx** open, click the tab labeled *Sheet1* near the bottom left corner of the window above the Status bar.

2 If necessary, click in any cell to deselect the range that was used to generate the column chart in the previous activity.

3 Select the range A5:A12, hold down the Ctrl key, and then select the range H5:H12.

4 Click the Insert tab.

5 Click the Pie button in the Charts group.

6 Click *Pie in 3-D*, the first pie chart in the *3-D Pie* section in the drop-down list.

7 Point to the border of the chart object until the pointer displays with the four-headed arrow move icon, hold down the left mouse button, and then drag the chart below the worksheet. Position the chart approximately centered below columns A–H with the top edge in row 22.

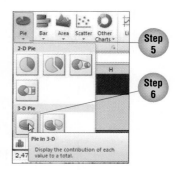

Need Help?

You may find it helpful to scroll the worksheet until you see several blank rows below row 22 before moving the chart.

8 With the chart object still selected, click the Chart Tools Layout tab.

9 Click the Data Labels button in the Labels group and then click *More Data Label Options* at the drop-down list.

10 At the Format Data Labels dialog box with *Label Options* selected in the left pane, click the *Value* check box in the *Label Contains* section to clear the box and then click the *Percentage* check box to add a check mark.

11 Click *Outside End* in the *Label Position* section.

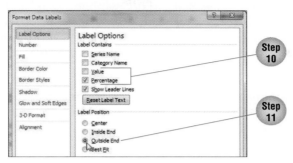

Step 10

Step 11

> **In Brief**
> **Create Pie Chart**
> 1. Select cells.
> 2. Click Insert tab.
> 3. Click Pie button.
> 4. Click desired pie type.
> 5. Move and/or resize chart as required.
> 6. Apply design options.

12 Click *Number* in the left pane, click *Percentage* in the *Category* list box, select the number in the *Decimal places* text box, and then type **1**.

Step 12

13 Close the Format Data Labels dialog box.

14 Click the Chart Tools Design tab.

15 Click the More arrow button in the Chart Styles group and then click *Style 10* at the drop-down list (second option in second row).

16 Change the chart title to **Total Operating Expenses Forecast**. Refer to Activity 3.7, Steps 9–10, if you need assistance with this step.

19	Minimum expense		$	183.75	$	189.00	$	201.25	$	199.50	$	773.50
20	Count of expense items		7					

Step 16

Total Operating Expenses Forecast

31.3% Advertising
29.8% Bank charges
Cleaning
Linens
3.6% 7.3% Office supplies
2.5% Telephone
16.0% 9.5% Utilities

17 Click in the worksheet area outside the chart to deselect the chart.

18 Save and then close **ES3-WBQtrExpBudg.xlsx**.

In Addition

Sparklines

A new Sparklines group was added to the Insert tab in Excel 2010. Sparklines are miniature charts that you can add to a cell. These miniature charts illustrate changes from a specified row or column of data. For example, in the worksheet shown, the sparkline chart was created in F4 based on the range of values in B4:E4. Click the Insert tab and then click Line, Column, or Win/Loss in the Sparklines group. At the Create Sparklines dialog box, select the data range that contains the values you want to base the chart upon (B4:E4), select the cell in which to draw the chart (F4), and then click OK.

	A	B	C	D	E	F
1	**The Waterfront Bistro**					
2	Quarterly Performance Benchmarks					
3		Qtr1	Qtr2	Qtr3	Qtr4	
4	Daily sales per seat	150.00	275.00	190.00	225.00	

Sparkline Column Chart

Activity 3.9

Creating a Line Chart; Drawing Shapes

A line chart shows trends and change over time at even intervals. Line charts emphasize the rate of change over time rather than the magnitude of the change. You can easily spot a trend in a line chart, look for unusual points in the data series, or even predict future values based on the line's shape and direc- tion. The Shapes button in the Insert tab includes buttons with which you can draw lines, rectangles, basic shapes, block arrows, equation shapes, flow- chart symbols, stars and banners, and callouts. Enclosed shapes can also contain text. Draw shapes, arrows, or add text boxes to add emphasis or insert explanatory notes in a worksheet.

Project

SNAP

Tutorial 3.6
Creating Charts in Excel

Dana has created a worksheet with the bistro's performance statistics by quarter along with the National Restaurant Association's statistics. Dana would like you to create charts in order to compare the data visually.

1. Open **WBPerfStats.xlsx**. Save the workbook in the ExcelS3 folder and name it **ES3-WBPerfStats**.

2. Select A3:E4, hold down the Ctrl key, and then select A8:E8.

3. Click the Insert tab, click the Line button in the Charts group, and then click *Line with Markers* in the *2-D Line* section at the drop-down list (first option in second row).

   Notice the line chart clearly shows that the bistro performed below the association's average check per person for the first half of the year but finished the year well above the association's statistics.

   Step 3

4. Point to the border of the chart object until the pointer displays with the four-headed arrow move icon and then drag the chart below the worksheet approximately centered below columns A–E and with the top edge in row 11.

5. Select A3:E3, A5:E5, and A9:E9 and then create a Line chart similar to the line chart created at Step 3.

6. Move the new line chart below the first one, leaving one blank row between the two charts.

   In the next steps you will draw shapes and add text to the shapes to add emphasis in the two line charts.

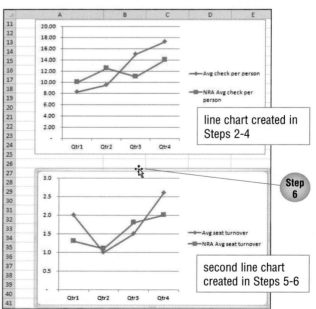

line chart created in Steps 2-4

Step 6

second line chart created in Steps 5-6

7. If necessary, click the Insert tab. Click the Shapes button in the Illustrations group.

   The Shapes drop-down list contains shape buttons grouped by category.

8 Click the *12-Point Star* button  in the *Stars and Banners* group (fourth from right in first row).

> When a shape object tool has been selected, the pointer changes to a crosshairs.

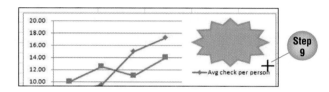

Step 8

9 Position the crosshairs in the white space above the legend in the first line chart near the top of the chart just right of the 20.00 grid line, drag the crosshairs down and right as shown, and then release the mouse. If you are not happy with the shape, press Delete to remove the star and then try again.

> When you release the mouse, the shape is positioned with eight white sizing handles around the perimeter of the shape as well as a green rotation handle and a yellow diamond center point. The Drawing Tools Format tab becomes active with options to customize the shape.

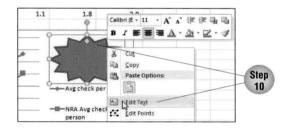

Step 9

10 Right-click the shape and then click *Edit Text* at the shortcut menu.

> An insertion point appears inside the shape indicating you can begin typing.

Step 10

11 Type **A Strong Finish!**, press Ctrl + E to center the text, and then click in the worksheet outside the chart.

Step 11

12 If necessary, click the Insert tab. Click the Shapes button and then click the *Wave* button in the *Stars and Banners* group (second from right in second row).

13 Draw a wave shape in the white space above the legend in the second line chart similar to the one shown.

14 Right-click the shape and then click *Edit Text* at the shortcut menu.

Steps 12-15

15 Type **Qtr 4 30% above NRA!**, click the Home tab, click the Middle Align button in the Alignment group, and then click in the worksheet outside the chart.

16 Print the worksheet.

17 Save and then close **ES3-WBPerfStats.xlsx**.

In Brief

Create Line Chart
1. Select cells.
2. Click Insert tab.
3. Click Line button.
4. Click desired line type.
5. Move and/or resize chart as required.
6. Apply design options.

Draw Shape
1. Click Insert tab.
2. Click Shapes button.
3. Click desired shape.
4. Drag to create shape.
5. Move, resize, or format shape as required.

Add Text to Shape
1. Right-click shape.
2. Click *Edit Text*.
3. Type text.
4. Click outside shape.

Activity 3.10

Modifying and Formatting Charts

To make changes to an existing chart, click inside a chart or chart element to display the translucent border around the perimeter of the chart object. Point to the border to move the chart or point to one of the eight sizing handles to resize the chart. When the chart is selected, the Chart Tools Design, Layout, and Format tabs become available. Use these tabs to add, delete, or modify the chart or chart elements.

Project

You will modify the charts created for the quarterly expense budget forecast worksheet by formatting the legend, changing the font in the chart title, and changing the chart type.

The Waterfront
B·I·S·T·R·O

SNAP

Tutorial 3.7
Changing a Chart Type

1. Open **ES3-WBQtrExpBudg.xlsx** and then click anywhere inside the pie chart to select the chart object.

   Once a chart is selected, the three contextual Chart Tools tabs become available—Design, Layout, and Format.

2. Click inside the pie chart legend.

   Eight sizing handles appear around the legend indicating the object is selected. You can drag the legend to another location or resize the legend using one of the handles.

3. Click the Chart Tools Format tab.

4. Click the Shape Outline button in the Shape Styles group and then click the *Light Blue* color box in the color palette (fourth from right in *Standard Colors* section).

   This adds a thin, light blue border around the legend.

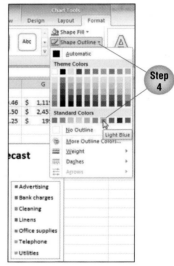

5. Right-click the chart title and then use the Font and Font Size buttons in the Mini toolbar to change the title to 14-point Verdana.

6. Click inside the chart area to deselect the chart title.

7. Click inside any one of the percent values around the edge of the pie.

   This selects all seven data labels.

8. Click the Home tab and then click the Bold button in the Font group.

9. Click in the worksheet area outside the pie chart.

10. Click the ColumnChart tab located near the bottom left corner of the window above the Status bar and then click inside the column chart to select the chart.

11. Click the Chart Tools Design tab and then click the Change Chart Type button in the Type group.

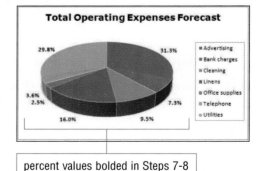

percent values bolded in Steps 7-8

12 At the Change Chart Type dialog box, click *Bar* in the left pane and then click *Clustered Bar in 3-D* in the *Bar* section in the right pane (fourth option in first row).

13 Click OK.

14 Click *Layout 1* in the Chart Layouts group.

> This layout moves the legend to the right side of the chart where there is more room.

15 Click the More arrow button in the Chart Styles group and then click *Style 2* in the drop-down list (second option in first row).

16 Print the chart.

17 Click the Sheet1 tab, click the File tab, and then click Print.

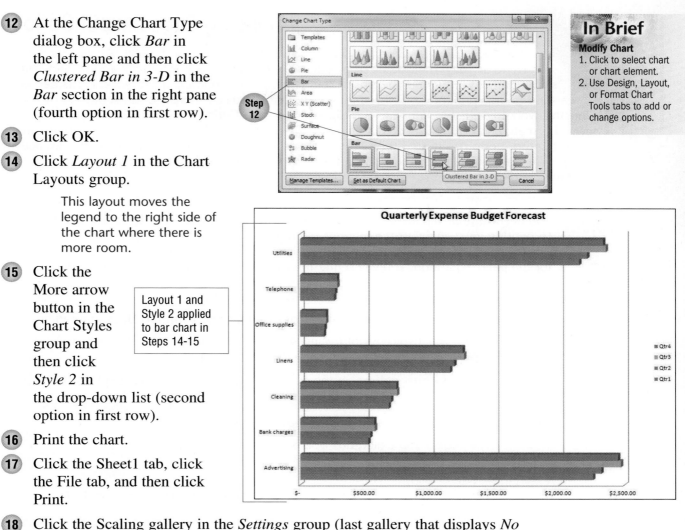

In Brief

Modify Chart
1. Click to select chart or chart element.
2. Use Design, Layout, or Format Chart Tools tabs to add or change options.

Step 12

Layout 1 and Style 2 applied to bar chart in Steps 14-15

18 Click the Scaling gallery in the *Settings* group (last gallery that displays *No Scaling*), click *Fit Sheet on One Page* at the drop-down list, and then click the Print button.

> Scaling a worksheet means Excel will decrease the size of print proportionately in order to fit a worksheet to the specified number of pages (in this case one page).

19 Save and then close **ES3-WBQtrExpBudg.xlsx**.

In Addition

Chart Elements

Another method to edit a chart is to right-click a chart element to display a context-sensitive shortcut menu. For example, right-clicking the axis labels in the bar chart displays the shortcut menu shown at the right. The bottom section of the shortcut menu changes depending on the element you clicked.

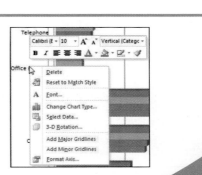

Activity
3.11

Changing Page Layout Options

The Page Layout tab contains buttons to modify the page setup and scaling options for printing purposes. You can also change print options while previewing the worksheet in the Print tab Backstage view. The margin on a worksheet is the blank space at the top, bottom, left, and right edges of the page and the beginning of the printed text. The default margins are 0.75 inch top and bottom and 0.7 inch left and right. Smaller worksheets can be centered horizontally and/or vertically to improve the printed appearance. For larger worksheets, you can choose to shrink the text by scaling the size of printed text to force the printout to a minimum number of pages such as the quarterly expense budget forecast printed in the last activity which you scaled to fit one page.

Project

You need to print the invoice to Performance Threads completed in an earlier activity. Prior to printing you will adjust the margins to improve the worksheet's appearance using the Print tab Backstage view. Dana would also like the worksheet printed with the loan analysis for the patio expansion. You will center the worksheet horizontally before printing.

SNAP

Tutorial 3.8
Changing Page
Margins and Layout
Options

1. Open **ES3-WBInvPTDirMtg.xlsx**.

2. Click the File tab and then click Print to open the Print tab Backstage view.

   Notice the invoice is not balanced on the page. In the next steps you will change the margins to improve the page layout.

3. Click the Margins gallery in the *Settings* category (currently displays *Normal Margins*).

4. Click *Custom Margins* at the drop-down list.

   The Page Setup dialog box opens with the Margins tab active.

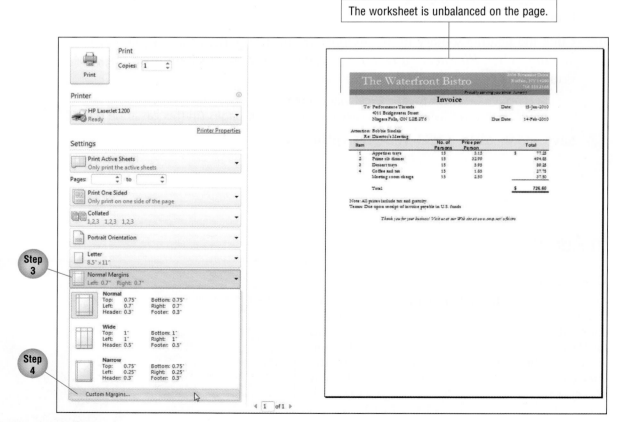

The worksheet is unbalanced on the page.

5 Select the current entry in the *Top* text box, type **1.25**, select the current entry in the *Left* text box, type **1.25**, and then click OK.

Step 5

> The preview pane in Backstage view shows the worksheet with the new margins applied. The page layout is improved for printing.

6 Click the Print button.

7 Save and then close **ES3-WBInvPTDirMtg.xlsx**.

8 Open **ES3-WBPatioLoan.xlsx**.

9 Click the Page Layout tab, click the Orientation button in the Page Setup group, and then click *Landscape*.

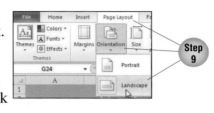

Step 9

10 Click the Margins button in the Page Setup group and then click *Custom Margins* at the drop-down list.

> The Page Setup dialog box opens with the Margins tab active. This is another way to open the same Page Setup dialog box you accessed using the Margins gallery in Print tab Backstage view.

11 Change the *Top* margin to *1.25*.

Step 11

12 Click the *Horizontally* check box in the *Center on page* section and then click OK.

Step 12

> Centering the worksheet horizontally is another method that can be used to ensure the worksheet prints balanced between the left and right edges of the page. You can choose both the *Horizontally* and *Vertically* check boxes to print a worksheet that is centered between both the left and right edges (horizontally), and the top and bottom edges (vertically) of the page.

13 Print the worksheet.

14 Save and then close **ES3-WBPatioLoan.xlsx**.

In Addition

Printing Column or Row Headings on Multiple Pages

Use the Print Titles button in the Page Setup group in the Page Layout tab to define column or row headings that you want repeated at the top or left edge of each page to make the data in rows and columns in a multipage printout easier to identify.

Activity 3.12

Using Page Layout View; Inserting Headers and Footers

Page Layout view allows you to view the worksheet along with the print settings. Page Layout view also displays horizontal and vertical rulers to assist with measurements. A header is text that prints at the top of each work-sheet and a footer is text that prints at the bottom of each worksheet. Excel includes pre-defined headers and footers that can be selected from a drop-down list or you can create your own custom header or footer text.

Project

Tutorial 3.9
Adding Headers and Footers

Before printing the profit-sharing bonus worksheet completed earlier, you want to add identifying information in a custom header and footer and check other print options using Page Layout view.

1. Open **ES3-WBEmpBonus.xlsx**.

2. Click the Page Layout button located at the right side of the Status bar near the Zoom slider bar.

Step 2

3. If necessary, use the horizontal and vertical scroll bars to adjust the window so that the worksheet including the white space for the top, left, and right margins is entirely visible.

4. Click over the text *Click to add header* near the top center of the page.

Step 4

A header and footer are divided into three sections. Click at the left or right side of the header area to open the left or right section text box in which you can type or insert header and footer elements. By default, text in the left section is left-aligned, text in the center section is centered, and text in the right section is right-aligned.

5. Click at the left edge of the Header area to open the left section text box and then type your first and last names.

Step 5

6. Click at the right edge of the Header area to open the right section text box, type **Date Printed:**, and then press the spacebar once.

7. Click the Current Date button in the Header & Footer Elements group in the Header & Footer Tools Design tab.

Excel inserts the code *&[Date]*, which causes the current date to be inserted at the location of the code when the worksheet is printed.

Step 7

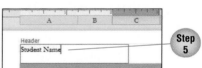

Step 6

In Brief

Insert Header or Footer
1. Switch to Page Layout view.
2. Click over *Click to add header* or *Click to add footer*.
3. Insert desired header and footer elements and/or type text in left, center, or right section.
4. Click in the worksheet area to end header or footer editing.

8 Click the Go to Footer button 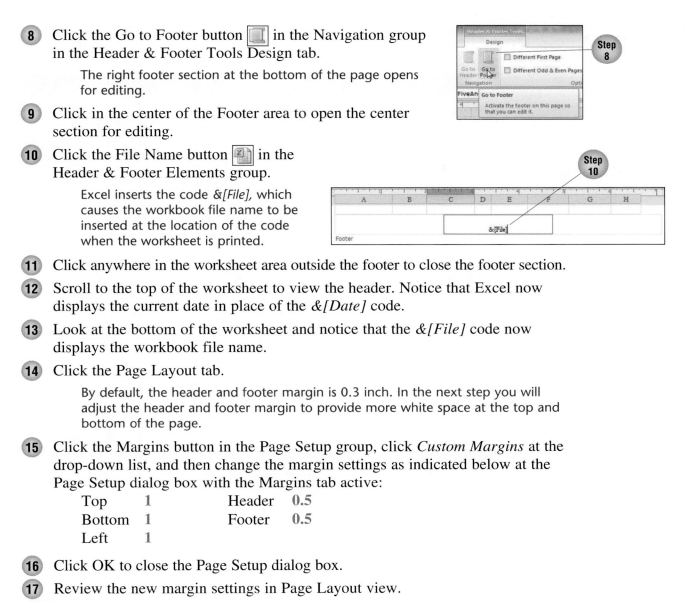 in the Navigation group in the Header & Footer Tools Design tab.

> The right footer section at the bottom of the page opens for editing.

9 Click in the center of the Footer area to open the center section for editing.

10 Click the File Name button in the Header & Footer Elements group.

> Excel inserts the code *&[File]*, which causes the workbook file name to be inserted at the location of the code when the worksheet is printed.

11 Click anywhere in the worksheet area outside the footer to close the footer section.

12 Scroll to the top of the worksheet to view the header. Notice that Excel now displays the current date in place of the *&[Date]* code.

13 Look at the bottom of the worksheet and notice that the *&[File]* code now displays the workbook file name.

14 Click the Page Layout tab.

> By default, the header and footer margin is 0.3 inch. In the next step you will adjust the header and footer margin to provide more white space at the top and bottom of the page.

15 Click the Margins button in the Page Setup group, click *Custom Margins* at the drop-down list, and then change the margin settings as indicated below at the Page Setup dialog box with the Margins tab active:

Top	1	Header	0.5
Bottom	1	Footer	0.5
Left	1		

16 Click OK to close the Page Setup dialog box.

17 Review the new margin settings in Page Layout view.

18 Print the worksheet.

Review new margin settings in Page Layout view in Step 17.

Your date will vary.

19 Click the Normal button located at the right side of the Status bar near the Zoom slider bar (immediately left of the Page Layout View button).

20 Save and then close **ES3-WBEmpBonus.xlsx**.

Features Summary

Feature	Ribbon Tab, Group	Button
change margins	Page Layout, Page Setup OR File, Print	
create a column chart	Insert, Charts	
create a line chart	Insert, Charts	
create a pie chart	Insert, Charts	
Date & Time functions	Formulas, Function Library	
draw a shape	Insert, Illustrations	
Financial functions	Formulas, Function Library	
insert function	Formulas, Function Library	f_x
insert header or footer	Insert, Text OR Page Layout View	
Logical functions	Formulas, Function Library	
Page Layout view	View, Workbook Views	OR
scale page width and/or height	Page Layout, Scale to Fit OR File, Print	
Statistical functions	Formulas, Function Library	

Knowledge Check

Completion: In the space provided at the right, indicate the correct term, command, or option.

1. This symbol next to a column or row number means the reference is absolute.
2. AVERAGE and COUNT are two of the functions grouped in this function category.
3. This Date and Time function inserts the current date (without the time) in the active cell.
4. This financial function returns the payment for a loan based on a constant interest rate and period of time for repayment.
5. A range name is typed in this box at the left end of the Formula bar.
6. The IF function is found in this category of functions in the Function Library.
7. This type of chart is used to illustrate each data point as a proportion of the total.
8. When a chart is selected, these three contextual Chart Tools tabs appear.

9. This button in the Illustrations group is used when you want
to draw a star. _____

10. Page Setup options such as custom margins can be changed
using the Page Layout tab or while viewing a preview of how
the worksheet will print in this view. _____

11. You can type header or footer text directly in the worksheet
while viewing the worksheet in this view. _____

12. This code is inserted in the header or footer when you click
the File Name button in the Header & Footer Elements group. _____

Skills Review

Review 1 Creating Range Names; Inserting Statistical, Date, and IF Functions; Changing Page Layout Options

1. Open **WBQtrRev.xlsx** and then save the workbook in the ExcelEOS
folder and name it **ES3-R1-WBQtrRev**.

2. Select and name the ranges indicated.

| B4:B8 | *Quarter1* | C4:C8 | *Quarter2* | D4:D8 | *Quarter3* |
| E4:E8 | *Quarter4* | F4:F8 | *TotalRev* | | |

3. Type labels in the cells indicated.

    A14   Average revenue   A15   Maximum revenue   A16   Minimum revenue

4. In B14, B15, and B16, enter the functions that will calculate the average, maximum, and
minimum revenue values using the Quarter1 range name in each function.

5. Insert average, maximum, and minimum functions in C14:F16 using the Quarter2,
Quarter3, Quarter4, and TotalRev range names, respectively, in each column's functions.

6. Make A18 the active cell and then type **Date created**.

7. Enter in B18 a DATE function that will insert the current date. ***Note: You do not want to
use TODAY or NOW functions, because the date will update each time you open the file***.

8. Format B18 to display the date in the format *14-Mar-2001*.

9. Type the label **Next revision date** in A19 and then enter a formula in B19 that will add
350 days to the date in B18.

10. Type the label **Quarterly minimum target** in A21 and the value **350000** in B21.

11. Format B21 to Comma Style with no decimals and name the cell *MinTarget*.

12. Type the label **Revenue target not met by** in A22.

13. Dana Hirsch set the minimum target of $350,000 for each quarter's revenue. Calculate
in B22 the amount under target the quarter's total revenue is by entering the IF formula:
=if(b10<mintarget,b10-mintarget,0).

14. Drag the fill handle from B22 to C22:E22.

15. Change the page orientation to landscape, change the top margin to 1.5 inches, and center
the worksheet horizontally.

16. Create a header that will print your first and last names at the left margin and the current
date and time separated by one space at the right margin.

17. Create a footer that will print the file name at the right margin.

18. Save and print **ES3-R1-WBQtrRev.xlsx**. ***Note: If you submit your work in hard copy,
check with your instructor to see if you need to print two copies of this worksheet with
one of the copies showing the cell formulas instead of the calculated results***.

Review 2 Creating Charts; Drawing Shapes

1. With **ES3-R1-WBQtrRev.xlsx** open, select the range A3:E8 and then create a column chart with the following options:
   a. Choose the *Clustered Column* in the *2-D Column* section (first chart option).
   b. Move the chart to a new sheet with the sheet label *ColumnChart*.
   c. Apply the Layout 1 chart layout.
   d. Apply the Style 34 chart style.
   e. Change the chart title to *Quarterly Revenue Budget Forecast*.
2. Print the ColumnChart sheet.
3. Make Sheet1 the active sheet, select the ranges A3:A8 and F3:F8, and then create a Pie chart with the following options.
   a. Choose the *Exploded Pie in 3-D* in the *3-D Pie* section (second chart option).
   b. Move the chart to a new sheet with the sheet label *PieChart*.
   c. Apply the Layout 6 chart layout.
   d. Apply the Style 34 chart style.
   e. Change the chart title to *Total Revenue Budget Forecast*.
4. With PieChart the active sheet, draw an *Up Arrow Callout* shape (last shape in second row in the *Block Arrows* group) in the white space below the pie chart. Draw the shape approximately 1 inch wide and 1.5 inches high with the top of the arrow pointing up towards 55% in the Dining room pie slice.
5. Add the text **This is a 10% increase over last year!** inside the up arrow callout shape.
6. Select the shape, click the Home tab, and click the Center button and the Middle Align button in the Alignment group.
7. Print the PieChart sheet.
8. Save and then close **ES3-R1-WBQtrRev.xlsx**.

Skills Assessment

Note: If you submit your work in hard copy, check with your instructor before completing these Assessments to find out if you need to print two copies of each worksheet with one of the copies showing the cell formulas instead of the calculated results.

Assessment 1 Creating Statistical and IF Functions; Using Absolute References

1. Alex Torres, manager of the Toronto office for First Choice Travel, has started a workbook to calculate sales commission for the Toronto sales agents. First Choice Travel has implemented a new bonus commission based upon the number of cruises booked. Alex has asked for your help in writing the correct formulas to calculate the commission owed to the agents and analyze the results. To begin, open **FCTSalesComm.xlsx** and then save the workbook in the ExcelEOS folder naming it **ES3-A1-FCTSalesComm**.

2. Create an IF function to calculate the commission for Lopez in D4 using the information in the Commission Parameters table in F2:G5 and in the box below the table. When writing your IF statement, use references to the percent values in G4 and G5 so that when Alex revises the percents the worksheet will automatically recalculate commissions correctly. *Hint: The formula will be copied in the next step, so G4 and G5 need to be absolute references*.
3. Copy the IF function in D4 to the remaining rows in column D.
4. Format the values in column D to an appropriate number style.
5. Enter **Average commission** in B20 and create a function in D20 to calculate the average commission paid. Enter **Maximum commission** in B21 and create a function in D21 to show the highest commission paid. Enter **Minimum commission** in B22 and create a function to show the lowest commission paid.
6. Change the top margin to 1.25 inches and the left margin to 1.5 inches.
7. Save, print, and then close **ES3-A1-FCTSalesComm.xlsx**.

Assessment 2 Applying the PMT Function

1. You are the assistant to Sam Vestering, manager of North American Distribution for Worldwide Enterprises. Sam has entered in a workbook details on financing from two companies for an office expansion loan. Sam would like you to enter the formulas to calculate the estimated monthly loan payments and the total cost of each loan. To begin, open **WELoan.xlsx** and then save the workbook in the ExcelEOS folder naming it **ES3-A2-WELoan**.
2. Calculate the monthly payments on the loan in B7 and D7.
3. Calculate the total payments required for each loan in B11 and D11.
4. Save, print, and then close **ES3-A2-WELoan.xlsx**.

Assessment 3 Creating Charts; Drawing Shapes

1. Cal Rubine, chair of the Theatre Arts Division at Niagara Peninsula College, has asked you to create charts from the grades analysis report to present at a divisional meeting. After reviewing the grades, you decide to create a line chart depicting the grades for all of the courses and a pie chart summarizing the total grades. To begin, open **NPCGrades.xlsx** and then save the workbook in the ExcelEOS folder naming it **ES3-A3-NPCGrades**.
2. Create a line chart in a new sheet labeled *LineChart* that displays the A+ through F grades for all five courses. Include an appropriate chart title. You determine the line chart style, layout, and any other chart elements and formats that will make the chart easy to interpret.
3. Create a 3-D pie chart that displays the total of each grade as a percentage of 100. *Hint: Select the ranges B4:G4 and B11:G11 to create the chart*. Include an appropriate chart title and display percents around the outside of the pie slices as well as the Category names. Position the pie chart below the grades worksheet starting in row 14.
4. In the white space at the top left of the chart draw a right-pointing block arrow pointing to the percent value above the pie slice for the F grade. Inside the block arrow type the text **Lowest failure rate since 2008!** If necessary, format the text to a smaller font to fit the text within the available space.
5. Print the worksheet centered horizontally and print the line chart.
6. Save and then close **ES3-A3-NPCGrades.xlsx**.

Assessment 4 Creating Charts; Changing Page Layout; Inserting a Footer

1. Melissa Gehring, manager of the Los Angeles office for First Choice Travel, has prepared a workbook with European destinations and current package pricing options. Melissa wants you to create two charts and improve the appearance of the worksheet before she presents it at the next staff meeting. To begin, open **FCTEurope. xlsx** and then save the workbook in the ExcelEOS folder naming it **ES3-A4-FCTEurope**.
2. Insert a new row above the worksheet and add the title *European Packages* merged and centered over the worksheet.
3. Increase the height of row 1 to *27.00 (36 pixels)*.
4. Apply the Opulent theme to the worksheet.
5. Apply the Title style to A1, the Accent2 style to the range A2:G2, and the Accent1 cell style to the range A3:G3.
6. Format the values in B4:G13 to Comma Style with zero decimals.
7. Create a *Clustered bar in 3-D* bar chart in a new sheet labeled *14NightsChart* that graphs the standard and deluxe rates for all of the destinations for 14 nights. Add an appropriate title to the chart and make any other formatting choices you think would enhance the chart.
8. Print the 14NightsChart sheet.
9. Create a *Clustered bar in 3-D* bar chart in a new sheet labeled *21NightsChart* that graphs the standard and deluxe rates for all of the destinations for 21 nights. Add an appropriate title to the chart and make any other formatting choices you think would enhance the chart.
10. Print the 21NightsChart sheet.
11. Make Sheet1 the active sheet, change the page orientation to landscape, change the top margin to 1.5 inches, and center the worksheet horizontally.
12. Create a custom footer that prints your name at the left margin and the file name at the right margin.
13. Print Sheet1.
14. Save and then close **ES3-A4-FCTEurope.xlsx**.

Assessment 5 Finding Information on Chart Axis Options

1. Use the Help feature to find information on changing the vertical axis scale options in a chart.
2. Open **ES3-A4-FCTEurope.xlsx**.
3. Save the workbook in the ExcelEOS folder and name it **ES3-A5-FCTEurope**.
4. Make the 14NightsChart sheet active.
5. Using the information you learned in Help, change the value axis options so that the minimum value is fixed at 1000 and the major unit is fixed at 500. This means the value axis will start at $1,000 instead of zero and gridlines will show at every $500 interval.
6. Print the 14NightsChart sheet.
7. Save and then close **ES3-A5-FCTEurope.xlsx**.

Assessment 6 Individual Challenge
Social Networking Survey

1. You want to know which social networking tool and which social activity is the most popular among your friends, family, and classmates. Ask 10 to 20 friends, family, or classmates the following two questions and collect the responses in an Excel worksheet.
   a. Which of the following social networking sites do you use?

Facebook	LinkedIn
MySpace	Flixster
Twitter	HI5

   b. Which social networking activities do you do at these sites?

Share photos	Share updates about me or my family
Write a blog	Write reviews
Connect with people	

2. Create a chart in a new sheet labeled *SocialNetSites* that displays the total users for each of the social networking sites in the first survey question. You determine the most appropriate chart type to display the survey results. Add an appropriate chart title and any other chart formatting options to enhance the chart's appearance.

3. Print the SocialNetSites sheet.

4. Create a chart in a new sheet labeled *SocialNetAct* that displays the total participants for each type of social networking activity in the second survey question. You determine the appropriate chart type to display the survey results. Add an appropriate chart title and any other chart formatting options to enhance the chart's appearance.

5. Print the SocialNetAct sheet.

6. Save the workbook and name it **ES3-A6-SocialNetSurvey**.

7. Print the worksheet with the source data for the two charts and then close **ES3-A6-SocialNetSurvey.xlsx**.

Marquee Challenge

Challenge 1 Creating Charts on Movie Attendance Statistics

1. You are working with Shannon Grey, president of Marquee Productions, on presentation materials for an upcoming staff development workshop on producing and marketing movies. As part of Shannon's research for the workshop, she compiled a workbook with statistics related to movie attendance by age group and by household income. Shannon has asked you to create two charts for the workshop based on this source data. To begin, open **MPMovieStats.xlsx** and then save the workbook in the ExcelEOS folder naming it **ES3-C1-MPMovieStats**.
2. Using the data in the workbook, create the two charts shown in Figure 3.1.
3. The font for the title and axis text is Impact. Use your best judgment to determine chart style, layout, and other formatting options. Explore the various formatting options for elements such as the chart area, walls, axes, and gridlines.
4. Position the bar chart in a new sheet with the label *AgeChart*.
5. Position the doughnut chart in a new sheet with the label *IncomeChart*.
6. Save the revised workbook.
7. Print each chart and then close **ES3-C1-MPMovieStats.xlsx**.

FIGURE 3.1 Challenge 1

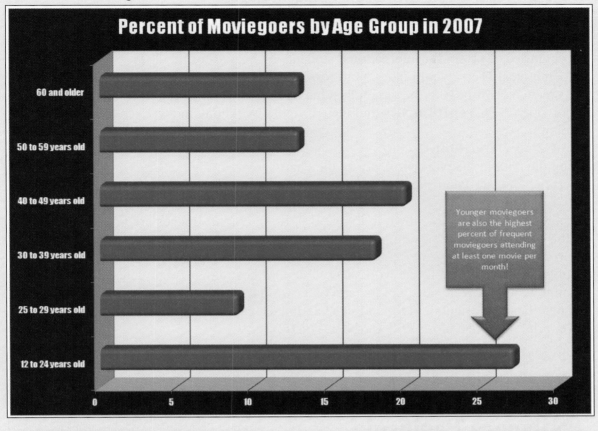

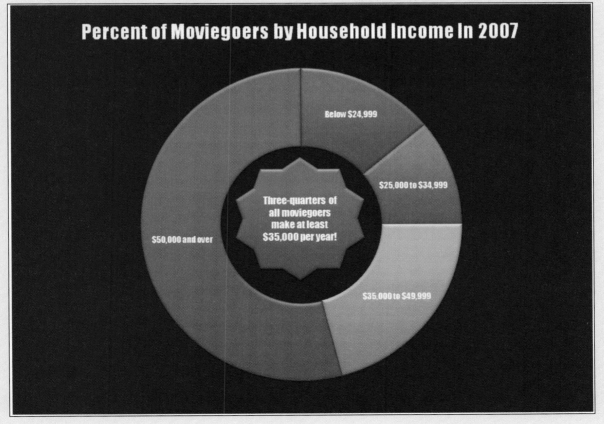

Challenge 2 Preparing an International Student Report

1. You work in the Registrar's Office at Niagara Peninsula College. Terri VanDaele, the registrar, has sent you a workbook with the top ten countries of origin for international students registered for the 2011 academic year. Terri would like you to format the workbook to improve the appearance and create a chart next to the data for inclusion with the annual report to the board. To begin, open **NPCTop10Int.xlsx** and then save the workbook in the ExcelEOS folder naming it **ES3-C2-NPCTop10Int**.
2. Using the data in the workbook, create the chart shown in Figure 3.2.
3. Insert the Niagara Peninsula College logo as shown in Figure 3.2 using the file named **NPCLogo.jpg**.
4. Format the worksheet as shown in Figure 3.2. If the clip art images are not available on the computer you are using, select an appropriate alternative image. *Hint: Use the keyword* **diversity** *when searching for the picture at the top right of the worksheet.* Apply the Verve theme to the worksheet. Use your best judgment to determine font size, column widths, row heights, colors, and other formatting elements.
5. Change the page orientation to landscape and make sure the workbook fits on one page.
6. Save, print, and then close **ES3-C2-NPCTop10.xlsx**.

FIGURE 3.2 Challenge 2

Australia	10	
Bahamas	9	
China	85	
Hong Kong	41	
India	65	
Italy	12	
Japan	47	
Korea	33	
Pakistan	24	
United Kingdom	12	

Niagara Peninsula College
International Student Registrations by Country for 2011

Excel SECTION 4

Working with Multiple Worksheets, Tables, and Other File Formats

Skills

- Insert, delete, and rename a worksheet
- Format sheet tabs
- Move and copy a worksheet
- Group and ungroup worksheets
- Create 3-D references in formulas
- Link cells between worksheets
- Print multiple worksheets
- Use Page Break Preview to manipulate page breaks
- Format data as a table
- Apply table design options
- Insert rows and columns into a table
- Add a total row to a table
- Sort and filter a table by single and multiple criteria
- Insert, edit, delete, and print comments
- Create a new workbook using a template
- Open and save a workbook in a different file format
- Create a PDF/XPS copy of a worksheet

Projects Overview

Complete the quarterly sales report and the payroll report; format, sort, filter, and insert comments in the special events and inventory workbooks; create an invoice and billing statement for catering services; convert to and from Excel versions and text file formats an employee schedule, investment summary, and special events file.

Create a grade summary worksheet for the Theatre Arts Co-op Internships report.

Produce a list of costumes with a final delivery date of July 9; insert comments in the production schedule in preparation for the design team meeting; format the costume rentals report, calculate the rental fees, and convert the file to Excel 2010 file format.

Import U.S. and Canadian distributor information from text files, combine the information into one workbook, and then format and sort the report.

Model Answers for Projects

These model answers for the projects that you complete in Section 4 provide a preview of the finished projects before you begin working and also allow you to compare your own results with these models to ensure you have created the materials accurately.

ES4-WBQtrlySales.xlsx is the project in Activities 4.1 to 4.4.

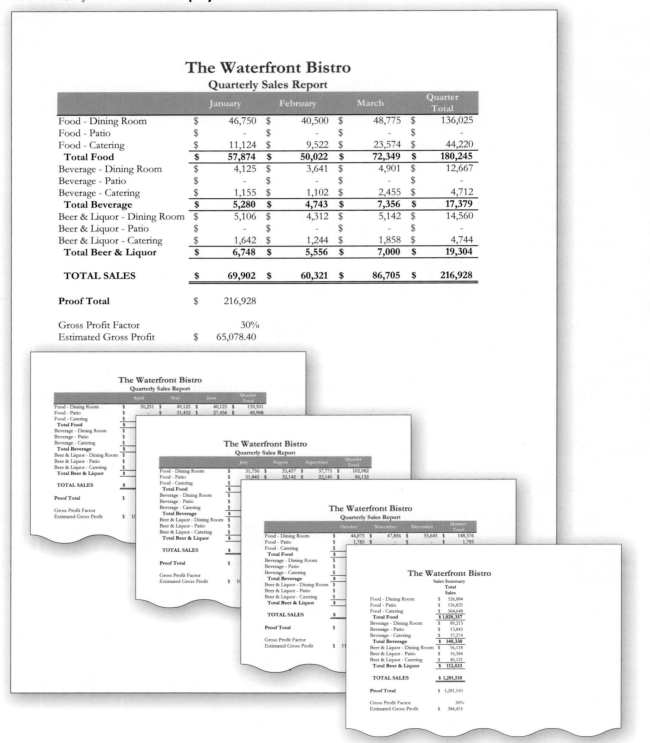

The Waterfront Bistro
Quarterly Sales Report

	January	February	March	Quarter Total
Food - Dining Room	$ 46,750	$ 40,500	$ 48,775	$ 136,025
Food - Patio	$ -	$ -	$ -	$ -
Food - Catering	$ 11,124	$ 9,522	$ 23,574	$ 44,220
Total Food	**$ 57,874**	**$ 50,022**	**$ 72,349**	**$ 180,245**
Beverage - Dining Room	$ 4,125	$ 3,641	$ 4,901	$ 12,667
Beverage - Patio	$ -	$ -	$ -	$ -
Beverage - Catering	$ 1,155	$ 1,102	$ 2,455	$ 4,712
Total Beverage	**$ 5,280**	**$ 4,743**	**$ 7,356**	**$ 17,379**
Beer & Liquor - Dining Room	$ 5,106	$ 4,312	$ 5,142	$ 14,560
Beer & Liquor - Patio	$ -	$ -	$ -	$ -
Beer & Liquor - Catering	$ 1,642	$ 1,244	$ 1,858	$ 4,744
Total Beer & Liquor	**$ 6,748**	**$ 5,556**	**$ 7,000**	**$ 19,304**
TOTAL SALES	**$ 69,902**	**$ 60,321**	**$ 86,705**	**$ 216,928**

Proof Total	$	216,928
Gross Profit Factor		30%
Estimated Gross Profit	$	65,078.40

The Waterfront Bistro
Quarterly Sales Report

	April	May	June	Quarter Total
Food - Dining Room	$ 50,251	$ 49,125	$ 40,125	$ 139,501
Food - Patio	$ -	$ 21,452	$ 27,456	$ 48,908
Food - Catering	$			
Total Food	$			
Beverage - Dining Room	$			
Beverage - Patio	$			
Beverage - Catering	$			
Total Beverage	$			
Beer & Liquor - Dining Room	$			
Beer & Liquor - Patio	$			
Beer & Liquor - Catering	$			
Total Beer & Liquor	$			
TOTAL SALES	$			

Proof Total $

Gross Profit Factor
Estimated Gross Profit $ 10

The Waterfront Bistro
Quarterly Sales Report

	July	August	September	Quarter Total
Food - Dining Room	$ 31,750	$ 33,457	$ 37,775	$ 102,982
Food - Patio	$ 31,845	$ 32,142	$ 22,145	$ 86,132
Food - Catering	$			
Total Food	$			
Beverage - Dining Room	$			
Beverage - Patio	$			
Beverage - Catering	$			
Total Beverage	$			
Beer & Liquor - Dining Room	$			
Beer & Liquor - Patio	$			
Beer & Liquor - Catering	$			
Total Beer & Liquor	$			
TOTAL SALES	$			

Proof Total $

Gross Profit Factor
Estimated Gross Profit $ 10

The Waterfront Bistro
Quarterly Sales Report

	October	November	December	Quarter Total
Food - Dining Room	$ 44,875	$ 47,856	$ 55,645	$ 148,376
Food - Patio	$ 1,785	$ -	$ -	$ 1,785
Food - Catering	$			
Total Food	$			
Beverage - Dining Room	$			
Beverage - Patio	$			
Beverage - Catering	$			
Total Beverage	$			
Beer & Liquor - Dining Room	$			
Beer & Liquor - Patio	$			
Beer & Liquor - Catering	$			
Total Beer & Liquor	$			
TOTAL SALES	$			

Proof Total $

Gross Profit Factor
Estimated Gross Profit $ 11

The Waterfront Bistro
Sales Summary

	Total Sales
Food - Dining Room	$ 526,884
Food - Patio	$ 136,825
Food - Catering	$ 364,648
Total Food	**$ 1,028,357**
Beverage - Dining Room	$ 89,213
Beverage - Patio	$ 13,843
Beverage - Catering	$ 37,274
Total Beverage	**$ 140,330**
Beer & Liquor - Dining Room	$ 56,118
Beer & Liquor - Patio	$ 16,584
Beer & Liquor - Catering	$ 40,121
Total Beer & Liquor	**$ 112,823**
TOTAL SALES	**$ 1,281,510**

Proof Total $ 1,281,510

Gross Profit Factor 30%
Estimated Gross Profit $ 384,453

ES4-WBCatering.xlsx is the project in Activities 4.5 and 4.6 and part of the project in Activity 4.7.

First Name	Last Name	Contact Phone	Event	Date	Room	Guests	Special Menu	Price Per Person	Contract Total
\multicolumn{10}{c}{The Waterfront Bistro}									

The Waterfront Bistro
Catering Contracts

First Name	Last Name	Contact Phone	Event	Date	Room	Guests	Special Menu	Price Per Person	Contract Total
Weston	Kressman	716 555 4219	Wedding	2/28/2011	Sunset	266	Yes	28.95	$ 7,700.70
Alfonso	Ramirez	716 555 3488	Wedding	12/31/2011	Westview	160	Yes	35.95	$ 5,752.00
Mario	Fontaine	716 555 1886	Engagement Party	1/20/2011	Westview	177	Yes	28.95	$ 5,124.15
Zack	Doucet	716 555 3488	Wedding	6/20/2011	Sunset	168	Yes	28.95	$ 4,863.60
Matteo	Limardi	716 555 9447	50th Wedding Anniversary	12/24/2011	Westview	125	Yes	35.95	$ 4,493.75
Bahurai	Omkar	905 555 3411	Wedding	8/30/2011	Westview	155	Yes	28.95	$ 4,487.25
Max	Santore	905 555 3264	Wedding	4/28/2011	Westview	157	Yes	25.95	$ 4,074.15
Reed	Pavelich	716 555 2286	Wedding	7/25/2011	Starlake	110	Yes	31.95	$ 3,514.50
Tao	Okinawa	716 555 1665	Wedding	12/21/2011	Westview	110	Yes	27.95	$ 3,074.50
Orlando	Fagan	716 555 3694	25th Wedding Anniversary	3/10/2011	Westview	88	Yes	28.95	$ 2,547.60
Omar	Hamid	716 555 8796	Engagement Party	5/8/2011	Sunset	85	Yes	28.95	$ 2,460.75
Raji	Jai	716 555 6885	Baby Shower	11/6/2011	Westview	85	No	28.95	$ 2,460.75
Corina	Guzman	716 555 4112	Wedding	12/22/2011	Westview	85	Yes	28.95	$ 2,460.75
Elena	Alvarez	905 555 4884	Wedding	11/19/2011	Westview	112	No	21.95	$ 2,458.40
Sonora	Yee	716 555 2668	Birthday Party	12/31/2011	Starlake	73	Yes	31.95	$ 2,332.35
Kim	Pockovic	905 555 3698	Birthday Party	3/18/2011	Westview	62	Yes	35.95	$ 2,228.90
Frances	Corriveau	716 555 3256	Birthday Party	1/23/2011	Westview	85	Yes	25.95	$ 2,205.75
Elizabeth	McMaster	716 555 9442	Engagement Party	7/11/2011	Sunset	75	Yes	27.95	$ 2,096.25
Percy	Bresque	716 555 1248	50th Wedding Anniversary	4/12/2011	Westview	62	Yes	32.95	$ 2,042.90
Mahika	Kapoor	716 555 3669	Birthday Party	10/5/2011	Sunset	68	Yes	28.95	$ 1,968.60
Nicole	Griffin	905 555 4166	25th Wedding Anniversary	6/17/2011	Starlake	54	Yes	31.95	$ 1,725.30
Bogdana	Petrov	716 555 6889	Birthday Party	12/20/2011	Sunset	51	Yes	31.95	$ 1,629.45
Carlotta	Balducci	716 555 9665	Birthday Party	8/22/2011	Starlake	62	Yes	25.95	$ 1,608.90
Liana	Fantino	716 555 9648	25th Wedding Anniversary	11/30/2011	Sunset	54	No	28.95	$ 1,563.30
Lane	Gill	416 555 3264	Business Meeting	3/29/2011	Starlake	71	No	21.95	$ 1,558.45
Jesse	Golinsky	716 555 4218	Business Meeting	6/26/2011	Westview	57	No	24.95	$ 1,422.15
Su-Lin	Ping	716 555 7774	Baby Shower	7/10/2011	Sunset	62	Yes	21.95	$ 1,360.90
Bianca	Vargas	716 555 3884	Engagement Party	10/15/2011	Starlake	40	Yes	31.95	$ 1,278.00
Walter	Szucs	905 555 6998	Birthday Party	6/10/2011	Starlake	42	No	28.95	$ 1,215.90
Sofia	Delgado	716 555 8465	Birthday Party	8/10/2011	Starlake	55	No	21.95	$ 1,207.25
Alfredo	Juanitez	716 555 4668	Business Meeting	7/31/2011	Westview	49	No	23.95	$ 1,173.55
Franco	Costa	716 555 3345	Business Meeting	9/30/2011	Sunset	32	No	31.95	$ 1,022.40
Carlo	Sanchez	905 555 6344	Business Meeting	9/10/2011	Westview	45	No	21.95	$ 987.75
Dana	Russell	716 555 4965	Birthday Party	5/30/2011	Starlake	36	No	26.95	$ 970.20
Mei-Yin	Zhang	716 555 2121	Business Meeting	12/1/2011	Starlake	28	Yes	31.95	$ 894.60
Guido	Donato	716 555 8444	Business Meeting	10/22/2011	Westview	30	No	25.95	$ 778.50
Cecily	Hillmore	716 555 6598	Business Meeting	1/15/2011	Starlake	35	No	21.95	$ 768.25
Jack	Torrance	716 555 1469	Business Meeting	5/15/2011	Westview	26	No	23.95	$ 622.70
Cristian	Martinez	716 555 4331	Business Meeting	12/15/2011	Starlake	18	No	31.95	$ 575.10
Total						3155		28.36	$ 90,710.25

ES4-WBCatering.xlsx is part of the project in Activity 4.7.

First Name	Last Name	Contact Phone	Event	Date	Room	Guests	Special Menu	Price Per Person	Contract Total	
Weston	Kressman	716 555 4219	Wedding	2/28/2011	Sunset	266	Yes	28.95	$	7,700.70
Alfonso	Ramirez	716 555 3488	Wedding	12/31/2011	Westview	160	Yes	35.95	$	5,752.00
Mario	Fontaine	716 555 1886	Engagement Party	1/20/2011	Westview	177	Yes	28.95	$	5,124.15
Zack	Doucet	716 555 3488	Wedding	6/20/2011	Sunset	168	Yes	28.95	$	4,863.60
Matteo	Limardi	716 555 9447	50th Wedding Anniversary	12/24/2011	Westview	125	Yes	35.95	$	4,493.75
Bahurai	Omkar	905 555 3411	Wedding	8/30/2011	Westview	155	Yes	28.95	$	4,487.25
Max	Santore	905 555 3264	Wedding	4/28/2011	Sunset	157	Yes	25.95	$	4,074.15
Reed	Pavelich	716 555 2286	Wedding	7/25/2011	Starlake	110	Yes	31.95	$	3,514.50
Tao	Okinawa	716 555 1665	Wedding	12/21/2011	Westview	110	Yes	27.95	$	3,074.50
Orlando	Fagan	716 555 3694	25th Wedding Anniversary	3/10/2011	Westview	88	Yes	28.95	$	2,547.60
Omar	Hamid	716 555 8796	Engagement Party	5/8/2011	Sunset	85	Yes	28.95	$	2,460.75
Raji	Jai	716 555 6885	Baby Shower	11/6/2011	Westview	85	No	28.95	$	2,460.75
Corina	Guzman	716 555 4112	Wedding	12/22/2011	Westview	85	Yes	28.95	$	2,460.75
Elena	Alvarez	905 555 4884	Wedding	11/19/2011	Westview	112	No	21.95	$	2,458.40
Sonora	Yee	716 555 2668	Birthday Party	12/31/2011	Starlake	73	Yes	31.95	$	2,332.35
Kim	Pockovic	905 555 3698	Birthday Party	3/18/2011	Westview	62	Yes	35.95	$	2,228.90
Frances	Corriveau	716 555 3256	Birthday Party	1/23/2011	Westview	85	Yes	25.95	$	2,205.75
Elizabeth	McMaster	716 555 9442	Engagement Party	7/11/2011	Sunset	75	Yes	27.95	$	2,096.25
Percy	Bresque	716 555 1248	50th Wedding Anniversary	4/12/2011	Westview	62	Yes	32.95	$	2,042.90
Mahika	Kapoor	716 555 3669	Birthday Party	10/5/2011	Sunset	68	Yes	28.95	$	1,968.60
Nicole	Griffin	905 555 4166	25th Wedding Anniversary	6/17/2011	Starlake	54	Yes	31.95	$	1,725.30
Bogdana	Petrov	716 555 6889	Birthday Party	12/20/2011	Sunset	51	Yes	31.95	$	1,629.45
Carlotta	Balducci	716 555 9665	Birthday Party	8/22/2011	Starlake	62	Yes	25.95	$	1,608.90
Liana	Fantino	716 555 9648	25th Wedding Anniversary	11/30/2011	Sunset	54	No	28.95	$	1,563.30
Lane	Gill	416 555 3264	Business Meeting	3/29/2011	Starlake	71	No	21.95	$	1,558.45
Jesse	Golinsky	716 555 4218	Business Meeting	6/26/2011	Sunset	57	No	24.95	$	1,422.15
Su-Lin	Ping	716 555 7774	Baby Shower	7/10/2011	Sunset	62	Yes	21.95	$	1,360.90
Bianca	Vargas	716 555 3884	Engagement Party	10/15/2011	Starlake	40	Yes	31.95	$	1,278.00
Walter	Szucs	905 555 6998	Birthday Party	6/10/2011	Starlake	42	No	28.95	$	1,215.90
Sofia	Delgado	716 555 8465	Birthday Party	8/10/2011	Starlake	55	No	21.95	$	1,207.25
Alfredo	Juanitez	716 555 4668	Business Meeting	7/31/2011	Westview	49	No	23.95	$	1,173.55
Franco	Costa	716 555 3345	Business Meeting	9/30/2011	Sunset	32	No	31.95	$	1,022.40
Carlo	Sanchez	905 555 6344	Business Meeting	9/10/2011	Westview	45	No	21.95	$	987.75
Dana	Russell	716 555 4965	Birthday Party	5/30/2011	Starlake	36	No	26.95	$	970.20
Mei-Yin	Zhang	716 555 2121	Business Meeting	12/1/2011	Starlake	28	Yes	31.95	$	894.60
Guido	Donato	716 555 8444	Business Meeting	10/22/2011	Westview	30	No	25.95	$	778.50
Cecily	Hillmore	716 555 6598	Business Meeting	1/15/2011	Starlake	35	No	21.95	$	768.25
Jack	Torrance	716 555 1469	Business Meeting	5/15/2011	Westview	26	No	23.95	$	622.70
Cristian	Martinez	716 555 4331	Business Meeting	12/15/2011	Starlake	18	No	31.95	$	575.10
Total						3155		28.36	$	90,710.25

ES4-WBCatering.xlsx is part of the project in Activity 4.8.

			The Waterfront Bistro					
			Catering Contracts					
First Name	Last Name	Contact Phone	Event	Date	Room	Guests	Special Menu	Price Per Person	Contract Total
Nicole	Griffin	905 555 4166	25th Wedding Anniversary	6/17/2011	Starlake	54	Yes	31.95	$ 1,725.30
Orlando	Fagan	716 555 3694	25th Wedding Anniversary	3/10/2011	Westview	88	Yes	28.95	$ 2,547.60
Percy	Bresque	716 555 1248	50th Wedding Anniversary	4/12/2011	Westview	62	Yes	32.95	$ 2,042.90
Matteo	Limardi	716 555 9447	50th Wedding Anniversary	12/24/2011	Westview	125	Yes	35.95	$ 4,493.75
Su-Lin	Ping	716 555 7774	Baby Shower	7/10/2011	Sunset	62	Yes	21.95	$ 1,360.90
Carlotta	Balducci	716 555 9665	Birthday Party	8/22/2011	Starlake	62	Yes	25.95	$ 1,608.90
Sonora	Yee	716 555 2668	Birthday Party	12/31/2011	Starlake	73	Yes	31.95	$ 2,332.35
Mahika	Kapoor	716 555 3669	Birthday Party	10/5/2011	Sunset	68	Yes	28.95	$ 1,968.60
Bogdana	Petrov	716 555 6889	Birthday Party	12/20/2011	Sunset	51	Yes	31.95	$ 1,629.45
Frances	Corriveau	716 555 3256	Birthday Party	1/23/2011	Westview	85	Yes	25.95	$ 2,205.75
Kim	Pockovic	905 555 3698	Birthday Party	3/18/2011	Westview	62	Yes	35.95	$ 2,228.90
Mei-Yin	Zhang	716 555 2121	Business Meeting	12/1/2011	Starlake	28	Yes	31.95	$ 894.60
Bianca	Vargas	716 555 3884	Engagement Party	10/15/2011	Starlake	40	Yes	31.95	$ 1,278.00
Omar	Hamid	716 555 8796	Engagement Party	5/8/2011	Sunset	85	Yes	28.95	$ 2,460.75
Elizabeth	McMaster	716 555 9442	Engagement Party	7/11/2011	Sunset	75	Yes	27.95	$ 2,096.25
Mario	Fontaine	716 555 1886	Engagement Party	1/20/2011	Westview	177	Yes	28.95	$ 5,124.15
Reed	Pavelich	716 555 2286	Wedding	7/25/2011	Starlake	110	Yes	31.95	$ 3,514.50
Weston	Kressman	716 555 4219	Wedding	2/28/2011	Sunset	266	Yes	28.95	$ 7,700.70
Max	Santore	905 555 3264	Wedding	4/28/2011	Sunset	157	Yes	25.95	$ 4,074.15
Zack	Doucet	716 555 3488	Wedding	6/20/2011	Sunset	168	Yes	28.95	$ 4,863.60
Bahurai	Omkar	905 555 3411	Wedding	8/30/2011	Westview	155	Yes	28.95	$ 4,487.25
Tao	Okinawa	716 555 1665	Wedding	12/21/2011	Westview	110	Yes	27.95	$ 3,074.50
Corina	Guzman	716 555 4112	Wedding	12/22/2011	Westview	85	Yes	28.95	$ 2,460.75
Alfonso	Ramirez	716 555 3488	Wedding	12/31/2011	Westview	160	Yes	35.95	$ 5,752.00
Total						2408		29.99	$ 71,925.60

ES4-WBCatering.xlsx is part of the project in Activity 4.8.

			The Waterfront Bistro					
			Catering Contracts					
First Name	Last Name	Contact Phone	Event	Date	Room	Guests	Special Menu	Price Per Person	Contract Total
Nicole	Griffin	905 555 4166	25th Wedding Anniversary	6/17/2011	Starlake	54	Yes	31.95	$ 1,725.30
Dana	Russell	716 555 4965	Birthday Party	5/30/2011	Starlake	36	No	26.95	$ 970.20
Walter	Szucs	905 555 6998	Birthday Party	6/10/2011	Starlake	42	No	28.95	$ 1,215.90
Sofia	Delgado	716 555 8465	Birthday Party	8/10/2011	Starlake	55	No	21.95	$ 1,207.25
Carlotta	Balducci	716 555 9665	Birthday Party	8/22/2011	Starlake	62	Yes	25.95	$ 1,608.90
Sonora	Yee	716 555 2668	Birthday Party	12/31/2011	Starlake	73	Yes	31.95	$ 2,332.35
Cecily	Hillmore	716 555 6598	Business Meeting	1/15/2011	Starlake	35	No	21.95	$ 768.25
Lane	Gill	416 555 3122	Business Meeting	3/29/2011	Starlake	71	No	21.95	$ 1,558.45
Mei-Yin	Zhang	716 555 2121	Business Meeting	12/1/2011	Starlake	28	Yes	31.95	$ 894.60
Cristian	Martinez	716 555 4331	Business Meeting	12/15/2011	Starlake	18	No	31.95	$ 575.10
Bianca	Vargas	716 555 3884	Engagement Party	10/15/2011	Starlake	40	Yes	31.95	$ 1,278.00
Reed	Pavelich	716 555 2286	Wedding	7/25/2011	Starlake	110	Yes	31.95	$ 3,514.50
Total						624		28.28	$ 17,648.80

ES4-WBCatering.xlsx is part of the project in Activity 4.8.

			The Waterfront Bistro					
			Catering Contracts					
First Name	Last Name	Contact Phone	Event	Date	Room	Guests	Special Menu	Price Per Person	Contract Total
Weston	Kressman	716 555 4219	Wedding	2/28/2011	Sunset	266	Yes	28.95	$ 7,700.70
Max	Santore	905 555 3264	Wedding	4/28/2011	Sunset	157	Yes	25.95	$ 4,074.15
Zack	Doucet	716 555 3488	Wedding	6/20/2011	Sunset	168	Yes	28.95	$ 4,863.60
Total						591		27.95	$ 16,638.45

ES4-WBCatering.xlsx is the project in Activity 4.9.

The Waterfront Bistro
Catering Contracts

First Name	Last Name	Contact Phone	Event	Date	Room	Guests	Special Menu	Price Per Person	Contract Total
Nicole	Griffin	905 555 4166	25th Wedding Anniversary	6/17/2011	Starlake	54	Yes	31.95	$ 1,725.30
Liana	Fantino	716 555 9648	25th Wedding Anniversary	11/30/2011	Sunset	54	No	28.95	$ 1,563.30
Orlando	Fagan	716 555 3694	25th Wedding Anniversary	3/10/2011	Westview	88	Yes	28.95	$ 2,547.60
Percy	Bresque	716 555 1248	50th Wedding Anniversary	4/12/2011	Westview	62	Yes	32.95	$ 2,042.90
Matteo	Limardi	716 555 9447	50th Wedding Anniversary	12/24/2011	Westview	125	Yes	35.95	$ 4,493.75
Su-Lin	Ping	716 555 7774	Baby Shower	7/10/2011	Sunset	62	Yes	21.95	$ 1,360.90
Raji	Jai	716 555 6885	Baby Shower	11/6/2011	Westview	85	Yes	28.95	$ 2,460.75
Dana	Russell	716 555 4965	Birthday Party	5/30/2011	Starlake	36	Yes	26.95	970.20
Walter	Szucs	905 555 6998	Birthday Party	6/10/2011	Starlake	42	Yes	28.95	$ 1,215.90
Sofia	Delgado	716 555 8465	Birthday Party	8/10/2011	Starlake	55	No	21.95	$ 1,207.25
Carlotta	Balducci	716 555 9665	Birthday Party	8/22/2011	Starlake	62	Yes	25.95	$ 1,608.90
Sonora	Yee	716 555 2668	Birthday Party	12/31/2011	Starlake	73	Yes	31.95	$ 2,332.35
Mahika	Kapoor	716 555 3669	Birthday Party	10/5/2011	Sunset	68	Yes	28.95	$ 1,968.60
Bogdana	Petrov	716 555 6889	Birthday Party	12/20/2011	Sunset	51	Yes	31.95	$ 1,629.45
Frances	Corriveau	716 555 3256	Birthday Party	1/23/2011	Westview	85	Yes	25.95	2,205.75
Kim	Pockovic	905 555 3698	Birthday Party	3/18/2011	Westview	62	Yes		2,228.90
Cecily	Hillmore	716 555 6598	Business Meeting	1/15/2011	Starlake	35	No		768.25
Lane	Gill	416 555 3264	Business Meeting	3/29/2011	Starlake	71	No		1,558.45
Mei-Yin	Zhang	716 555 2121	Business Meeting	12/1/2011	Starlake	28	Yes	31.95	894.60
Cristian	Martinez	716 555 4331	Business Meeting	12/15/2011	Starlake	18	No	31.95	$ 575.10
Franco	Costa	716 555 3345	Business Meeting	9/30/2011	Sunset	32	No	31.95	$ 1,022.40
Jack	Torrance	716 555 1469	Business Meeting	5/15/2011	Westview	26	No	23.95	$ 622.70
Jesse	Golinsky	716 555 4218	Business Meeting	6/26/2011	Westview	57	No	24.95	$ 1,422.15
Alfredo	Juanitez	716 555 4668	Business Meeting	7/31/2011	Westview	49	No	23.95	$ 1,173.55
Carlo	Sanchez	905 555 6344	Business Meeting	9/10/2011	Westview	45	No	21.95	$ 987.75
Guido	Donato	716 555 8444	Business Meeting	10/22/2011	Westview	30	No	25.95	$ 778.50
Bianca	Vargas	716 555 3884	Engagement Party	10/15/2011	Starlake	40	Yes	31.95	$ 1,278.00
Omar	Hamid	716 555 8796	Engagement Party	5/8/2011	Sunset	85	Yes	28.95	$ 2,460.75
Elizabeth	McMaster	716 555 9442	Engagement Party	7/11/2011	Sunset	75	Yes	27.95	$ 2,096.25
Mario	Fontaine	716 555 1886	Engagement Party	1/20/2011	Westview	177	Yes	28.95	$ 5,124.15
Reed	Pavelich	716 555 2286	Wedding	7/25/2011	Starlake	110	Yes	31.95	$ 3,514.50
Weston	Kressman	716 555 4219	Wedding	2/28/2011	Sunset	266	Yes	28.95	$ 7,700.70
Max	Santore	905 555 3264	Wedding	4/28/2011	Sunset	157	Yes	25.95	$ 4,074.15
Zack	Doucet	716 555 3488	Wedding	6/20/2011	Sunset	168	Yes	28.95	$ 4,863.60
Bahurai	Omkar	905 555 3411	Wedding	8/30/2011	Westview	155	Yes	28.95	$ 4,487.25
Elena	Alvarez	905 555 4884	Wedding	11/19/2011	Westview	112	No	21.95	$ 2,458.40
Tao	Okinawa	716 555 1665	Wedding	12/21/2011	Westview	110	Yes	27.95	$ 3,074.50
Corina	Guzman	716 555 4112	Wedding	12/22/2011	Westview	85	Yes	28.95	$ 2,460.75
Alfonso	Ramirez	716 555 3488	Wedding	12/31/2011	Westview	160	Yes	35.95	$ 5,752.00
Total						3155		28.36	$ 90,710.25

Student Name:
Waiting for Frances to confirm the final number of guests.

Student Name:
Remind Pierre that six guests require a diabetic menu.

ES4-AP_WENov13_2011.xlsx is the project in Activity 4.10.

Time Card

Employee	Aparna Patel			Manager:	Dana Hirsch
[Street Address]	15 Pearl Street			Employee phone:	716 555 3381
[Address 2]				Employee e-mail:	
[City, ST ZIP Code]	Buffalo, NY 14202				

Week ending: 11/13/2011

Day	Date	Regular Hours	Overtime	Sick	Vacation	Total
Monday	11/7/2011	8.00	1.75			9.75
Tuesday	11/8/2011	7.00				7.00
Wednesday	11/9/2011	8.00				8.00
Thursday	11/10/2011	8.00				8.00
Friday	11/11/2011	7.00				7.00
Saturday	11/12/2011					
Sunday	11/13/2011					
Total hours		38.00	1.75			39.75
Rate per hour		$ 15.25	$ 22.88			
Total pay		$ 579.50	$ 40.04	$ -	$ -	$ 619.54

Employee signature   Date

Manager signature   Date

This document grouping demonstrates some of the different file formats you will convert to and from during Activity 4.11.

The Waterfront Bistro
Catering Contracts

First Name	Last Name	Contact Phone	Event	Date	Room	Guests	Special Menu	Price Per Person
Cecily	Hillmore	716 555 6598	Business Meeting	1/15/2011	Starlake	35	No	21.95
Mario	Fontaine	716 555 1886	Engagement Party	1/20/2011	Westview	177	Yes	28.95
Frances	Corriveau	716 555 3256	Birthday Party	1/23/2011	Westview	85	Yes	25.95
Weston	Kressman	716 555 4219	Wedding	2/28/2011	Sunset	266	Yes	28.95
Orlando	Fagan	716 555 3694	25th Wedding Anniversary	3/10/2011	Westview	88	Yes	28.95
Kim	Pockovic	905 555 3698	Birthday Party	3/18/2011	Westview	62	Yes	35.95
Lane	Gill	416 555 3264	Business Meeting	3/29/2011	Starlake	71	No	21.95
Percy	Bresque	716 555 1248	50th Wedding Anniversary	4/12/2011	Westview	62	Yes	32.95
Max	Santore	905 555 3264	Wedding	4/28/2011	Sunset	157	Yes	25.95
Omar	Hamid	716 555 8796	Engagement Party	5/8/2011	Sunset	85	Yes	28.95
Jack	Torrance	716 555 1469	Business Meeting	5/15/2011	Westview	26	No	23.95
Dana	Russell	716 555 4965	Birthday Party	5/30/2011	Starlake	36	No	26.95
Walter	Szucs	905 555 6998	Birthday Party	6/10/2011	Starlake	42	No	28.95
Nicole	Griffin	905 555 4166	25th Wedding Anniversary	6/17/2011	Starlake	54	Yes	31.95
Zack	Doucet	716 555 3488	Wedding	6/20/2011	Sunset	168	Yes	28.95
Jesse	Golinsky	716 555 4218	Business Meeting	6/26/2011	Westview	57	No	24.95
Su-Lin	Ping	716 555 7774	Baby Shower	7/10/2011	Sunset	62	Yes	21.95
Elizabeth	McMaster	716 555 9442	Engagement Party	7/11/2011	Sunset	75	Yes	27.95
Reed	Pavelich	716 555 2286	Wedding	7/25/2011	Starlake	110	Yes	31.95
Alfredo	Juanitez	716 555 4668	Business Meeting	7/31/2011	Westview	49	No	23.95
Sofia	Delgado	716 555 8465	Birthday Party	8/10/2011	Starlake	55	No	21.95
Carlotta	Balducci	716 555 9665	Birthday Party	8/22/2011	Starlake	62	Yes	25.95
Bahurai	Omkar	905 555 3411						
Carlo	Sanchez	905 555 6344						
Franco	Costa	716 555 3345						
Mahika	Kapoor	716 555 3669						
Bianca	Vargas	716 555 3884						
Guido	Donato	716 555 8444						
Raji	Jai	716 555 6885						
Elena	Alvarez	905 555 4884						
Liana	Fantino	716 555 9648						
Mei-Yin	Zhang	716 555 2121						
Cristian	Martinez	716 555 4331						
Bogdana	Petrov	716 555 6889						
Tao	Okinawa	716 555 1665						
Corina	Guzman	716 555 4112						
Matteo	Limardi	716 555 9447						
Alfonso	Ramirez	716 555 3488						

```
                              ES4-WBCatering.csv
The Waterfront Bistro,,,,,,,,
Catering Contracts,,,,,,,,
First Name,Last Name,Contact Phone,Event,Date,Room,Guests,Special Menu,Price Per
Person
Cecily,Hillmore,716 555 6598,Business Meeting,1/15/2011,Starlake,35,No,21.95
Mario,Fontaine,716 555 1886,Engagement Party,1/20/2011,Westview,177,Yes,28.95
Frances,Corriveau,716 555 3256,Birthday Party,1/23/2011,Westview,85,Yes,25.95
Weston,Kressman,716 555 4219,Wedding,2/28/2011,Sunset,266,Yes,28.95
Orlando,Fagan,716 555 3694,25th Wedding Anniversary,3/10/2011,Westview,88,Yes,28.95
Kim,Pockovic,905 555 3698,Birthday Party,3/18/2011,Westview,62,Yes,35.95
Lane,Gill,416 555 3264,Business Meeting,3/29/2011,Starlake,71,No,21.95
Percy,Bresque,716 555 1248,50th Wedding Anniversary,4/12/2011,Westview,62,Yes,32.95
Max,Santore,905 555 3264,Wedding,4/28/2011,Sunset,157,Yes,25.95
Omar,Hamid,716 555 8796,Engagement Party,5/8/2011,Sunset,85,Yes,28.95
Jack,Torrance,716 555 1469,Business Meeting,5/15/2011,Westview,26,No,23.95
Dana,Russell,716 555 4965,Birthday Party,5/30/2011,Starlake,36,No,26.95
Walter,Szucs,905 555 6998,Birthday Party,6/10/2011,Starlake,42,No,28.95
Nicole,Griffin,905 555 4166,25th Wedding Anniversary,6/17/2011,Starlake,54,Yes,31.95
Zack,Doucet,716 555 3488,Wedding,6/20/2011,Sunset,168,Yes,28.95
Jesse,Golinsky,716 555 4218,Business Meeting,6/26/2011,Westview,57,No,24.95
Su-Lin,Ping,716 555 7774,Baby Shower,7/10/2011,Sunset,62,Yes,21.95
Elizabeth,McMaster,716 555 9442,Engagement Party,7/11/2011,Sunset,75,Yes,27.95
Reed,Pavelich,716 555 2286,Wedding,7/25/2011,Starlake,110,Yes,31.95
Alfredo,Juanitez,716 555 4668,Business Meeting,7/31/2011,Westview,49,No,23.95
Sofia,Delgado,716 555 8465,Birthday Party,8/10/2011,Starlake,55,No,21.95
Carlotta,Balducci,716 555 9665,Birthday Party,8/22/2011,Starlake,62,Yes,25.95
Bahurai,Omkar,905 555 3411,Wedding,8/30/2011,Westview,55,Yes,28.95
Carlo,Sanchez,905 555 6344,Business Meeting,9/10/2011,Westview,45,No,21.95
Franco,Costa,716 555 3345,Business Meeting,9/30/2011,Starlake,32,No,31.95
Mahika,Kapoor,716 555 3669,Birthday Party,10/5/2011,Sunset,68,Yes,28.95
Bianca,Vargas,716 555 3884,Engagement Party,10/15/2011,Starlake,40,Yes,31.95
Guido,Donato,716 555 8444,Business Meeting,10/22/2011,Westview,30,No,25.95
Raji,Jai,716 555 6885,Baby Shower,11/6/2011,Westview,85,No,28.95
Elena,Alvarez,905 555 4884,Wedding,11/19/2011,Westview,112,No,21.95
Liana,Fantino,716 555 9648,25th Wedding Anniversary,11/30/2011,Sunset,54,No,28.95
Mei-Yin,Zhang,716 555 2121,Business Meeting,12/1/2011,Starlake,28,Yes,31.95
Cristian,Martinez,716 555 4331,Business Meeting,12/15/2011,Starlake,18,No,31.95
Bogdana,Petrov,716 555 6889,Birthday Party,12/20/2011,Sunset,51,Yes,31.95
Tao,Okinawa,716 555 1665,Wedding,12/21/2011,Westview,110,Yes,27.95
Corina,Guzman,716 555 4112,Wedding,12/22/2011,Westview,85,Yes,28.95
Matteo,Limardi,716 555 9447,50th Wedding
Anniversary,12/24/2011,Westview,125,Yes,35.95
Alfonso,Ramirez,716 555 3488,Wedding,12/31/2011,Westview,160,Yes,35.95
```

Employee Schedule
Pier Dining Room
For the Week of February 14-20, 2011

Time	Monday	Tuesday	Wednesday	Thursday	Friday	Saturday	Sunday
7am - 3pm	Cortez Hill Modano	Cortez Hill Soulliere	Cortez Hill Soulliere	Cortez Hill Santini	Cortez Hill Cortez	Soulliere Santini Modano	Soulliere Santini Modano
3pm - 11pm	Su-Lin	Modano	Modano	Su-Lin	Santini Modano	Su-Lin Modano	Su-Lin
6pm - 2am					Su-Lin	Su-Lin	

All schedule changes must be approved in advance by Dana Hirsch.

ES4-WBInvestment.xlsx is the project in Activity 4.12.

The Waterfront B·I·S·T·R·O

Investment Scenario for Cash Surplus		
Basic savings account interest rate	1.15%	per annum
Number of investment payments	8	years
Cash surplus available each year	($55,000)	per annum

Future Value of Investment: $458,123.24

Activity 4.1

Inserting, Deleting, and Renaming a Worksheet; Formatting Sheet Tabs

A new workbook initially contains three sheets named Sheet1, Sheet2, and Sheet3. Additional sheets can be added or deleted as needed. Organizing large amounts of data by grouping related topics in individual worksheets makes the task of creating, editing, and analyzing data more manageable. For example, you could keep track of your test grades in one worksheet and assignment grades in another. A summary sheet at the beginning or end of the workbook would be used to consolidate the test and assignment grades and calculate a final mark. By breaking down the data into smaller units, you are able to view, enter, and edit cells quickly. Format sheet tabs using different colors to visually group related sheets.

Project

Dana Hirsch has asked you to complete the quarterly sales report workbook. To begin this project, you will insert, rename, and delete a worksheet and then organize the sheets by applying color to the sheet tabs.

The Waterfront B·I·S·T·R·O

SNAP

Tutorial 4.1
Inserting, Moving, Renaming, and Hiding a Worksheet

1. Open **WBQtrlySales.xlsx**.

2. Save the workbook in the ExcelS4 folder naming it **ES4-WBQtrlySales**.

3. Click the Qtr2 tab and then view the worksheet.

   Step 3

4. Click the Sheet3 tab and then view the worksheet.

   The quarterly sales report has been organized with each quarter's sales in a separate worksheet. In the next step, you will insert a worksheet for the fourth quarter.

5. Click the Insert Worksheet button located at the end of the sheet tabs (immediately right of Sheet3).

   Step 5

   Clicking the Insert Worksheet button inserts a new worksheet at the end of the existing sheets. In the next step, you will insert at the beginning of the workbook a new worksheet that will be used to summarize the sales data from the four quarters.

   new worksheet inserted at Step 5

6. Right-click the Qtr1 tab.

   Right-clicking a worksheet tab activates the worksheet and displays the worksheet shortcut menu.

   Step 7

   Step 6

7. Click *Insert* at the shortcut menu.

8. With *Worksheet* already selected in the General tab in the Insert dialog box, click OK.

   Five worksheets now exist in the workbook: Sheet2, Qtr1, Qtr2, Sheet3, and Sheet1.

9. Right-click the Sheet2 tab and then click *Rename* at the shortcut menu.

   This selects the current worksheet name in the sheet tab.

10. Type **Summary** and then press Enter.

    Step 10

11 Double-click the Sheet3 tab.

> You can also rename a worksheet by double-clicking the sheet tab.

12 Type **Qtr3** and then press Enter.

13 Right-click the Sheet1 tab and then click *Delete* at the shortcut menu.

> You can also click the Delete button arrow in the Cells group of the Home tab and then click *Delete Sheet* at the drop-down list to delete the active worksheet from the workbook. If the worksheet selected for deletion contains data, a message box appears warning you that data may exist in the sheet and you will have to confirm the deletion. Be careful when deleting worksheets since Undo does not restore a deleted sheet.

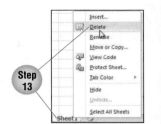

Step 13

In Brief

Insert Worksheet
1. Right-click sheet tab.
2. Click *Insert*.
3. Click OK.
OR
Click Insert Worksheet button.

Rename a Worksheet
1. Right-click sheet tab.
2. Click *Rename*.
3. Type new name.
4. Press Enter.
OR
Double-click sheet tab, type new name, and then press Enter.

Delete Worksheet
1. Right-click sheet tab.
2. Click *Delete*.

14 Right-click the Summary tab to activate the Summary worksheet and display the shortcut menu.

15 Point to *Tab Color* and then click *Dark Red* in the *Standard Colors* section of the color palette (first color square).

> Changing the color of sheet tabs can help to visually identify related worksheets or the organizational structure of the workbook.

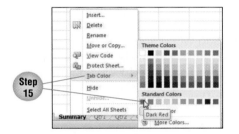

Step 15

16 Right-click the Qtr1 tab, point to *Tab Color*, and then click *Purple* in the *Standard Colors* section of the color palette (last color square).

17 Repeat Step 16 for the Qtr2 and Qtr3 sheet tabs.

> The three worksheets containing the quarterly sales data are now organized with the same tab color (purple). The worksheet that will later contain the summary data for the entire year is differentiated by the dark red tab color.

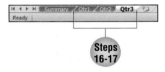

Steps 16-17

18 Save **ES4-WBQtrlySales.xlsx**.

In Addition

Tab Scrolling Buttons

The tab scrolling buttons are located at the left edge of the horizontal scroll bar as shown below. Use these buttons to scroll the worksheet tabs if there are more tabs than currently displayed. Drag the tab split box to the right or left to increase or decrease the number of worksheet tabs displayed or to change the size of the horizontal scroll bar.

tab scrolling buttons

tab split box

Activity 4.2

Moving and Copying Worksheets; Grouping and Ungrouping Worksheets

Drag a sheet tab to move a worksheet to a different position within the workbook. Hold down the Ctrl key while dragging a worksheet tab to copy it. Exercise caution when moving or copying a worksheet since calculations may become inaccurate after the worksheet has been repositioned or copied. A workbook with multiple worksheets that all have similar column and row structure can have formatting options applied to all sheets in one step by first grouping the worksheets.

Project

Tutorial 4.1
Inserting, Moving, Renaming, and Hiding a Worksheet

Continue your work on the quarterly sales report by copying the Qtr3 worksheet, renaming the sheet, and then entering data for the fourth quarter's sales. Next, you will move the Summary sheet after the Qtr4 sheet. Finally, you will apply formatting options to all four quarters by grouping the sheets.

1. With **ES4-WBQtrlySales.xlsx** open and Qtr3 the active sheet, position the mouse pointer over the Qtr3 tab, hold down the Ctrl key, drag the pointer to the right (on top of the Insert Worksheet button), release the mouse button, and then release the Ctrl key.

   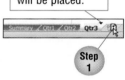

   Black arrow indicates position where worksheet will be placed.

   Step 1

   Ctrl + dragging a tab copies a worksheet. As you drag the pointer to the right, a black down-pointing arrow and a white page with a plus sign display with the pointer, indicating the position where the copied worksheet will be placed. The copied worksheet is labeled the same as the source worksheet with *(2)* added to the end of the name.

2. Double-click *Qtr3 (2)*, type **Qtr4**, and then press Enter.

3. With Qtr4 the active worksheet, select and delete the following ranges to remove the copied Qtr3 sales data, thereby preventing potential data entry errors when you add the Qtr4 sales data later.
   B4:D6
   B8:D10
   B12:D14

4. Change B3 from *July* to *October*; C3 from *August* to *November*; and D3 from *September* to *December*.

   The worksheet is now cleared of the third quarter's data. As new data is typed, the totals will automatically update. First, you will move the Summary worksheet after the four quarterly sales worksheets.

5. Position the pointer over the Summary tab, hold down the left mouse button and drag the pointer right after Qtr4 (on top of the Insert Worksheet button), and then release the mouse button.

   Step 5

   Dragging a tab moves the worksheet. As you drag the pointer to the right, a black down-pointing arrow and a white page display with the pointer, indicating the position where the worksheet will be repositioned.

6. Click Qtr4 and enter the data for the fourth quarter as shown in Figure 4.1 on the following page. You do not need to type the dollar symbols, commas, or zeros after decimals since the cells are already formatted. Type a zero in the cells displayed with a dash.

FIGURE 4.1 Data for Fourth Quarter

	A	B	C	D	E
1	The Waterfront Bistro				
2	Quarterly Sales Report				
3		October	November	December	Quarter Total
4	Food - Dining Room	$ 44,875	$ 47,856	$ 55,645	$ 148,376
5	Food - Patio	$ 1,785	$ -	$ -	$ 1,785
6	Food - Catering	$ 30,254	$ 33,746	$ 65,245	$ 129,245
7	**Total Food**	**$ 76,914**	**$ 81,602**	**$ 120,890**	**$ 279,406**
8	Beverage - Dining Room	$ 41,623	$ 4,687	$ 5,642	$ 51,952
9	Beverage - Patio	$ 245	$ -	$ -	$ 245
10	Beverage - Catering	$ 3,245	$ 3,165	$ 6,452	$ 12,862
11	**Total Beverage**	**$ 45,113**	**$ 7,852**	**$ 12,094**	**$ 65,059**
12	Beer & Liquor - Dining Room	$ 3,856	$ 4,962	$ 5,179	$ 13,997
13	Beer & Liquor - Patio	$ 215	$ -	$ -	$ 215
14	Beer & Liquor - Catering	$ 3,167	$ 3,563	$ 6,538	$ 13,268
15	**Total Beer & Liquor**	**$ 7,238**	**$ 8,525**	**$ 11,717**	**$ 27,480**
16					
17	**TOTAL SALES**	**$ 129,265**	**$ 97,979**	**$ 144,701**	**$ 371,945**

(7) Click Qtr1, hold down the Shift key, and then click Qtr4.

> The four worksheets are now grouped. Notice that *[Group]* appears next to the file name in the Title bar. Any formatting options that you change apply to all four worksheets. Use the Shift key to select a group of sheets starting with the first tab selected through to the last tab selected. Use the Ctrl key to group nonadjacent sheets.

(8) Select A1:A2 and then change the Fill Color to White (click *White, Background 1* in the *Theme Colors* section of the Fill Color palette).

(9) Select A3:E3, apply the Accent2 cell style (second option in the bottom row in the *Themed Cell Styles* section of the Cell Styles drop-down gallery), and then click the Bold button **B**.

(10) Click any cell to deselect the range, right-click any of the Qtr sheet tabs and then click *Ungroup Sheets* at the shortcut menu.

> The worksheets are no longer grouped and can be individually formatted.

(11) Click Qtr1 and view the formatting applied in Steps 8–9. Click each of the other quarterly sales worksheets to view the same formats.

(12) Save **ES4-WBQtrlySales.xlsx**.

In Addition

Move or Copy Dialog Box

In Steps 1 and 5 you copied and moved a worksheet by dragging the sheet tab with the pointer. You can also use the Move or Copy dialog box (shown at the right) to move or copy worksheets within the active workbook or to another open workbook. Right-click the sheet to be moved or copied and then click *Move* or *Copy* at the shortcut menu. Click the worksheet in front of which you want to place the moved or copied worksheet in the *Before sheet* list box and click OK to move, or click the *Create a copy* check box and then click OK to copy. To move or copy to another open workbook, select the destination file name in the *To book* drop-down list.

Activity 4.3

Using 3-D References

A formula that references the same cell in a range that extends over two or more worksheets is called a 3-D reference. A formula with **3-D references** is used to consolidate data from several worksheets into one worksheet. Worksheets that will use 3-D references should have the data set up the same in each sheet. For example, if E4 in the Qtr1 sheet contains the total dining room sales, then E4 in the remaining sheets should contain the same value. In this project you will create the following 3-D reference in a SUM formula: *=SUM('Qtr1:Qtr4'!E4)*. The range *Qtr1:Qtr4* within the SUM argument is the 3-D reference that instructs Excel to add the contents of E4 starting in the worksheet labeled *Qtr1* and ending with the worksheet labeled *Qtr4*. The 3-D range is enclosed in single quotes and an exclamation point separates the worksheet range from the cell reference.

Project

SNAP

Tutorial 4.2
Linking Data and Using 3-D References

To continue the quarterly sales report, you will copy labels from the Qtr1 worksheet to the Summary sheet and enter 3-D formulas that reference the total sales cells in the four quarterly sales worksheets.

1. With **ES4-WBQtrlySales.xlsx** open, click the Qtr1 tab.

2. Select A4:A22 and then click the Copy button in the Clipboard group in the Home tab.

3. Make Summary the active worksheet and click A4.

4. Click the Paste button arrow in the Clipboard group and then click the Keep Source Column Widths button (second option in second row) in the *Paste* section of the Paste gallery.

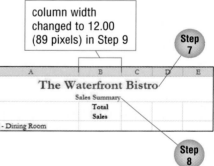

5. Make B3 the active cell, type **Total**, press Alt + Enter, type **Sales**, and then press Enter.

6. Bold and center B3.

7. Make Qtr1 the active worksheet, copy A1, and then paste to A1 in the Summary worksheet.

8. Create the subtitle **Sales Summary** merged and centered in A2:E2. Apply bold and the *Gray-80%, Text 2* font color (fourth color box in first row of *Theme Colors* section) to the subtitle.

9. Change the width of column B to *12.00 (89 pixels)*.

10. Save **ES4-WBQtrlySales.xlsx**.

   Saving the workbook before consolidating data using 3-D references is a good idea in case you encounter difficulties when performing the consolidation. In Steps 11–14, you will enter a 3-D formula using the point-and-click method.

11. With Summary still the active worksheet, make B4 the active cell.

12. Type **=sum(**.

13. Click the Qtr1 tab, hold down the Shift key, and then click the Qtr4 tab.

   This groups the four quarterly sales worksheets and Qtr1 is the worksheet now displayed. Watch the formula bar each time you click the mouse to view the formula that is being built.

14 Click E4 and then press Enter.

15 Press the Up Arrow key to return the active cell back to B4 and then read the completed formula in the Formula bar, *=SUM('Qtr1:Qtr4'!E4)*.

> Notice Excel inserted the closing bracket automatically. The result, *526884*, appears in B4, which is the total of the values in E4 in all four quarterly sales worksheets.

Step 14

In Brief

Create Formula with 3-D Reference
1. Make desired cell active.
2. Type =sum(.
3. Click first sheet tab.
4. Shift + click last sheet tab.
5. Click cell containing data to be summed in all sheets.
6. Press Enter.

	B	C
	fx	=SUM('Qtr1:Qtr4'!E4)
1	The Waterfront Bistro	
2	Sales Summary	
3	Total Sales	
4 Food - Dining Room	526884	

Step 15

16 Drag the fill handle from B4 down through B15 to copy the 3-D formula to the remaining rows.

17 Make B17 the active cell, type the formula **=b7+b11+b15**, and then press Enter.

		Total Sales
3		
4	Food - Dining Room	526884
5	Food - Patio	136825
6	Food - Catering	364648
7	Total Food	1028357
8	Beverage - Dining Room	89213
9	Beverage - Patio	13843
10	Beverage - Catering	37274
11	Total Beverage	140330
12	Beer & Liquor - Dining Room	56118
13	Beer & Liquor - Patio	16584
14	Beer & Liquor - Catering	40121
15	Total Beer & Liquor	112823
16		
17	TOTAL SALES	1281510

Step 16

Step 17

18 Apply the Accounting Number Format to B4:B17 and then decrease the decimals so that zero decimals display.

19 Deselect the range and then save **ES3-WBQtrlySales.xlsx**.

In Addition

Using 3-D References in Dissimilar Worksheets

You can consolidate data in multiple worksheets where the worksheets are not structured the same. For example, assume that you want to add two salary values from two worksheets. In the first worksheet (labeled Marketing) the salary value resides in D6 and in the second worksheet (labeled Finance) the salary value resides in H12. The following formula entered into the desired cell in the summary worksheet adds the two values: =Marketing!D6+Finance!H12.

Activity 4.4

Linking Cells; Printing Multiple Worksheets

In Section 2, you learned how to use Copy and Paste to link two cells. Recall that the Paste gallery includes a Paste Link button which establishes a link between the source and destination cell(s). You can also link cell(s) within the same workbook or between different workbooks by entering a formula that references the source cell. If the source data changes, the cell that is linked to the source will automatically update to reflect the change. To print more than one worksheet at once, group the worksheets prior to printing, or display the Print tab Backstage view and change the Print gallery in the Settings category to *Print Entire Workbook*.

Project

SNAP

Tutorial 4.2
Linking Data and Using 3-D References

Tutorial 4.3
Setting a Print Area and Printing Multiple Worksheets

To finish the quarterly sales report, you will link to a cell in another worksheet to enter the percent of gross profit and then copy formatting to ensure consistency before setting the page layout options and printing the entire workbook.

1. With **ES4-WBQtrlySales.xlsx** open and with Summary the active worksheet, make B21 the active cell.

2. Type =.

3. Click the Qtr1 tab, click B21, and then press Enter.

   The value *30%* displays in B21 of the Summary sheet.

4. Press the Up Arrow key to return the active cell back to B21 and then look at the formula that was entered in the Formula bar from Steps 2–3.

   The formula =*'Qtr1'!B21* means that the contents of B21 in the Summary worksheet are drawn from the contents of B21 in the Qtr1 worksheet. Any change made to B21 in Qtr1 automatically causes B21 in Summary to update as well.

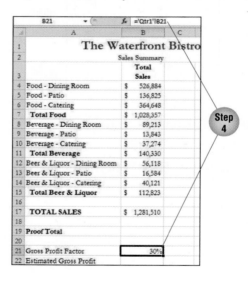

5. Make B22 the active cell, type **=b17*b21**, and then press Enter.

   Estimated Gross Profit is calculated by multiplying Total Sales (B17) times the Gross Profit Factor (B21).

6. Format B22 to Accounting Number Format with no decimals.

7 Make B19 the active cell and then type a formula that will check the accuracy of the total sales in cell B17. ***Hint: Look at the proof total formulas in the Qtr1– Qtr4 worksheets as an example.***

As you near completion of the quarterly sales report, in Steps 8–11 you will use the Format Painter feature to ensure formatting in the Summary worksheet is consistent with formatting in the other worksheets before you print the report. Recall from Section 2 that Format Painter is a feature that allows you to copy formatting attributes from one cell to other cells in the worksheet.

17	TOTAL SALES	$ 1,281,510
18		
19	Proof Total	$ 1,281,510	**Step 7**
20		
21	Gross Profit Factor	30%
22	Estimated Gross Profit	$ 384,453

Steps 5-6

8 Make E7 in the Qtr4 worksheet the active cell and then double-click the Format Painter button ⬚ in the Clipboard group.

Double-clicking the Format Painter button toggles the copy format feature on so that you can paste formats multiple times. Notice that the pointer has a paint brush icon attached to it as you move the mouse over the worksheet in the next step.

9 Click the Summary tab, click B7, click B11, and then click B15.

Step 8

Step 9

continues

10 Click the Format Painter button to turn off the feature.

11 Make E17 in the Qtr4 worksheet the active cell, click the Format Painter button, click the Summary tab, and then click B17.

> Single-clicking the Format Painter turns the feature on only for the next mouse click. Notice the feature has been automatically turned off after clicking B17.

12 Click the Qtr1 sheet tab, hold down the Shift key, and then click the Summary sheet tab.

> All of the worksheets are now grouped. In the next step you will create a footer which will be applied to each worksheet because they are grouped.

13 Click the Insert tab and then click the Header & Footer button [icon] in the Text group.

14 Click the Go to Footer button [icon] in the Navigation group of the Header & Footer Tools Design tab.

15 With the insertion point positioned in the center section of the footer, click the Sheet Name button [icon] in the Header & Footer Elements group in the Header & Footer Tools Design tab.

> Excel inserts the code *&[Tab]* in the footer, which will be replaced with the worksheet name when the worksheet is viewed in Page Layout view or printed.

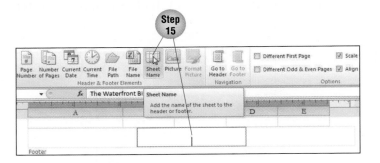

16 Click in the worksheet area outside the footer.

17 Click the File tab and then click the Print tab.

18 Since all of the worksheets were grouped when you opened the Print tab Backstage view, notice the page navigation in the Print Preview section indicates that 5 pages will print.

19 Click the Next Page button ▶ four times, viewing each page in Print Preview.

20 Click the Print button.

Step 20

Print	
🖨️ Print	Copies: 1

Printer ⓘ

HP LaserJet 1200
Ready

Printer Properties

Settings

Print Active Sheets
Only print the active sheets

Pages: ___ to ___

Print One Sided
Only print on one side of the page

Collated
1,2,3 1,2,3 1,2,3

Portrait Orientation

Letter
8.5" x 11"

Normal Margins
Left: 0.7" Right: 0.7"

No Scaling
Print sheets at their actual size

Page Setup

The Waterfront Bistro
Quarterly Sales Report

	January	February	March	Quarter Total
Food - Dining Room	$ 46,750	$ 40,500	$ 48,775	$ 136,025
Food - Patio	$ -	$ -	$ -	$ -
Food - Catering	$ 11,124	$ 9,522	$ 23,574	$ 44,220
Total Food	$ 57,874	$ 50,022	$ 72,349	$ 180,245
Beverage - Dining Room	$ 4,125	$ 3,641	$ 4,901	$ 12,667
Beverage - Patio	$ -	$ -	$ -	$ -
Beverage - Catering	$ 1,155	$ 1,102	$ 2,455	$ 4,712
Total Beverage	$ 5,280	$ 4,743	$ 7,356	$ 17,379
Beer & Liquor - Dining Room	$ 5,106	$ 4,312	$ 5,142	$ 14,560
Beer & Liquor - Patio	$ -	$ -	$ -	$ -
Beer & Liquor - Catering	$ 1,642	$ 1,244	$ 1,858	$ 4,744
Total Beer & Liquor	$ 6,748	$ 5,556	$ 7,000	$ 19,304
TOTAL SALES	$ 69,902	$ 60,321	$ 86,705	$ 216,928

Proof Total $ 216,928

Gross Profit Factor   30%
Estimated Gross Profit $ 65,078.40

Qtr1

Next Page ◀ 1 of 5 ▶

Step 19

In Brief

Link Worksheet
1. Make destination cell active.
2. Type =.
3. Click sheet tab for source cell.
4. Click source cell.
5. Press Enter.

Print Multiple Worksheets
1. Click first sheet tab.
2. Shift + click last sheet tab.
3. Click File tab.
4. Click Print tab.
5. Click Print button.

21 Click the View tab and then click the Normal button ▦ in the Workbook Views group.

22 Right-click any of the grouped sheet tabs and then click *Ungroup Sheets* at the shortcut menu.

23 Save and then close **ES4-WBQtrlySales.xlsx**.

Activity 4.5

Using Page Break Preview

A page break displays in the worksheet as a broken line along cell borders between columns or rows. Excel inserts the page breaks automatically based on the margin settings, page orientation, and paper size. You can adjust the page break positions if you do not like where the page break has occurred. Display the worksheet in Page Break Preview to view the worksheet with page numbers behind the cells indicating the number of pages required to print the entire worksheet and a blue broken line indicating page break locations. Unused cells outside the printing area are grayed out but still accessible if you want to add additional data. You can adjust the page breaks by dragging the blue broken line to the preferred location. Excel automatically adjusts scaling options to accommodate the cells within the revised page break location.

Project

In your next project you will be working with a catering contract summary. As your first task, you will view the worksheet in Page Break Preview to make adjustments to page layout options and page break locations.

The Waterfront B·I·S·T·R·O

SNAP

Tutorial 4.4
Inserting a Page Break

1. Open **WBCatering.xlsx**.

2. Save the workbook in the ExcelS4 folder and name it **ES4-WBCatering**.

3. Spend a moment reviewing the column headings and the data stored in the worksheet.

4. Click the View tab and then click the Page Break Preview button in the Workbook Views group. If necessary, click OK if a Welcome to Page Break Preview message box displays.

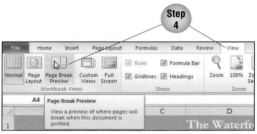
Step 4

5. Change the Zoom setting to 90%.

In Page Break Preview, page breaks are shown as broken or solid blue lines. A broken line indicates an automatic page break inserted by Excel. A solid blue line indicates a manual page break. You can adjust a page break by dragging the blue line to the desired position.

6. Notice that two pages are required to print the worksheet with the current page layout settings. Click the Page Layout tab and then change the orientation to landscape.

Your screen may vary from the one shown, depending on your display settings and monitor size.

The worksheet requires more pages to print when the orientation is changed to landscape at Step 6.

7 Scroll the worksheet to view the changes to the page breaks in landscape orientation. Notice that the worksheet now requires more pages to print.

In Brief

Page Break Preview
1. Click View tab.
2. Click Page Break Preview.
OR
Click Page Break Preview button on Status bar.

8 Look at the *Scale* number in the Scale to Fit group of the Page Layout tab. Notice the current value is *100%*.

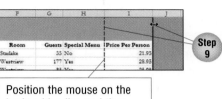

In Steps 9–11, you will adjust the position of the page breaks and then see how the scaling percentage is automatically adjusted to accommodate more cells printed in the page.

9 Position the mouse pointer on the blue broken line between columns H and I until the pointer displays as a left- and right-pointing arrow, drag the mouse to the right of column I, and then release the mouse.

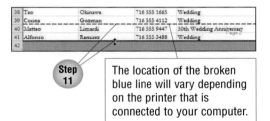

Position the mouse on the broken blue line and then drag to the right of column I.

10 View the bottom of the worksheet. Notice that only a few lines have been moved to page 2.

11 Position the mouse pointer on the broken blue line between rows near the bottom of the worksheet until the pointer displays as an up- and down-pointing arrow, and then drag the broken line below row 41.

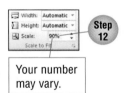

The location of the broken blue line will vary depending on the printer that is connected to your computer.

Notice that the entire worksheet now fits on one page. When you drag an automatic page break to a new location, the page break changes to a solid blue line indicating the break is a manual page break.

12 Look at the revised value in the *Scale* text box in the Scale to Fit group. Notice the value has been reduced from 100%.

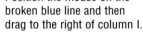

Your number may vary.

Excel automatically adjusts the scaling percent downward when you adjust a break page that causes more cells to print on the page.

13 Click the View tab and then click the Normal button in the Workbook Views group.

14 Save **ES4-WBCatering.xlsx**.

In Addition

Inserting or Removing a Page Break in Normal View

Page breaks generally do not appear in Normal view until you have displayed the worksheet in the Print tab Backstage view. Broken lines appear between column or row borders to indicate automatic page breaks. To insert a manual page break in Normal view, position the active cell in the row below or the column to the right of which you want the page break to occur, click the Page Layout tab, click the Breaks button in the Page Setup group and then click *Insert Page Break* at the drop-down list (shown at the right).

Activity 4.6

Formatting Data as a Table; Applying Table Design Options

Create a table in Excel to manage data independently from other cells in the worksheet, or to filter and sort a list. A worksheet can contain more than one range formatted as a table. By default, filter arrows appear in the first row of the table and a border surrounds the table range with a sizing arrow at the bottom right corner. Excel includes a variety of predefined table styles to apply professional quality formatting features to the range within a table. The contextual Table Tools Design tab becomes available when a range of cells is defined as a table.

Project You will format the catering contract list as a table, add a record to the list, and create a new calculated column to extend the catering contract amounts. Finally, you will add a totals row to the bottom of the table to sum the catering contracts.

The Waterfront B·I·S·T·R·O

SNAP

Tutorial 4.5
Formatting Data as a Table

Tutorial 4.6
Adding Rows to a Table

1. With **ES4-WBCatering.xlsx** open, select A3:I41.

2. Click the Home tab and then click the Format as Table button in the Styles group.

3. Click *Table Style Medium 17* (third option in third row in *Medium* section) at the drop-down gallery.

> Excel includes several predefined table styles grouped into *Light*, *Medium*, and *Dark* categories with which you can add color, borders, and shading formats to cells within the table. In addition, you can create your own custom table style saved with the current workbook. The table styles shown in the drop-down gallery are dependent on the worksheet's current theme.

4. At the Format As Table dialog box, with *=$A$3:$I$41* selected in the *Where is the data for your table?* text box, click OK.

> Excel applies the table style formats to the range, displays filter arrows in the first row of the table, and adds a border to the table, including a sizing handle to the bottom right cell.

5. Click in any cell to deselect the range.

> In the next step, you will add a new record to the table.

6. Make A42 the active cell and then type a new row in the columns indicated. Press Enter after typing the price per person.

First Name	Sonora
Last Name	Yee
Contact Phone	716 555 2668
Event	Birthday Party
Date	12/31/2011

Room	Starlake
Guests	73
Special Menu	Yes
Price per Person	31.95

Since you typed data in the row immediately below the table, Excel automatically expands the table to include the new row and applies the table style formats. You can also insert a new row by pressing Tab at the last cell in the table to insert a new blank row below and then type the data.

In Brief

Format Table
1. Select range.
2. Click Format as Table button.
3. Click desired table style.
4. Click OK.

Add Total Row
1. Click Table Tools Design tab.
2. Click *Total Row* check box.
3. If necessary, choose desired function in numeric columns.

| 41 | Alfonso | Ramirez | 716 555 3488 | Wedding | 12/31/2011 | Westview | 160 | Yes | 35.95 |
| 42 | Sonora | Yee | 716 555 2668 | Birthday Party | 12/31/2011 | Starlake | 73 | Yes | 31.95 |

Step 6

7 Make J3 the active cell, type **Contract Total**, and then press Enter.

Typing new data in a column immediately right of the table also automatically expands the table list range.

8 With J4 the active cell, type the formula **=g4*i4** and then press Enter.

Typing a formula in a table column causes Excel to automatically categorize the column as a calculated column and duplicate the formula in the remainder of the table.

Contract Total
$ 768.25
$ 5,124.15
$ 2,205.75
$ 7,700.70
$ 2,547.60
$ 2,228.90
$ 1,558.45
$ 2,042.90
$ 4,074.15
$ 2,460.75
$ 622.70
$ 970.20
$ 1,215.90
$ 1,725.30
$ 4,863.60
$ 1,422.15

Step 9

9 Select J4:J42, apply the Accounting Number Format, and then change the column width to *16.00 (117 pixels)*.

10 Deselect the range and then click the Table Tools Design tab.

11 Click the *Total Row* check box in the Table Style Options group.

Excel adds the word *Total* in the leftmost cell in the row below the table and sums the cells in column J.

Step 11

Table Tools ES4-WBCatering
iew | Design

☑ Header Row ☐ First Column
☑ Total Row ☐ Last Column
☑ Banded Rows ☐ Banded Columns
Table Style Options

Total Row (Ctrl+Shift+T)

Turn on or off the total row of the table.

The total row is a row at the end of the table which displays totals for each column.

12 Make G43 the active cell, click the list arrow that appears, and then click *Sum* at the pop-up list.

13 Make I43 the active cell, click the list arrow that appears, and then click *Average* at the pop-up list.

14 Decrease the decimals in I43 to two decimal places.

12/15/2011	Starlake	18	No	31.95	$ 575.10
12/20/2011	Sunset	51	Yes	31.95	$ 1,629.45
12/21/2011	Westview	110	Yes	27.95	$ 3,074.50
12/22/2011	Westview	85	Yes	28.95	$ 2,460.75
12/24/2011	Westview	125	Yes	35.95	$ 4,493.75
12/31/2011	Westview	160	Yes	35.95	$ 5,752.00
12/31/2011	Starlake	73	Yes	31.95	$ 2,332.35
		3155		28.36	$ 90,710.25

Step 12   **Steps 13-14**

15 Select A1:J1 and then click the Merge & Center button ⊞ in the Alignment group in the Home tab to remove the merging of columns A through I.

16 With A1:J1 still selected, click the Merge & Center button a second time to merge columns A through J.

17 Correct the centering of the title in row 2 by completing steps similar to those in Steps 15–16.

18 Save **ES4-WBCatering.xlsx**.

Activity
4.7

Sorting a Table by Single and Multiple Criteria

In Section 1 you learned to sort the payroll worksheet alphabetically by last names. To sort rows in a table by single or multiple criteria involves the same process as the one used in Section 1. To sort by a single column, click in any cell in the column by which you wish to sort and then use the *Sort A to Z* or *Sort Z to A* options at the Sort & Filter drop-down list. To group the rows first by one column and then sort the rows within each group by another column, open the Sort dialog box. You can continue to group and sort by multiple criteria as needed.

Project

SNAP

Tutorial 4.7
Using the Sort Feature in Tables

You decide to print the catering data sorted in descending order by the contract total. Next, you want a printout of the catering list grouped first by the event, then by room, and then by date.

1. With **ES4-WBCatering.xlsx** open, click any cell in column J within the table range.

2. Click the Sort & Filter button in the Editing group in the Home tab.

3. Click *Sort Largest to Smallest* at the drop-down list.

   The table is rearranged in descending order by contract total with the highest contract amount at the top of the list. Excel displays a down-pointing black arrow in the filter arrow button to indicate that the table is ordered by the *Contract Total* column.

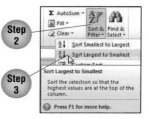

4. Select H4:I43 and center the cells within the range.

5. Deselect the range and then click the View tab.

6. Display the worksheet in Page Break Preview and adjust the page breaks so that the worksheet fits on one page.

7. Print the worksheet.

8. Display the worksheet in Normal view and then click the Home tab.

9. Click the Sort & Filter button and then click *Custom Sort* at the drop-down list.

10. At the Sort dialog box, click the down-pointing arrow at the right of *Sort by* in the *Column* section (currently reads *Contract Total*) and then click *Event* at the drop-down list.

11. Click the down-pointing arrow at the right of the list box in the *Order* section (currently reads *Z to A*) and then click *A to Z* at the drop-down list.

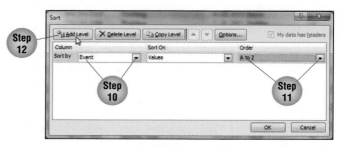

12. Click the Add Level button in the Sort dialog box.

13. Click the down-pointing arrow at the right of *Then by* in the *Column* section and then click *Room* at the drop-down list.

   The default entries of *Values* for *Sort On* and *A to Z* for *Order* are correct since you want the cells sorted by the room names in ascending order.

136 **EXCEL** Section 4

14 Click the Add Level button.

15 Click the down-pointing arrow at the right of the second *Then by* list box in the *Column* section and then click *Date* at the drop-down list.

> The default entries of *Values* for *Sort On* and *Oldest to Newest* for *Order* are correct since you want to sort the dates in ascending order.

16 Click OK to perform the sort.

17 Examine the sorted worksheet and compare your results with the partial worksheet shown below. Notice the rows are grouped and sorted first by event starting with *25th Wedding Anniversary*. Within each event group, the rows are next arranged by room and then within each room group the rows are arranged by date.

Step 13
Step 15
Step 16
Step 17

Sort

Column		Sort On		Order	
Sort by	Event	Values		A to Z	
Then by	Room	Values		A to Z	
Then by	Date	Values		Oldest to Newest	

My data has headers

The Waterfront Bistro
Catering Contracts

	First Name	Last Name	Contact Phone	Event	Date	Room	Guests	Special Menu	Price Per Person	Contract Total
4	Nicole	Griffin	905 555 4166	25th Wedding Anniversary	6/17/2011	Starlake	54	Yes	31.95	$ 1,725.30
5	Linna	Fantino	716 555 9648	25th Wedding Anniversary	11/30/2011	Sunset	54	No	28.95	$ 1,563.30
6	Orlando	Fagan	716 555 3694	25th Wedding Anniversary	3/10/2011	Westview	88	Yes	28.95	$ 2,547.60
7	Percy	Bresque	716 555 1248	50th Wedding Anniversary	4/12/2011	Westview	62	Yes	32.95	$ 2,042.90
8	Matteo	Limardi	716 555 9447	50th Wedding Anniversary	12/24/2011	Westview	125	Yes	35.95	$ 4,493.75
9	Su-Lin	Ping	716 555 7774	Baby Shower	7/10/2011	Sunset	62	Yes	21.95	$ 1,360.90
10	Raji	Jai	716 555 6885	Baby Shower	11/6/2011	Westview	85	No	28.95	$ 2,460.75
11	Dana	Russell	716 555 4965	Birthday Party	5/30/2011	Starlake	36	No	26.95	$ 970.20
12	Walter	Szucs	905 555 6998	Birthday Party	6/10/2011	Starlake	42	No	28.95	$ 1,215.90
13	Sofia	Delgado	716 555 8465	Birthday Party	8/10/2011	Starlake	55	No	21.95	$ 1,207.25
14	Carlotta	Balducci	716 555 9665	Birthday Party	8/22/2011	Starlake	62	Yes	25.95	$ 1,608.90
15	Sonora	Yee	716 555 2668	Birthday Party	12/31/2011	Starlake	73	Yes	31.95	$ 2,332.35
16	Mishika	Kapoor	716 555 3669	Birthday Party	10/5/2011	Sunset	68	Yes	28.95	$ 1,968.60
17	Bogdana	Petrov	716 555 6889	Birthday Party	12/20/2011	Sunset	51	Yes	31.95	$ 1,629.45
18	Frances	Corriveau	716 555 3256	Birthday Party	1/23/2011	Westview	85	Yes	25.95	$ 2,205.75
19	Kim	Pockovic	905 555 3698	Birthday Party	3/18/2011	Westview	62	Yes	35.95	$ 2,228.90
20	Cecily	Hillmore	716 555 6598	Business Meeting	1/15/2011	Starlake	35	No	21.95	$ 768.25
21	Lane	Gill	416 555 3264	Business Meeting	3/29/2011	Starlake	71	No	21.95	$ 1,558.45
22	Mei-Yin	Zhang	716 555 2121	Business Meeting	12/1/2011	Starlake	28	Yes	31.95	$ 894.60
23	Cristian	Martinez	716 555 4331	Business Meeting	12/15/2011	Starlake	18	No	31.95	$ 575.10
24	Franco	Costa	716 555 3345	Business Meeting	9/30/2011	Sunset	32	No	31.95	$ 1,022.40
25	Jack	Torrance	716 555 1469	Business Meeting	5/15/2011	Westview	26	No	23.95	$ 622.70
26	Jesse	Golinsky	716 555 4218	Business Meeting	6/26/2011	Westview	57	No	24.95	$ 1,422.15
27	Alfredo	Juanitez	716 555 4668	Business Meeting	7/31/2011	Westview	49	No	23.95	$ 1,173.55
28	Carlo	Sanchez	905 555 6344	Business Meeting	9/10/2011	Westview	45	No	21.95	$ 987.75
29	Guido	Donato	716 555 8444	Business Meeting	10/22/2011	Westview	30	No	25.95	$ 778.50

18 Print the worksheet.

19 Save **ES4-WBCatering.xlsx**.

In Brief

Sort Table by Single Column
1. Click in any row within column by which to sort.
2. Click the Sort & Filter button.
3. Click *Sort A to Z,* or *Sort Smallest to Largest* or *Sort Z to A,* or *Sort Largest to Smallest.*

Sort Table by Multiple Columns
1. Click Sort & Filter button.
2. Click *Custom Sort.*
3. Select first column to sort by.
4. Select sort order.
5. Click Add Level.
6. Repeat Steps 3–5 for each sort column.
7. Click OK.

In Addition

More about Sorting

By default, Excel sorts the data in a column alphanumerically. Alphanumeric sorting arranges rows with entries that begin with symbols first, then numbers, then letters. Notice in the catering events workbook that the events beginning with numbers, such as *25th Wedding Anniversary* and *50th Wedding Anniversary*, are the first rows in the sorted worksheet.

Activity 4.8

Filtering a Table

A *filter* is used to display only certain records within the table that meet specified criteria. The records that do not meet the filter criteria are temporarily hidden from view. Using a filter, you can view and/or print a subset of rows within a table. For example, you might want to print a list of catering events that have been booked into a certain room. Once you have printed the list, removing the filter redisplays all of the rows. Excel displays filter arrows in the first row of the table with which you specify the filter criteria.

Project

To prepare for an upcoming meeting with the executive chef, Dana has asked for a printout of the catering events that require a special menu. Another printout of the events booked into the Starlake Room is needed for planning staff requirements. Finally, Dana wants a printed list of the weddings booked into the Sunset Room.

SNAP

Tutorial 4.8
Filtering a Table

1 With **ES4-WBCatering.xlsx** open, click the filter arrow button ▼ next to the label *Special Menu* in H3.

> Filter a table by selecting the criterion from a drop-down list. For each column in the table, a filter arrow button appears. Excel looks in the active column and includes in the filter drop-down list each unique field value that exists within the column. In addition, the entries *Sort A to Z, Sort Z to A,* and *Sort by Color* appear at the top of the list.

2 Click the check box next to *No* in the drop-down list to remove the check mark.

> Clearing a check mark for a check box instructs Excel to hide those rows within the table that match the check box entry. Since the only other entry in the column is *Yes*, the criterion for the filter is to display only those rows within the table that have the text entry *Yes* in column H.

3 Click OK.

> Excel hides any records that have a value other than *Yes* in the column as shown below. The row numbers of the matching items that were found are displayed in blue and a filter icon appears in the filter arrow button in H3 to indicate H is the column that was used to filter the rows. The Status bar also shows the message that 24 of 39 records were found. A filtered worksheet can be edited, formatted, charted, or printed.

4 Print the filtered worksheet.

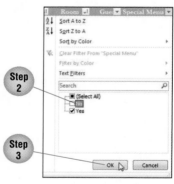

> **Step 2**
>
> **Step 3**

> Filter icon indicates the column used to filter the table.

> Excel hides rows that do not meet the criterion. Matching row numbers are displayed in blue.

	First Name	Last Name	Contact Phone	Event	Date	Room	Gue	Special Menu
4	Nicole	Griffin	905 555 4166	25th Wedding Anniversary	6/17/2011	Starlake	54	Yes
6	Orlando	Fagan	716 555 3694	25th Wedding Anniversary	3/10/2011	Westview	88	Yes
7	Percy	Bresque	716 555 1248	50th Wedding Anniversary	4/12/2011	Westview	62	Yes
8	Matteo	Limardi	716 555 9447	50th Wedding Anniversary	12/24/2011	Westview	125	Yes
9	Su-Lin	Ping	716 555 7774	Baby Shower	7/10/2011	Sunset	62	Yes
14	Carlotta	Balducci	716 555 9665	Birthday Party	8/22/2011	Starlake	62	Yes
15	Sonora	Yee	716 555 2668	Birthday Party	12/31/2011	Starlake	73	Yes
16	Mahika	Kapoor	716 555 3669	Birthday Party	10/5/2011	Sunset	68	Yes
17	Bogdana	Petrov	716 555 6889	Birthday Party	12/20/2011	Sunset	51	Yes
18	Frances	Cozzireau	716 555 3256	Birthday Party	1/23/2011	Westview	85	Yes
19	Kim	Pockovic	905 555 3698	Birthday Party	3/18/2011	Westview	62	Yes
22	Mei-Yin	Zhang	716 555 2121	Business Meeting	12/1/2011	Starlake	28	Yes
30	Bianca	Vargas	716 555 3884	Engagement Party	10/15/2011	Starlake	40	Yes
31	Omar	Hamid	716 555 8796	Engagement Party	5/8/2011	Sunset	85	Yes
32	Elizabeth	McMaster	716 555 9442	Engagement Party	7/11/2011	Sunset	75	Yes
33	Mario	Fontaine	716 555 1886	Engagement Party	1/20/2011	Westview	177	Yes
34	Reed	Pavelich	716 555 2286	Wedding	7/25/2011	Starlake	110	Yes
35	Weston	Kressman	716 555 4219	Wedding	2/28/2011	Sunset	266	Yes
36	Max	Santore	905 555 3264	Wedding	4/28/2011	Sunset	157	Yes
37	Zack	Doucet	716 555 3488	Wedding	6/20/2011	Sunset	168	Yes
38	Bahurai	Omkar	905 555 3411	Wedding	8/30/2011	Westview	155	Yes
40	Tao	Okinawa	716 555 1665	Wedding	12/21/2011	Westview	110	Yes
41	Corina	Guzman	716 555 4112	Wedding	12/22/2011	Westview	85	Yes
42	Alfonso	Ramirez	716 555 3488	Wedding	12/31/2011	Westview	160	Yes
43	Total						2408	

(5) Point to the filter icon in the filter arrow button in H3. Notice the filter criterion displays in the ScreenTip.

(6) Click the filter arrow button in H3.

(7) Click *Clear Filter From "Special Menu"* at the filter drop-down list.

All rows within the table are restored to view.

(8) Click the filter arrow button in F3.

(9) Clear the check marks in the *Westview* and *Sunset* check boxes at the drop-down list and then click OK.

Only the catering events where Starlake is the specified room are displayed.

(10) Print the filtered worksheet.

(11) Click the filter arrow button in F3.

(12) Click the *(Select All)* check box to insert a check mark and then click OK.

Choosing the *(Select All)* check box is another method to redisplay the entire table. In the next steps, you will filter by the event and then filter the subset of rows again to further refine a report.

(13) Click the filter arrow button in D3.

(14) Click the *(Select All)* check box to clear the check marks from all check boxes in the drop-down list, click the *Wedding* check box to insert a check mark, and then click OK.

(15) Click the filter arrow button in F3.

(16) Clear the check mark from the *Starlake* and the *Westview* check boxes and then click OK.

table filtered first by Wedding *Event* and then by Sunset *Room* in Steps 13-16

3	First Name	Last Name	Contact Phone	Event		Date	Room
35	Weston	Kressman	716 555 4219	Wedding		2/28/2011	Sunset
36	Max	Santore	905 555 3264	Wedding		4/28/2011	Sunset
37	Zack	Doucet	716 555 3488	Wedding		6/20/2011	Sunset
43	Total						

(17) Print the filtered worksheet.

(18) Redisplay all records for both filtered columns.

(19) Save **ES4-WBCatering.xlsx**.

In Brief

Filter Table
1. Click desired filter arrow button.
2. Clear check boxes for items you do not want to view.
3. Click OK.

Remove Filter
1. Click desired filter arrow button.
2. Click *Clear Filter from (column title)*.

Step 5

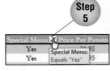

Step 7

table filtered by *Starlake* in Step 9

3	First Name	Last Name	Contact Phone	Event		Date	Room
4	Nicole	Griffin	905 555 4166	25th Wedding Anniversary		6/17/2011	Starlake
11	Dana	Russell	716 555 4965	Birthday Party		5/30/2011	Starlake
12	Walter	Szucs	905 555 6998	Birthday Party		6/10/2011	Starlake
13	Sofia	Delgado	716 555 8465	Birthday Party		8/10/2011	Starlake
14	Carlotta	Balducci	716 555 9665	Birthday Party		8/22/2011	Starlake
15	Sonora	Yee	716 555 2668	Birthday Party		12/31/2011	Starlake
20	Cecily	Hillmore	716 555 6598	Business Meeting		1/15/2011	Starlake
21	Lane	Gill	416 555 3264	Business Meeting		3/29/2011	Starlake
22	Mei-Yin	Zhang	716 555 2121	Business Meeting		12/1/2011	Starlake
23	Cristian	Martinez	716 555 4331	Business Meeting		12/15/2011	Starlake
30	Bianca	Vargas	716 555 3884	Engagement Party		10/15/2011	Starlake
34	Reed	Pavelich	716 555 2286	Wedding		7/25/2011	Starlake
43	Total						

Step 14

In Addition

Filtering Data Not Formatted as a Table

Data in a worksheet that has not been formatted as a table can also be filtered using techniques similar to those you learned in this activity. Select the range of cells that you wish to filter, click the Sort & Filter button in the Editing group in the Home tab, and then click *Filter* at the drop-down list. Excel adds filter arrows in each column of the first row of the selected range.

Activity 4.9

Inserting, Editing, Deleting, and Printing Comments

A *comment* is a pop-up box containing text that displays when the cell pointer is positioned over a cell with an attached comment. A diagonal red triangle in the upper right corner of the cell alerts the reader that a comment exists. The Review tab contains buttons to insert and delete comments, show or hide all comment boxes, and scroll through comments within a worksheet. Use comments to provide instructions, ask questions, or add other explanatory text to a cell.

Project

Dana has given you two notes and a reminder that should be inserted into the appropriate event information in the catering contracts workbook.

Tutorial 4.9
Inserting and Editing
Comments

1 With **ES4-WBCatering.xlsx** open, make G10 the active cell.

2 Click the Review tab.

3 Click the New Comment button in the Comments group.

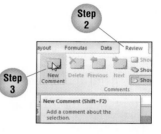

> A comment box displays anchored to the active cell with the user's name inserted in bold text at the top of the box. In worksheets accessed by multiple people, the name helps the reader identify the person who made the comment.

4 Type **Waiting for Frances to confirm the final number of guests.**

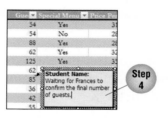

5 Click in the worksheet outside the comment box.

> A diagonal red triangle appears in the upper right corner of G10 indicating a comment exists for the cell.

6 Right-click H19 and then click *Insert Comment* at the shortcut menu.

7 Type **Remind Pierre that five guests require a diabetic menu.**

1/23/2011 Westview	85	Yes
3/18/2011 Westview	62	Yes
1/15/2011 Starlake	35	No
3/29/2011 Starlake	71	No
12/1/2011 Starlake	28	Yes

Student Name:
Remind Pierre that five guests require a diabetic menu.

Step 7

8 Click in the worksheet outside the comment box.

9 Hover the cell pointer over G10.

> Hovering the cell pointer over a cell that contains a comment causes the comment box to pop up.

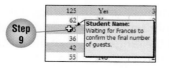

10 Click I24, click the New Comment button in the Comments group, type **Signed contract not yet received. Follow-up in two weeks.**, and then click in the worksheet outside the comment box.

11 Right-click H19 and then click *Edit Comment* at the shortcut menu.

12 Move the cursor and insert and delete text as necessary to change the comment text from *five* to *six* guests require a diabetic menu.

13 Click in the worksheet outside the comment box and then press Ctrl + Home to move the active cell to A1.

14 Click the Next button  in the Comments group.

Excel opens the comment box in G10.

15 Click the Next button to scroll to the next comment box in H19.

16 Click the Next button to scroll to the third comment box and then click the Delete button in the Comments group.

By default, comments do not print with the worksheet. In the next steps, you will print the worksheet with the comment text displayed next to the cells.

17 Click the Show All Comments button in the Comments group.

18 Click the Page Layout tab.

19 Click the Page Setup group dialog box launcher located at the bottom right corner of the Page Setup group.

20 Click the Sheet tab at the Page Setup dialog box, click the down-pointing arrow next to *Comments* in the *Print* section, click *As displayed on sheet*, and then click OK.

21 Print the worksheet.

22 Click the Review tab and then click the Show All Comments button to remove the display of the comment boxes.

23 Save and then close **ES4-WBCatering.xlsx**, leaving Excel open for the next activity.

In Brief

Insert Comment
1. Make active cell in which to insert comment.
2. Click Review tab.
3. Click New Comment button.
4. Type comment text.
5. Click in worksheet outside comment box.

Print Comments with Worksheet
1. Click Page Layout tab.
2. Click Page Setup dialog box launcher.
3. Click Sheet tab in Page Setup dialog box.
4. Click down-pointing arrow to right of Comments.
5. Click *As displayed on sheet* or *At end of sheet*.
6. Click OK.
7. Print worksheet.

Activity 4.10

Creating a Workbook from a Template

Excel includes worksheets that are formatted and have text and formulas created for specific uses such as creating sales invoices, expenses, timecards, and financial statements. These preformatted worksheets are called *templates*. Templates can be customized and saved with a new name to reflect individual company data. Additional templates can be downloaded from Office Online.

Project Aparna Patel, the administrative assistant to Dana Hirsch, has provided her hours worked for submission to payroll. You will use the Time Card template to fill out the paperwork.

Tutorial 4.10
Using Templates

1 Click the File tab and then click the New tab.

2 At the New tab Backstage view, click *Sample templates* in the *Available Templates* section in the center pane.

> The sample templates installed on the computer you are using are shown in the center pane.

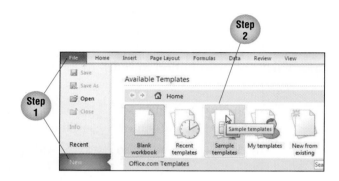

3 Double-click the *Time Card* template in the center pane.

4 Scroll down the template to view the type of information required and the way the data is arranged on the page.

5 If necessary, click C7 (next to *Employee*), type **Aparna Patel**, and then press Enter twice.

> Pressing Enter twice moves the active cell next to *[Street Address]* (C9) in the template.

6 Type **15 Pearl Street** and then press Enter four times.

7 With the active cell next to *[City, ST ZIP Code]*, type **Buffalo, NY 14202** and then press Enter three times.

> The active cell moves next to *Week ending:* (C16).

8 Type **11/13/2011** and then click G7 (next to *Manager:*).

> Notice the dates in the table below *Week ending* update once you change the date in C16.

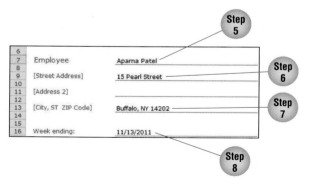

9 Type **Dana Hirsch** and then press Enter twice.

10 With the active cell next to *Employee phone:*, type **716 555 3381** and then click D21.

In Brief

Create Workbook from Template
1. Click File tab, then New tab.
2. Click *Sample templates* or an *Office.com* category.
3. Double-click desired template in center pane.
4. Fill in data or other information as needed.
5. Save, print, close.

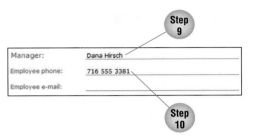

Manager:	Dana Hirsch
Employee phone:	716 555 3381
Employee e-mail:	

Step 9

Step 10

11 Type the remaining entries in the time card as shown below by typing the value and then pressing Enter or clicking the next cell as needed. The cells in the shaded *Total* column, and *Total hours* and *Total pay* rows calculate automatically.

Day	Date	Regular Hours	Overtime	Sick	Vacation	Total
Monday	11/7/2011	8.00	1.75			9.75
Tuesday	11/8/2011	7.00				7.00
Wednesday	11/9/2011	8.00				8.00
Thursday	11/10/2011	8.00				8.00
Friday	11/11/2011	7.00				7.00
Saturday	11/12/2011					
Sunday	11/13/2011					
Total hours		38.00	1.75			39.75
Rate per hour		$ 15.25	$ 22.88			
Total pay		$ 579.50	$ 40.04	$ -	$ -	$ 619.54

Step 11

12 Click the Save button.

13 At the Save As dialog box, navigate to the ExcelS4 folder on your storage medium, type **ES4-AP_WENov13_2011** in the *File name* text box, and then press Enter.

14 Print and then close **ES4-AP_WENov13_2011.xlsx**.

In Addition

Templates from Microsoft Office Online

Microsoft maintains a Templates page on Office Online from which you can browse hundreds of predesigned templates for all products in the Office 2010 suite. Browse for an Excel template in one of the categories in the *Office.com Templates* section in the center pane of the New tab Backstage view. For example, double-click the Expense Reports category and the available templates associated with expense reports in Office.com display in the center pane. Click a template to view a preview in the right pane. Click the Download button in the right pane to download the selected template to your computer.

Office.com Templates   Search Office.com for templates

Agendas   Budgets   Calendars   Expense reports   Forms   Inventories   Invoices   Lists   Memos

Plans   Planners   Receipts   Reports   Schedules   Statements   Stationery   Time sheets   More templates

Activity 4.11

Opening and Saving a Workbook in a Different File Format

The default file format for an Excel 2010 or Excel 2007 workbook is Extensible Markup Language (XML), which is different from the format used for earlier versions of Excel. Opening a file created in Excel from Excel 97 to Excel 2003 in Excel 2007 or Excel 2010 causes Excel to switch to compatibility mode. In this mode, you can edit and save the workbook retaining the original file format or convert the file to the new file format. You can save an Excel 2010 file in the Excel 97-2003 file format if you need to exchange the file with someone who does not have current software. A variety of other file formats are available to save workbooks for use in other applications.

Project

Tutorial 4.11
Converting a Workbook to a Different Format

You will open an employee schedule created in Excel 2003 by Aparna Patel and work in compatibility mode. An investment file on your system needs to be given to Aparna, so you will save the workbook in the earlier Excel version. Finally, the catering event workbook needs to be converted to another file format for the executive chef.

1 Open **WBSchedule-Feb14.xls**.

Notice the title bar displays *[Compatibility Mode]* next to the file name since the file you opened was created in a version of Excel prior to the new Excel 2007/Excel 2010 file format.

2 Insert a new row between rows 1 and 2 and then type the label **Pier Dining Room** merged and centered in columns A–H.

3 Change the font size of A2 to 16-point.

4 Make B9 the active cell, type **All schedule changes must be approved in advance by Dana Hirsch.**, and then press Enter.

5 Click the File tab and then click the Convert button at the Info tab Backstage view.

6 Click OK at the Microsoft Excel message stating that this action converts the workbook to the current file format.

When you click OK, the original file is deleted and replaced with the converted file with the file extension .xlsx.

Microsoft Excel

This action converts the workbook to the current file format, which allows you to use all of the new features of Excel, and it reduces the file size. The original workbook will be deleted and cannot be restored after this conversion.

☐ Do not ask me again about converting workbooks.
[Tell Me More...]

[OK] [Cancel]

Step 6

7 At the Microsoft Excel message that states the workbook conversion completed successfully and asking if you want to close and reopen the file, click Yes.

8 Look at the file name in the title bar and notice that the converted file now has the normal *.xlsx* file extension.

9 Close **WBSchedule-Feb14.xlsx**.

10 Open **WBInvestment.xlsx**.

11 Click the File tab, click the Save & Send tab, and then click *Change File Type* in the *File Types* section.

12 Double-click *Excel 97-2003 Workbook (*.xls)* in the *Change File Type* section of the Save & Send tab Backstage view.

13 At the Save As dialog box, type **ES4-WBInvestment** in the *File name* text box and then click the Save button.

continues

14 At the Microsoft Excel - Compatibility Checker dialog box advising you that some formatting is not supported in the selected file format, click the Continue button.

Earlier versions of Excel did not include the cell styles, themes, and table format galleries. Excel will match the formatting as closely as possible. When you know you have to exchange files with others that do not have Excel 2007, avoid using these features if possible or apply colors from the standard color palette.

Step 14

15 Close **ES4-WBInvestment.xls**.

The executive chef uses a special event planning software program that does not recognize Excel workbooks; however, the program can import data stored in the *comma delimited (csv)* file format. The csv format saves the data with a comma separating columns. Formulas are converted to text and all formatting within the worksheet is stripped from the file.

16 Open **WBCatering.xlsx**.

17 Click the File tab, click the Save & Send tab, and then click *Change File Type* in the *File Types* section of the Save & Send tab Backstage view.

18 Double-click *CSV (Comma delimited) (*.csv)* in the *Other File Types* section.

In Brief

Save Workbook in Excel 97-2003 File Format
1. Click File tab.
2. Click Save & Send tab.
3. Click *Change File Type.*
4. Double-click *Excel 97-2003 Workbook (*.xls).*
5. Type file name.
6. Click Save.
7. Click Continue at Compatibility Checker dialog box.

Save Workbook in Another File Format
1. Click File tab.
2. Click Save & Send tab.
3. Click *Change File Type.*
4. Double-click desired file type.
5. Type file name.
6. Click Save.
7. Respond to message boxes as they occur.

19 At the Save As dialog box, type **ES4-WBCatering** in the *File name* text box and then click Save.

20 Click OK at the Microsoft Excel message that says the selected file type does not support workbooks that contain multiple sheets and that clicking OK will save only the active worksheet.

21 Click Yes to save the workbook at the Microsoft Excel message that says **ES4-WBCatering.csv** may contain features that are not compatible with CSV (Comma delimited).

22 Close **ES4-WBCatering.csv**. Click *Don't Save* when prompted to save changes since the file has already been converted.

In Addition

More about File Format Converters in Excel

If the file type that you need to convert an Excel workbook to is not shown in the Save & Send tab Change File Type Backstage view, double-click the *Save as Another File Type* option to open the Save As dialog box. Open the *Save as type* list to view the complete list of file formats. Excel can convert only the active worksheet in most file formats. If a workbook contains multiple sheets, you may need to convert each sheet into a separate file.

Activity 4.12

Creating a PDF/XPS Copy of a Worksheet

PDF is a *Portable Document Format (PDF)* file that preserves fonts, formatting, and images in a printer friendly version that looks the same on most computers. The recipient of a PDF file needs to have installed the Adobe Reader application to open and view the file. Adobe Reader is available free of charge for download from Adobe's website. A person who receives an Excel file saved in PDF format does not need to have the Excel application on his or her computer in order to open, read, and print the file. Exchanging PDF files has become a popular method for collaborating with others since compatibility does not become an issue and each person keeps his/her original Excel file intact. The *XML Paper Specification (XPS)* format is a fixed-layout format with all formatting preserved (similar to PDF) that was developed by Microsoft. The XPS Viewer application is provided with Windows Vista and Windows 7.

Project

Dana has asked you to send the investment worksheet to the bistro's financial advisor. You decide to send her a PDF copy of the worksheet since you want to keep the original worksheet with the formulas intact.

(1) Open **WBInvestment.xlsx**.

(2) Click the File tab and then click the Save & Send tab.

(3) Click *Create PDF/XPS Document* in the *File Types* section.

(4) Click *Create PDF/XPS* in the *Create a PDF/XPS Document* section.

Tutorial 4.12
Creating a PDF/XPS
Copy of a Worksheet

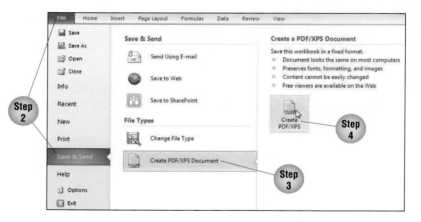

(5) At the Publish as PDF or XPS dialog box, with *WBInvestment.pdf* entered in the *File name* text box, and with the *Save as type* already set to *PDF (*.pdf)*, click the Publish button.

> The worksheet is converted to the PDF file format and, by default, the published file opens in an Adobe Reader window.

Need Help?

Adobe Reader not installed on your computer? Go to www.adobe.com and click the button labeled Get Adobe Reader to download and install the free program.

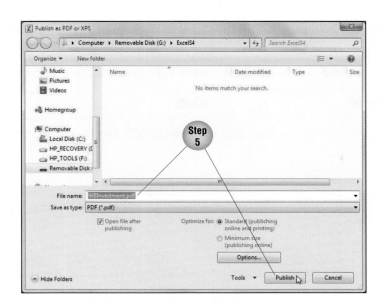

In Brief

Create PDF Copy of a Worksheet
1. Click File tab.
2. Click Share tab.
3. Click *Create PDF/XPS Document*.
4. Click *Create a PDF/XPS*.
5. Type file name.
6. Click Publish.

6 Print the document from the Adobe Reader window.

7 Close the Adobe Reader window.

In the next steps you will create another copy of the investment file in the XPS file format and compare how the two versions are viewed.

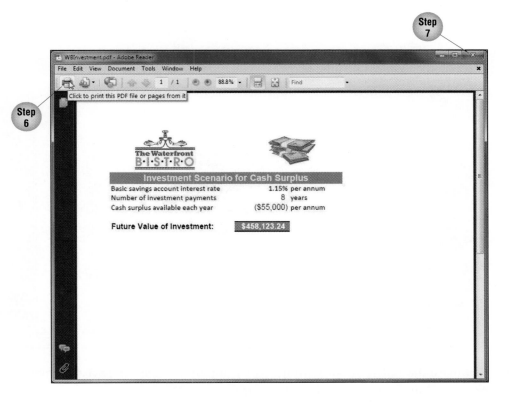

continues

8 At the Excel window with **WBInvestment.xlsx** open, click the File tab and then click the Save & Send tab.

9 Click *Create PDF/XPS Document* in the *File Types* section and then click *Create PDF/XPS*.

10 At the Publish as PDF or XPS dialog box, click the down-pointing arrow at the right of the *Save as type* box and then click *XPS Document (*.xps)* in the drop-down list.

Step 10

11 With the file name changed to *WBInvestment.xps*, click the Publish button.

The worksheet is converted to the XPS file format and by default, the published file opens in an XPS Viewer window.

12 Print the document from the XPS Viewer window.

13 Close the XPS Viewer window.

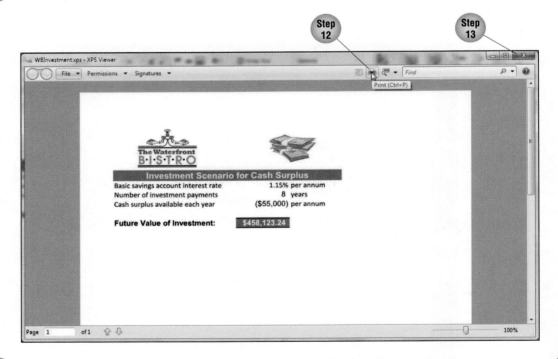

Step 12

Step 13

14 Compare the pdf printout with the xps printout. Notice the two documents preserved the Excel worksheet formatting.

15 Close **WBInvestment.xlsx**.

Features Summary

Feature	Ribbon Tab, Group	Button	File tab	Keyboard Shortcut
create PDF/XPS copy of worksheet			Save & Send	
delete comment	Review, Comments			
delete worksheet	Home, Cells			
edit comment	Review, Comments			
filter table	Home, Editing			
format sheet tab	Home, Cells			
format table	Home, Styles			
insert comment	Review, Comments			Shift + F2
Insert worksheet	Home, Cells			Shift + F11
move or copy worksheet	Home, Cells			
page break preview	View, Workbook Views			
print comments	Page Layout, Page Setup			
print multiple worksheets			Print	Ctrl + P
rename worksheet	Home, Cells			
save in different file format			Save & Send OR Save As	F12
save in earlier Excel version			Save & Send OR Save As, Excel 97-2003 Workbook	F12
show all comments	Review, Comments			
sort	Home, Editing			
templates			New	

Knowledge Check

Completion: In the space provided at the right, indicate the correct term, command, or option.

1. A new workbook initially contains this many sheets. _____

2. Perform this action with the mouse while pointing at a sheet tab to change the worksheet name. _____

3. Perform this action with multiple sheets to apply the same formatting options to all of them in one operation. _____

4. Hold down this key while dragging a sheet tab to copy the sheet. _____

5. The formula =*SUM('Jan:Jun'!G4)* includes this type of reference. _____

6. A link to a cell in another worksheet can be created by typing this kind of entry into the destination cell. _____

7. Page breaks are displayed as broken or solid blue lines in this view. _____

8. Click this button in the Styles group in the Home tab to define an area of a worksheet as an independent range that can be formatted and managed separately from the rest of the worksheet. _____

9. Select this option from the Sort & Filter list to open a dialog box in which to define more than one sort column. _____

10. This term refers to temporarily hiding rows that do not meet a specified criterion. _____

11. Use this feature to type additional information about a cell that appears in a pop-up box when the cell pointer is positioned over the cell. _____

12. Predesigned formatted worksheets that have labels and formulas created for specific uses can be accessed at this tab in Backstage view. _____

13. This is the default file format for Excel workbooks. _____

14. Opening a workbook created in an earlier version of Excel causes Excel to switch to this mode. _____

15. This type of file requires the Adobe Reader program to view. _____

Skills Review

Review 1 **Managing and Formatting Worksheets; Using 3-D References; Printing Multiple Worksheets**

1. Open **WBPayroll.xlsx** and then save the workbook in the ExcelEOS folder and name it **ES4-R1-WBPayroll**.
2. Delete the Week3 worksheet.
3. Copy the Week2 worksheet, positioning the new sheet after Week2, and then rename the *Week2 (2)* worksheet as Week3.
4. Copy the Week2 worksheet, positioning the new sheet after Week3, and then rename the *Week2 (2)* worksheet as Week4.
5. Make Week3 the active worksheet and then edit the following cells:
   Change E9 from *0* to *5*.
   Change I6 from *6* to *0*.
   Change H14 from *0* to *4*.
6. Make Week4 the active worksheet and then edit the following cells:
   Change C11 from *0* to *8*.
   Change G11 from *9* to *0*.
   Change I14 from *6* to *9*.
7. Apply a dark blue tab color to the Week1 through Week4 sheet tabs and a dark red tab color to the Summary tab.
8. With Summary the active worksheet, create a SUM formula with a 3-D reference in C6 that sums the hours for Lou Cortez for all four weeks.
9. Drag the fill handle in C6 to row 14.
10. Make Week1 the active sheet. Merge and center C3:D3 and then enter a DATE function in C3 to enter the date *November 6, 2011*.
11. Merge and center C4:D4 and then enter a formula in C4 that will add three days to the date in C3.
12. Complete steps similar to those in Steps 10–11 to enter the week ended and payment dates in the remaining worksheets as follows:
    C3 in Week2   **November 13, 2011**
    C3 in Week3   **November 20, 2011**
    C3 in Week4   **November 27, 2011**
13. Make Week1 the active sheet. In K6 enter the formula **=if(j6>40,j6-40,0)**, drag the fill handle from K6 to K14, and then calculate the total in K15. If you do not understand the formula in K6, talk with a classmate to work out the formula logic. *Note: A green error flag may appear in J15 if error checking is turned on for the computer you are using. You can ignore this inconsistent formula error which Excel has flagged as a potential error. The error alert occurs because the SUM function in column K is adding the cells above while the SUM function in column J adds the cells left*.
14. In L6 type the formula **=(j6*b17)+(k6*b17*.5)**, drag the fill handle from L6 to L14 and then calculate the total in L15. If you do not understand the formula in L6, talk with a classmate and work out the formula logic together. *Hint: The overtime hours in column K are paid a premium*.

15. Copy and paste the formulas in columns K and L to complete the *Overtime Hours* and *Gross Pay* column entries for Week2–Week4.

16. Make Summary the active worksheet and then enter the 3-D reference formulas in D6 and E6 to sum the overtime hours and gross pay for Lou Cortez from all four worksheets.

17. Copy the 3-D formulas in D6:E6 and paste to D7:E14.

18. Calculate the totals in C15:E15 and then format the *Gross Pay* column to Accounting Number Format.

19. Group and print all five worksheets. *Note: If you submit your work in hard copy, check with your instructor to see if you need to print two copies of the worksheets with one of the copies showing the cell formulas instead of the calculated results.*

20. Save and then close **ES4-R1-WBPayroll.xlsx**.

Review 2 Formatting a Table; Sorting; Filtering; and Inserting and Printing Comments

1. Open **WBInventory.xlsx** and then save the workbook in the ExcelEOS folder and name it **ES4-R2-WBInventory**.

2. Select A4:D45 and format the range as a table using *Table Style Medium 3* (third option in first row of *Medium* section).

3. Filter the table to display only those items that are purchased in units by the flat.

4. Print the filtered worksheet.

5. Redisplay all rows in the table.

6. Sort the table first by *Supplier Name* and then by *Item* with both levels in *A to Z* order.

7. Add a comment to B20 with the text **Dana, is this the right unit for this item?**

8. Add a comment to A23 with the text **This item is difficult to source. Dana, should we consider an alternative product?**

9. Show all comments in the worksheet and set comments to print *As displayed on sheet*.

10. Print the worksheet.

11. Save and then close **ES4-R2-WBInventory.xlsx**.

Review 3 Creating a Workbook Using a Template

1. Start a new workbook using the sample template *Billing Statement*.

2. Enter data into the template as shown in Figure 4.2.

3. Save the workbook in the ExcelEOS folder and name it **ES4-R3-PTStmntNov30**.

4. Print and then close **ES4-R3-PTStmntNov30.xlsx**.

FIGURE 4.2 Review 3

The Waterfront Bistro

3104 Rivermist Drive
Buffalo, NY 14280

Phone: (716) 555-3166
Fax: (716) 555-3190
E-mail: accounts@wfbistro.emcp.net

Statement

Statement #:   101
Date: November 30, 2011
Customer ID: PT-Sinclair

Bill To: Bobbie Sinclair

Performance Threads
4011 Bridgewater Street
NIAGARA FALLS, ON L2E 2T6

Date	Type	Invoice #	Description	Amount	Payment	Balance
11/10/2011	Dir Mtg	2462	Catering Services	$ 726.60		$ 726.60
					Total	$ 726.60

Reminder: Please include the statement number on your check.

Terms: Balance due in 30 days.

REMITTANCE

Customer Name:	Performance Threads
Customer ID:	PT-Sinclair
Statement #:	101
Date:	November 30, 2011
Amount Due:	$726.60
Amount Enclosed:	

Skills Assessment

Note: If you submit your work in hard copy, check with your instructor before completing these assessments to find out if you need to print two copies of each worksheet with one of the copies showing the cell formulas instead of the calculated results.

Assessment 1   Inserting, Deleting, and Renaming Worksheets; Linking Worksheets

1. You are the assistant to Cal Rubine, chair of the Theatre Arts Division at Niagara Peninsula College. The co-op consultant has entered grades for the internships at Marquee Productions and Performance Threads into separate worksheets in the same workbook. You need to create a worksheet to summarize the data. To begin, open **NPCInternGrades.xlsx** and then save the workbook in the ExcelEOS folder naming it **ES4-A1-NPCInternGrades**.
2. Insert a new worksheet before the MarqueeProductions worksheet, and rename the sheet *GradeSummary*.
3. Delete Sheet3.
4. Complete the GradeSummary worksheet by completing the following tasks:
   a. Copy A3:B7 in MarqueeProductions to A3:B7 in GradeSummary keeping the source column widths.
   b. Copy A4:B8 in PerformanceThreads to A8:B12 in GradeSummary.
   c. Copy G3:H3 in MarqueeProductions to C3:D3 in GradeSummary keeping the source column widths.

d. Link the cells in columns C and D of the GradeSummary worksheet to the corresponding grades and dates in MarqueeProductions and PerformanceThreads.

e. Copy the title and subtitle in rows 1 and 2 from MarqueeProductions to GradeSummary. Change the font size of rows 1 and 2 in GradeSummary to 12-point and then adjust the merge and center to columns A–D. Change the Fill Color in E1:H2 to *No Fill*.

f. Center the grades in column C.

5. Group the three worksheets and then change the page orientation to landscape.

6. Change the left margin for the GradeSummary sheet only to 3 inches.

7. Save, print all three worksheets, and then close **ES4-A1-NPCInternGrades.xlsx**.

Assessment 2 Formatting a Table; Filtering; Sorting

1. Bobbie Sinclair, business manager at Performance Threads, needs a list of costumes for Marquee Productions that have a final delivery date of July 9. You decide to format the list as a table and use sorting and filtering features to do this task. To begin, open **PTMarqueeSch.xlsx** and then save the workbook in the ExcelEOS folder naming it **ES4-A2-PTMarqueeSch**.

2. Select A10:H17 and then format the range as a table using *Table Style Light 15* (first option in third row of *Light* section).

3. Filter the table to show only those costumes with a final delivery date of July 9. *Note: Since Start Date and End Date are repeated as column headings in the table, Excel adds numbers after the first occurrences to make each column heading unique.*

4. Sort the filtered list by costume from A to Z.

5. Change the scaling option to fit the worksheet on one page and then print the filtered and sorted list.

6. Redisplay all rows in the table.

7. Sort the table first by the final delivery date from oldest to newest and then by costume from A to Z.

8. Save, print, and then close **ES4-A2-PTMarqueeSch.xlsx**.

Assessment 3 Inserting and Printing Comments

1. The costume design team at Performance Threads is meeting at the end of the week to discuss the production schedule for the Marquee Productions project. In preparation for this meeting, Bobbie Sinclair has asked you to review the schedule and send a copy with your comments inserted. To begin, open **PTMarqueeSch.xlsx** and then save the workbook in the ExcelEOS folder naming it **ES4-A3-PTMarqueeSch**.

2. Make D11 the active cell and then create the following comment:
   Sue is not yet done with the research. Design may not be able to start June 10.

3. Make D15 the active cell and then create the following comment:
   These dates may need adjustment due to overlapping projects.

4. Show all comments.

5. Turn on printing of comments *As displayed on sheet*.

6. Save, print, and then close **ES4-A3-PTMarqueeSch.xlsx**.

Formatting Columns and Formatting a Table; Opening an Excel 2003 Workbook and Saving as an Excel 2010 Workbook

1. Bobbie Sinclair of Performance Threads has a workbook file exported from the accounting system in Excel 2003 format with information on costume rentals. Bobbie has asked you to open the Excel 2003 workbook, modify the data to create a report, and save it in the 2010 file format. To begin, open **PTRentalCost.xls**.
2. Right-align column headings in columns C–E.
3. Insert two rows at the top of the worksheet and type the label Performance Threads in A1.
4. Type the subtitle Costume Rentals in A2.
5. Type the label DaysRented right-aligned in F3 and then AutoFit the column width.
6. Type the label TotalDue right-aligned in G3.
7. Enter the formula =e4-d4 in F4 and then format the result to Comma Style with no decimals.
8. Copy the formula in F4 to the remaining rows in column F.
9. Enter the formula =f4*c4 in G4 and then format the result to Accounting Number Format.
10. Copy the formula in G4 to the remaining rows in column G and then change the column width to *12.00 (89 pixels)*.
11. Select A3:G43 and then format the range as a table using *Table Style Light 9* (second option in second row of *Light* section).
12. Insert a total row at the bottom of the table.
13. Merge and center the title across columns A through G and then apply the Title cell style to A1. Merge and center the subtitle across columns A through G and then apply the Heading 1 style to A2.
14. Make sure the worksheet will print on one page.
15. Convert the workbook to an Excel 2010 file in the ExcelEOS folder and name it **ES4-A4-PTRentalCost**.
16. Print and then close **ES4-A4-PTRentalCost.xlsx**.

Assessment 5 Finding Information on File Formats Not Supported by Excel 2010

1. Use Excel Help to search for information on file formats that are not supported in Excel 2010.
2. Create a table in a new worksheet that provides the file format, the name of the software program with which the file format is associated, and the file extension that would be attached to the file. *Note: Copying and pasting information from the Excel Help window or a Microsoft website is not acceptable.*
3. Apply a table style to the table.
4. Make sure the information is easy to read and understand.
5. Make sure the table will fit on one page when printed.
6. Save the workbook in the ExcelEOS folder and name it **ES4-A5-FileFormats**.
7. Print and then close **ES4-A5-FileFormats.xlsx**.

Assessment 6 Individual Challenge
Smartphone Shopping

1. After graduation, your goal is to work independently as a consultant in your field of study. You plan to travel frequently in North America and Europe. You want to purchase a Smartphone to use while traveling for conference calling, email, web browsing, text messaging, and modifying Office documents. Research the latest product offerings for Smartphones on the Internet.
2. Select three phones from three different manufacturers for your short list comparison. Create a worksheet for analyzing the three Smartphones, organizing the information in a table so that the main features are categorized in the leftmost column with each phone's specification for that feature next to each category. Make sure each Smartphone's name or manufacturer is identified at the top of the respective columns. In the last row of the table insert the estimated cost for each Smartphone.
3. Based on your perception of the best value, select one of the phones as your recommendation and insert a comment in the phone's cost cell indicating your choice.
4. Add clip art or other enhancements to improve the worksheet's appearance.
5. Print the worksheet in landscape orientation scaled to fit on one page and with the comment cell printed as displayed on the sheet.
6. Save the workbook in the ExcelEOS folder and name it **ES4-A6-Smartphones**.
7. Close **ES4-A6-Smartphones.xlsx**.

Marquee Challenge

Challenge 1 Creating a Sales Invoice by Downloading a Template

1. Dana Hirsch of The Waterfront Bistro has asked you to find and download a professionally designed sales invoice template and then use the template to create an invoice to First Choice Travel for catering their business meeting.
2. Open the New tab Backstage view, click *Invoices* in the *Office.com Templates* section. Click the template named *Sales invoice (Blue Gradient design)* in the center pane and then click the Download button to download the template to your computer. If you cannot find the template shown in Figure 4.3, download another suitable template for a sales invoice.
3. Complete the customer invoice using information found in Figure 4.3.
4. To insert the logo, select the logo container object and then click the Picture Tools Format tab. Click the Change Picture button in the Adjust group. At the Insert Picture dialog box, navigate to the data file **TWBLogo.jpg**, and then double-click the file name. Move and resize the logo image as shown in Figure 4.3.
5. Delete the unused rows between the billing address and the body of the invoice.
6. Delete the unused rows between the last line item and the subtotal row.
7. Format the *QTY* column as shown in Figure 4.3.
8. Type **The Waterfront Bistro** next to *Make all checks payable to* near the bottom of the invoice.
9. Save the invoice in the ExcelEOS folder and name it **ES4-C1-WBInvFCT**.
10. Print and then close **ES4-C1-WBInvFCT.xlsx**.

FIGURE 4.3 Challenge 1

INVOICE

The Waterfront Bistro

3104 Rivermist Drive
Buffalo, NY 14280
P: 716.555.3166 F: 716.555.3190
www.emcp.net/wfbistro

INVOICE NO.	2463
DATE	(current date)
CUSTOMER ID	FCT-Torres

TO
Alex Torres
First Choice Travel
4277 Yonge Street
Toronto, ON M4P 2E6
416.555.9834

SHIP TO
2100 Victoria Street
Niagara-on-the-Lake, ON L0S 1J0

QTY	ITEM #	DESCRIPTION	UNIT PRICE	DISCOUNT	LINE TOTAL
16		Lunches	$ 18.23		$ 291.68
16		Desserts	5.31		84.96
16		Beverages	1.87		29.92
1		Delivery and setup	65.00		65.00
				SUBTOTAL	$ 471.56
				SALES TAX	6%
				TOTAL	$ 499.85

Challenge 2 Importing, Formatting and Sorting a Distributor List

1. Sam Vestering, manager of North American Distribution at Worldwide Enterprises, has provided you with two text files exported from the corporate head office computer. One file contains a list of U.S. distributors and the other contains a list of Canadian distributors. Sam would like a one-page list of all distributors.
2. Research in Help how to import a text file by opening the file. The files used in this challenge are delimited files with a comma as the delimiter character.
3. Open the text file named **WEUSDistributors.txt** and follow the steps in the Text Import Wizard as you learned in Help.
4. Open the file named **WECdnDistributors.txt** and follow the steps in the Text Import Wizard as you learned in Help.
5. Widen columns as necessary and then delete the second address and email address columns in both worksheets.
6. Move or copy the data from one of the worksheets to the bottom of the other worksheet.
7. Add the column labels above the data as shown in Figure 4.4.
8. Insert the logo named **WELogo.jpg**, add the title rows, and format the data as a table. Use your best judgment to determine the table style, column widths, and other formatting options to apply to the table as shown in Figure 4.4.
9. Look closely at Figure 4.4 to determine the sort order and then custom sort the table. *Hint: The table is sorted by three levels*.
10. Apply page layout options so that the worksheet prints centered on one page in landscape orientation.
11. Convert the worksheet to an Excel workbook in the ExcelEOS folder and name it **ES4-C2-WEDistributors**.
12. Create a PDF copy of the workbook, print the pdf document, and then close the Adobe Reader window.
13. Close **ES4-C2-WEDistributors.xlsx** and any other open workbooks without saving changes.

FIGURE 4.4 Challenge 2

Name	Mailing Address	City	State	ZIP code	Telephone	Fax
Worldwide Enterprises			**North American Distributor List**			
Olympic Cinemas	P. O. Box 1439	Calgary	AB	T2C 3P7	403-555-4587	403-555-4589
LaVista Cinemas	111 Vista Road	Phoenix	AZ	86355-6014	602-555-6231	602-555-6233
West Coast Movies	P. O. Box 298	Vancouver	BC	V6Y 1N9	604-555-3548	604-555-3549
Marquee Movies	1011 South Alameda Street	Los Angeles	CA	90045	612-555-2398	612-555-2377
Sunfest Cinemas	341 South Fourth Avenue	Tampa	FL	33562	813-555-3185	813-555-3177
Liberty Cinemas	P. O. Box 998	Atlanta	GA	73125	404-555-8113	404-555-2349
O'Shea Movies	59 Erie	Oak Park	IL	60302	312-555-7719	312-555-7381
Midtown Moviehouse	1033 Commercial Street	Emporia	KS	66801	316-555-7013	316-555-7022
All Nite Cinemas	2188 3rd Street	Louisville	KY	40201	502-555-4238	502-555-4240
Eastown Movie House	P. O. Box 722	Cambridge	MA	2142	413-555-0981	413-555-0226
Riverview Cinemas	1011-848 Sheppard Street	Winnipeg	MB	R2P 0N6	204-555-6538	204-555-6533
New Age Movies	73 Killarney Road	Moncton	NB	E1B 2Z9	506-555-8376	506-555-8377
EastCoast Cinemas	62 Mountbatten Drive	St.John's	NF	A1A 3X9	709-555-8349	709-555-8366
Hillman Cinemas	55 Kemble Avenue	Baking Ridge	NJ	7920	201-555-1147	201-555-1143
Seaboard Movie House Inc.	P. O. Box 1005	Dartmouth	NS	B2V 1Y8	902-555-3948	902-555-3950
Northern Reach Movies	P. O. Box 34	Yellowknife	NW	X1A 2N9	867-555-6314	867-555-6316
Mainstream Movies	P. O. Box 33	Buffalo	NY	14601	212-555-3269	212-555-3270
Victory Cinemas	12119 South 23rd	Buffalo	NY	14288	212-555-8746	212-555-8748
Waterfront Cinemas	P. O. Box 3255	New York	NY	14288	212-555-3845	212-555-3947
Westview Movies	1112 Broadway	New York	NY	10119	212-555-4875	212-555-4877
Mooretown Movies	P. O. Box 11	Dublin	OH	43107	614-555-8134	614-555-8339
Millennium Movies	4126 Yonge Street	Toronto	ON	M2P 2B8	416-555-9335	416-555-9338
Redwood Cinemas	P. O. Box 112F	Portland	OR	97466-3359	503-555-8641	503-555-8633
Wellington 10	1203 Tenth Southwest	Philadelphia	PA	19178	215-555-9045	215-555-9048
Waterdown Cinemas	575 Notre Dame Street	Summerside	PE	C1N 1T8	902-555-8374	902-555-8376
MountainView Movies	5417 RoyalMount Avenue	Montreal	PQ	H4P 1H8	514-555-3584	514-555-3585
Danforth Cinemas	P. O. Box 22	Columbia	SC	29201	803-555-3487	803-555-3421
Plains Cinema House	P. O. Box 209	Regina	SK	S4S 5Y9	306-555-1247	305-555-1248
Century Cinemas	3687 Avenue K	Arlington	TX	76013	817-555-2116	817-555-2119
Countryside Cinemas	22 Hillside Street	Bennington	VT	5201	802-555-1469	802-555-1470
Northern Stars Movies	811 Cook Street	Whitehorse	YK	Y1A 2S4	867-555-6598	867-555-6599

Integrating Programs
Word and Excel

Skills

- Copy and paste Word data into an Excel worksheet
- Link an Excel worksheet with a Word document
- Update linked data
- View linked data as an icon
- Link an Excel chart with a Word document
- Embed an Excel worksheet into a Word document
- Edit an embedded worksheet

Projects Overview

Copy data in a Word document on costume research, design, and sewing hours for employees into an Excel worksheet. Copy data in an Excel worksheet on employee payroll and then link the data to a Word document. Update the payroll hours for the employees for the next week. Copy employee payroll data in an Excel worksheet to a Word document and then update the data in Word.

Link a chart containing sales commissions for agents with a Word document and then update the sales commissions to reflect a higher percentage.

Copy Word data on student scores into an Excel worksheet. Copy an Excel chart containing data on student areas of emphasis in the Theatre Arts Division into a Word document and then update the chart in Excel.

Copy data in an Excel worksheet on theatre company revenues into a Word document and then update the data in Word.

Model Answers for Projects

These model answers for the projects that you complete in this section provide a preview of the finished projects before you begin working and also allow you to compare your own results with these models to ensure you have created the materials accurately.

Int1-PTExcelJuneHrs.xlsx is the project in Activity 1.1.

Employee	Research	Design	Sewing	Total
Scott Bercini	3	8	14	25
Terri Cantrell	5	10	18	33
Paul Gottlieb	2	7	10	19
Tae Jeong	6	12	20	38
Total	16	37	62	115

Int1-PTWordOctPay.docx is the project in Activity 1.2 and part of the project in Activity 1.3.

*Proudly serving the entertainment
industry for over 20 years!*

Employee Payroll

Week of October 15, 2012:

Employee	Hours	Pay Rate		Total	
Rosa Levens	20.0	$	14.65	$	293.00
Scott Bercini	40.0	$	15.10	$	604.00
Tae Jeong	25.5	$	12.40	$	316.20
Terri Cantrell	15.0	$	12.00	$	180.00
Paul Gottlieb	40.0	$	16.00	$	640.00

4011 Bridgewater Street ✂ Niagara Falls, ON L2E 2T6 ✂ (905) 555-2971

Int1-PTExcelOctPay.xlsx is part of the project in Activity 1.3.

Performance Threads

Employee Payroll, Week of October 15

Employee	Hours	Pay Rate	Total
Rosa Levens	20.0	$ 14.65	$ 293.00
Scott Bercini	40.0	$ 15.10	$ 604.00
Tae Jeong	25.5	$ 12.40	$ 316.20
Terri Cantrell	15.0	$ 12.00	$ 180.00
Paul Gottlieb	40.0	$ 16.00	$ 640.00

Int1-FCTWordSalesCom.docx is part of the project in Activity 1.4.

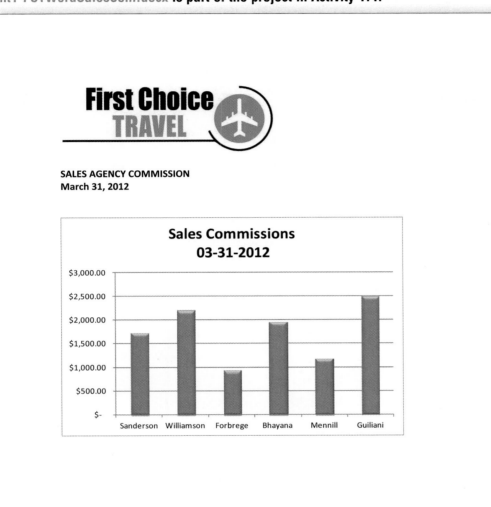

First Choice TRAVEL

SALES AGENCY COMMISSION
March 31, 2012

Sales Commissions
03-31-2012

Int1-FCTExcelSalesCom.xlsx is part of the project in Activity 1.4.

Sales Agent	Bookings	Commission
Sanderson	$ 43,189.00	$ 1,727.56
Williamson	$ 55,198.00	$ 2,207.92
Forbrege	$ 23,459.00	$ 938.36
Bhayana	$ 48,975.00	$ 1,959.00
Mennill	$ 29,657.00	$ 1,186.28
Guiliani	$ 63,198.00	$ 2,527.92

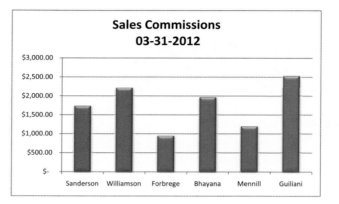

Int1-PTWordNovPay.docx is the project in Activity 1.5.

Proudly serving the entertainment
industry for over 20 years!

Employee Payroll

Week of November 12, 2012:

Employee	Hours	Pay Rate	Total
Rosa Levens	40.0	$ 14.65	$ 586.00
Scott Bercini	40.0	$ 15.10	$ 604.00
Tae Jeong	40.0	$ 12.40	$ 496.00
Terri Cantrell	40.0	$ 11.75	$ 470.00
Paul Gottlieb	40.0	$ 16.00	$ 640.00
Total			$ 2,796.00

4011 Bridgewater Street ✂ Niagara Falls, ON L2E 2T6 ✂ (905) 555-2971

Activity 1.1

Copying and Pasting Word Data into an Excel Worksheet

Microsoft Office is a suite that allows integration, which is the combining of data from two or more programs into one document. Integration can occur by copying and pasting data between programs. The program containing the data to be copied is called the *source* program and the program where the data is pasted is called the *destination* program. For example, you can copy data from a Word document into an Excel worksheet. Copy and paste data between programs in the same manner as you would copy and paste data within a program.

Project

You have been handed a Word document containing data on costume research, design, and sewing hours and need to copy the data to an Excel worksheet.

1. Open Word and then open the document named **PTWordJuneHrs.docx**.

2. Open Excel and then open the workbook **PTExcelJuneHrs.xlsx**.

3. Save the workbook with Save As and name it **Int1-PTExcelJuneHrs**.

4. Click the Word button on the Taskbar.

5. Select the five lines of text in columns as shown below.

6. Click the Copy button in the Clipboard group in the Home tab.

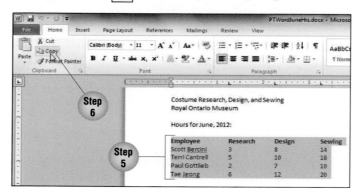

7. Click the Excel button on the Taskbar.

8. Make sure cell A2 is the active cell and then click the Paste button in the Clipboard group.

9. Click in cell E2 to deselect the text and then double-click the gray column boundary line between columns A and B.

> This increases the width of column A so the names display.

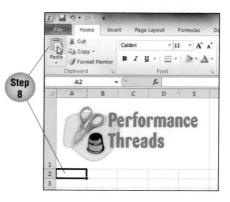

10 With cell E2 active, click the Bold button **B** and then type **Total**.

11 Make cell E3 the active cell, click the AutoSum button Σ in the Editing group, and then press Enter.

> This inserts a formula that calculates the total number of hours for Scott Bercini.

12 Copy the formula in cell E3 down to cells E4 through E6.

13 Make cell A7 active, click the Bold button, and then type **Total**.

14 Make cell B7 active, click the AutoSum button in the Editing group, and then press Enter.

> This inserts a formula that calculates the total number of research hours.

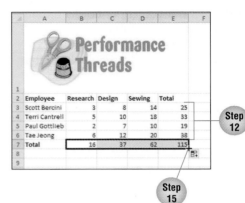

Step 12

Step 15

15 Copy the formula in cell B7 to cells C7 through E7.

16 Select cells A2 through E7.

17 Click the Format as Table button in the Styles group and then click *Table Style Light 11* (fourth option from the left in the second row in the *Light* section).

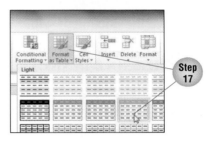

Step 17

18 At the Format As Table dialog box, click OK.

19 Remove the filtering arrows that display in cells A2 through E2. To do this, click the Home tab, click the Sort & Filter button in the Editing group, and then click *Filter* at the drop-down list.

20 Make any other changes needed to improve the visual display of the data in cells A2 through E7.

Step 19

21 Save, print, and then close **Int1-PTExcelJuneHrs.xlsx**.

22 Click the Word button on the Taskbar.

23 Close **PTWordJuneHrs.docx**.

> **In Brief**
>
> **Copy Data from One Program to Another**
> 1. Open desired programs and documents.
> 2. Select data in source program.
> 3. Click Copy button.
> 4. Click button on Taskbar representing destination program.
> 5. Click Paste button.

In Addition

Cycling between Open Programs

Cycle through open programs by clicking the button on the Taskbar representing the desired program. You can also cycle through open programs by pressing Alt + Tab. Pressing Alt + Tab causes a menu to display. Continue holding down the Alt key and pressing the Tab key until the desired program icon is selected by a border in the menu and then release the Tab key and the Alt key.

Linking an Excel Worksheet with a Word Document

In the previous activity, you copied data from a Word document and pasted it into an Excel worksheet. If you continuously update the data in the Word document, you would need to copy and paste the data each time into the Excel worksheet. If you update data on a regular basis that is copied to other programs, consider copying and linking the data. When data is linked, the data exists in the source program but not as separate data in the destination program. The destination program contains only a code that identifies the name and location of the source program, document, and the location in the document. Since the data is located only in the source program, changes made to the data in the source program are reflected in the destination program. Office updates a link automatically whenever you open the destination program or you edit the linked data in the destination program.

Project Copy data in an Excel worksheet on employee payroll for Performance Threads and then link the data to a Word document.

Performance Threads

1. With Word the active program, open the document named **PTWordOctPay.docx**.

2. Save the document with Save As and name it **Int1-PTWordOctPay**.

3. Make Excel the active program and then open the workbook named **PTExcelOctPay.xlsx**.

4. Save the workbook with Save As and name it **Int1-PTExcelOctPay**.

5. Link the data in cells in the worksheet into the Word document by selecting cells A3 through D8.

6. Click the Copy button in the Clipboard group in the Home tab.

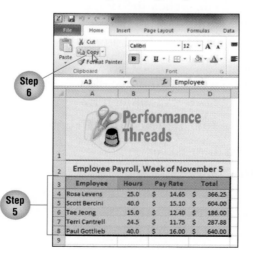

7. Click the Word button on the Taskbar.

8. Press Ctrl + End to move the insertion point to the end of the document (the insertion point is positioned a double space below *Week of October 8, 2012:*).

9 Click the Paste button arrow and then click *Paste Special* at the drop-down list.

Step 9

In Brief

Link Data between Programs
1. Open desired programs and documents.
2. Select data in source program.
3. Click Copy button.
4. Click button on Taskbar representing destination program.
5. Click Paste button arrow, *Paste Special*.
6. Click object in *As* list box.
7. Click *Paste link*.
8. Click OK.

10 At the Paste Special dialog box, click *Microsoft Excel Worksheet Object* in the *As* list box.

11 Click the *Paste link* option located at the left side of the dialog box.

12 Click OK to close the dialog box.

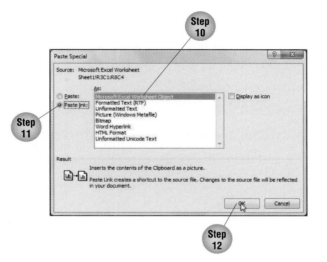

Step 10

Step 11

Step 12

13 Save, print, and then close **Int1-PTWordOctPay.docx**.

The table gridlines do not print.

14 Click the Excel button on the Taskbar.

15 Press the Esc key on the keyboard to remove the moving marquee around cells A3 through D8 and then click cell A3 to make it the active cell.

16 Close **Int1-PTExcelOctPay.xlsx**.

In Addition

Linking Data within a Program

Linking does not have to be between two different programs—you can link data between files in the same program. For example, you can create an object in a Word document such as a table or chart and then link the object with another Word document (or several Word documents). If you make a change to the object in the original document, the linked object in the other document (or documents) is automatically updated.

Updating Linked Data; Viewing a Link

The advantage of linking data over copying data is that editing the data in the source program will automatically update the data in the destination program. To edit linked data, open the document in the source program, make the desired edits, and then save the document. The next time you open the document in the destination program, the data is updated. The display of the linked data in the destination program can be changed to an icon. The icon represents the document and program to which the object is linked.

Project Update the payroll hours for the employees of Performance Threads in the Excel worksheet for the week of October 15.

1 With Excel the active program, open **Int1-PTExcelOctPay.xlsx**.

2 Make cell B4 the active cell and then change the number to *20.0*.

> Cells D4 through D8 contain a formula that multiplies the number in the cell in column B with the number in the cell in column C.

3 Make cell B6 the active cell and then change the number to *25.5*.

> When you make cell B6 the active cell, the result of the formula in cell D6 is updated to reflect the change you made to the number in cell B6.

4 Make cell B7 the active cell and then change the number to *15.0*.

5 Make cell C7 the active cell and then change the pay rate to *12.00*.

6 Double-click cell A2 and then change the date from *October 8* to *October 15*.

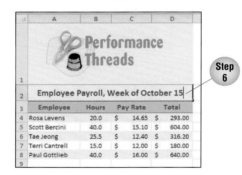

Step 6

7 Save, print, and then close **Int1-PTExcelOctPay.xlsx**.

8 Make Word the active program and then open **Int1-PTWordOctPay.docx**.

9 At the message asking if you want to update the document, click Yes.

> The document opens and is automatically updated to reflect the changes you made in **Int1-PTExcelOctPay.xlsx**.

10 Change the date above the table from *October 8* to *October 15*.

Step 10

Employee Payroll

Week of October 15, 2012:

Employee	Hours	Pay Rate	Total

11 Save and then print **Int1-PTWordOctPay.docx**.

12 Display the linked table as an icon. Begin by right-clicking in the table, pointing to *Linked Worksheet Object*, and then clicking *Convert*.

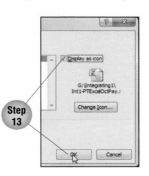

13 At the Convert dialog box, click the *Display as icon* check box to insert a check mark and then click OK.

Notice how the table changes to an icon representing the linked document.

14 Print **Int1-PTWordOctPay.docx**.

15 Make sure the linked object icon is still selected and then redisplay the table. To begin, right-click the icon, point to *Linked Worksheet Object*, and then click *Convert*.

16 At the Convert dialog box, click the *Display as icon* check box to remove the check mark and then click OK.

17 Save and then close **Int1-PTWordOctPay.docx**.

In Addition

Breaking a Link

The link between an object in the destination and source programs can be broken. To break a link, right-click on the object, point to *Linked Worksheet Object*, and then click *Links*. At the Links dialog box, click the Break Link button. At the question asking if you are sure you want to break the link, click the Yes button.

Activity 1.4

Linking an Excel Chart with a Word Document

While a worksheet does an adequate job of representing data, you can present some data more visually by charting the data. A chart is a visual representation of numeric data and, like a worksheet, can be linked to a document in another program. Link a chart in the same manner as you would link a worksheet.

Project

Link a chart containing sales commissions for agents of First Choice Travel with a Word document. Change the sales commission in the worksheet chart from 3% to 4%.

First Choice TRAVEL

1. Make Word the active program and then open **FCTWordSalesCom.docx**.

2. Save the document with Save As and name it **Int1-FCTWordSalesCom**.

3. Make Excel the active program and then open **FCTExcelSalesCom.xlsx**.

4. Save the workbook with Save As and name it **Int1-FCTExcelSalesCom**.

5. Click once in the chart area to select it. (A light gray border displays around the chart.)

   Make sure you do not select a specific chart element.

6. Click the Copy button in the Clipboard group in the Home tab.

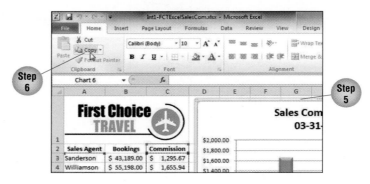

7. Click the Word button on the Taskbar.

8. Press Ctrl + End to move the insertion point to the end of the document.

9. Link the chart by clicking the Paste button arrow and then clicking *Paste Special* at the drop-down list.

10. At the Paste Special dialog box, click the *Microsoft Excel Chart Object* option in the *As* list box, click *Paste link*, and then click OK.

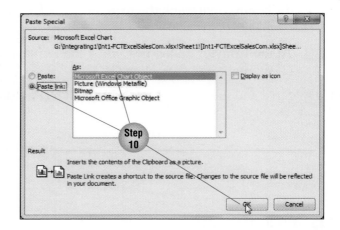

11. Save, print, and then close **Int1-FCTWordSalesCom.docx**.

12. Click the Excel button on the Taskbar.

13 The chart is based on a sales commission of 3 percent. Change the formula so it calculates a sales commission of 4 percent by double-clicking in cell C3 and then changing *0.03* in the formula to *0.04*.

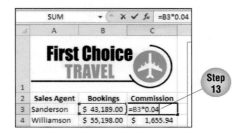

14 Press the Enter key.

> Pressing Enter displays the result of the formula calculating commissions at 4 percent.

15 Make cell C3 the active cell and then copy the new formula down to cells C4 through C8.

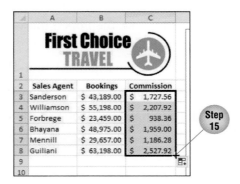

16 Save and then close **Int1-FCTExcelSalesCom.xlsx**.

17 Click the Word button on the Taskbar and then open the **Int1-FCTWordSalesCom.docx** document.

18 At the message asking if you want to update the document, click Yes.

> Notice the change in the amounts in the chart.

19 Save, print, and then close **Int1-FCTWordSalesCom.docx**.

In Addition

Customizing a Link

By default, a linked object is updated automatically and a linked object can be edited. You can change these defaults with options at the Links dialog box. Display this dialog box by right-clicking the linked object, pointing to *Linked Worksheet Object*, and then clicking *Links*. At the Links dialog box, click the *Manual update* option if you want to control when to update linked data. With the *Manual*

update option selected, update linked objects by clicking the Update Now button at the right side of the Links dialog box. If you do not want a linked object updated, click the *Locked* check box in the Links dialog box to insert a check mark.

Activity 1.5

Embedding an Excel Worksheet into a Word Document

You can copy an object between documents in a program, link an object, or embed an object. A linked object resides in the source program but not as a separate object in the destination program. An embedded object resides in the document in the source program as well as the destination program. If a change is made to an embedded object at the source program, the change is not made to the object in the destination program. Since an embedded object is not automatically updated as is a linked object, the only advantage to embedding rather than simply copying and pasting is that you can edit an embedded object in the destination program using the tools of the source program.

Project Copy data in an Excel worksheet on employee payroll for Performance Threads and then embed the data in a Word document. Update the payroll hours for the week of November 12 in the embedded Excel worksheet.

Performance Threads

1. With Word the active program, open the document named **PTWordNovPay.docx**.

2. Save the document with Save As and name it **Int1-PTWordNovPay**.

3. Make Excel the active program and then open the workbook named **PTExcelNovPay.xlsx**.

4. Save the workbook with Save As and name it **Int1-PTExcelNovPay**.

5. Embed cells into the Word document by selecting cells A3 through D8.

6. Click the Copy button in the Clipboard group in the Home tab.

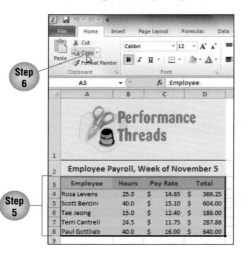

7. Click the Word button on the Taskbar.

8. Press Ctrl + End to move the insertion point to the end of the document (the insertion point is positioned a double space below *Week of November 5, 2012:*).

9. Click the Paste button arrow and then click *Paste Special* at the drop-down list.

10 At the Paste Special dialog box, click *Microsoft Excel Worksheet Object* in the *As* list box.

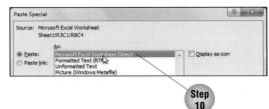

11 Click OK.

12 Save and print **Int1-PTWordNovPay.docx**.

13 Click the Excel button on the Taskbar.

14 Press the Esc key to remove the moving marquee around cells A3 through D8.

15 Click in cell A2 to make it the active cell and then close **Int1-PTExcelNovPay.xlsx**.

16 Click the Word button on the Taskbar.

17 Change the date above the table from *November 5* to *November 12*.

18 Position the arrow pointer anywhere in the worksheet and then double-click the left mouse button.

> In a few moments, the worksheet displays surrounded by column and row designations and the Excel tabs.

19 To produce the ordered costumes on time, the part-time employees worked a full 40 hours for the week of November 12. Make cell B4 the active cell and then change the number to *40*.

20 Make cell B6 the active cell and then change the number to *40*.

21 Make cell B7 the active cell and then change the number to *40*.

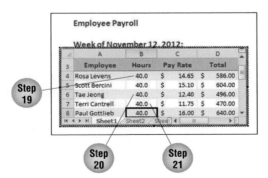

22 Bobbie Sinclair, Business Manager, wants to know the payroll total for the week of November 12 to determine the impact it has on the monthly budget. Add a new row to the table by making cell A8 the active cell and then pressing the down arrow key.

23 With cell A9 the active cell, type **Total**.

24 Make cell D9 the active cell and then click the AutoSum button in the Editing group.

25 Make sure D4:D8 displays in cell D9 and then press the Enter key.

continues

In Brief

Embed Data
1. Open desired programs and documents.
2. Select data in source program.
3. Click Copy button.
4. Click button on Taskbar representing destination program.
5. Click Paste button arrow, *Paste Special*.
6. Click object in *As* list box.
7. Click OK.

Edit Embedded Object
1. In source program, double-click embedded object.
2. Make desired edits.
3. Click outside object.

26 Increase the height of the worksheet by one row by positioning the arrow pointer on the bottom middle black sizing square until the pointer turns into a double-headed arrow pointing up and down. Hold down the left mouse button, drag down one row, and then release the mouse button.

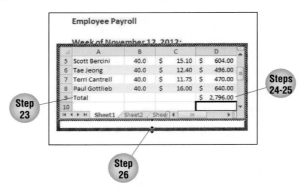

27 Using the arrow keys on the keyboard, make cell A3 the active cell and position cell A3 in the upper left corner of the worksheet. (This will display all cells in the worksheet containing data.)

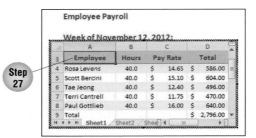

28 Click outside the worksheet to deselect it.

29 Save, print, and then close **Int1-PTWordNovPay.docx**.

The gridlines do not print.

In Addition

Inserting an Embedded Object from an Existing File

You embedded an Excel worksheet in a Word document using the Copy button and options at the Paste Special dialog box. Another method is available for embedding an object from an existing file. In the destination program document, position the insertion point where you want the object embedded and then click the Object button in the Text group. At the Object dialog box, click the Create from File tab. At the Object dialog box with the Create from File tab selected, type the desired file name in the *File name* text box or click the Browse button and then select the desired file from the appropriate folder. At the Object dialog box, make sure the *Link to file* check box does not contain a check mark and then click OK.

Troubleshooting Linking and Embedding Problems

If you double-click a linked or embedded object and a message appears telling you that the source file or source program cannot be opened, consider the following troubleshooting options. Check to make sure that the source program is installed on your computer. If the source program is not installed, convert the object to the file format of a program that is installed. Try closing other programs to free memory and make sure you have enough memory to run the source program. Check to make sure the source program does not have any dialog boxes open and, if it is a linked object, check to make sure someone else is not working in the source file.

Skills Review

Review 1 Copying and Pasting Data

1. Create a new folder on your storage medium and name it **IntegratingEOS**.
2. With Word the active program, open the document named **NPCWordScores.docx**.
3. Make Excel the active program and then open **NPCExcelScores.xlsx**.
4. Save the workbook in the IntegratingEOS folder and name it **Int1-R1-NPCExcelScores**.
5. Click the Word button on the Taskbar.
6. Select the nine lines of text in columns (the line beginning *Student* through the line beginning *Yiu, Terry*) and then click the Copy button in the Clipboard group in the Home tab.
7. Click the Excel button on the Taskbar.
8. With cell A5 active, paste the text into the worksheet.
9. Select cells A5 through A13, click the Delete button arrow, click *Delete Cells*, and then click OK at the Delete dialog box.
10. Increase the width of column A by double-clicking the gray column boundary line between columns A and B
11. Type the word **Average** in cell E5.
12. Make cell E6 active. Insert a formula that averages the numbers in cells B6 through D6.
13. Copy the formula in cell E6 down to cells E7 through E13.
14. With cells E6 through E13 selected, change the font to 12-point Cambria and then click four times on the Decrease Decimal button in the Number group in the Home tab.
15. Select cells B6 through D13 and then click once on the Increase Decimal button in the Number group in the Home tab. (This displays two numbers after the decimal point.)
16. Select cells B6 through E13, click the Center button in the Alignment group in the Home tab, and then deselect the cells.
17. Save, print, and then close **Int1-R1-NPCExcelScores.xlsx**.
18. Click the Word button on the Taskbar and then close the **NPCWordScores.docx** document.

Review 2 Linking an Object and Editing a Linked Object

1. With Word the active program, open the document named **NPCWordEnroll.docx**.
2. Save the document in the IntegratingEOS folder and name it **Int1-R2-NPCWordEnroll**.
3. Make Excel the active program and then open the workbook named **NPCExcelChart.xlsx**.
4. Save the workbook in the IntegratingEOS folder and name it **Int1-R2-NPCExcelChart**.
5. Link the chart to the Word document **Int1-R2-NPCWordEnroll.docx** a triple space below the *Student Enrollment* subtitle. (Make sure you use the Paste Special dialog box.)
6. Select the chart and then center it by clicking the Center button in the Paragraph group in the Home tab.
7. Save, print, and close **Int1-R2-NPCWordEnroll.docx**.
8. Click the Excel button on the Taskbar.
9. Click outside the chart to deselect it.
10. Print **Int1-R2-NPCExcelChart.xlsx**.
11. With **Int1-R2-NPCExcelChart.xlsx** open, make the following changes to the data in the specified cells:

A2   Change *Fall Term* to *Spring Term.*
B4   Change *75* to *98.*
B5   Change *30* to *25.*
B6   Change *15* to *23.*
B7   Change *38* to *52.*
B8   Change *25* to *10.*

12. Make cell A2 active.
13. Save, print, and then close **Int1-R2-NPCExcelChart.xlsx**.
14. Make Word the active program and then open **Int1-R2-NPCWordEnroll.docx**. (At the message asking if you want to update the document, click Yes.)
15. Save, print, and then close **Int1-R2-NPCWordEnroll.docx**.

Review 3 Embedding an Object

Worldwide Enterprises

1. With Word the active program, open the document named **WERevMemo.docx**.
2. Save the document in the IntegratingEOS folder and name it **Int1-R3-WERevMemo**.
3. Make Excel the active program and then open the workbook named **WEExcelRev.xlsx**.
4. Embed the data in cells A2 through D8 to the Word document **Int1-R3-WERevMemo.docx** a double space below the paragraph of text in the body of the memo.
5. Save and then print **Int1-R3-WERevMemo.docx**.
6. Click the Excel button on the Taskbar, close the **WEExcelRev.xlsx** workbook without saving it, and then exit Excel.
7. With **Int1-R3-WERevMemo.docx** open, double-click the worksheet and then make the following changes to the data in the specified cells:
   A2   Change *July Revenues* to *August Revenues.*
   B4   Change *1,356,000* to *1,575,000.*
   B5   Change *2,450,000* to *2,375,000.*
   B6   Change *1,635,000* to *1,750,000.*
   B7   Change *950,000* to *1,100,000.*
   B8   Change *1,050,000* to *1,255,000.*
8. Move the insertion point up to cell A2 and then click outside the worksheet to deselect it.
9. Make the following changes to the memo:
   Change the date from *August 13, 2012* to *September 3, 2012.*
   Change the subject from *July Revenues* to *August Revenues.*
10. Save, print, and then close **Int1-R3-WERevMemo.docx**.